JOINT EDITORS

PATRICK MILMO Q.C., M.A. (CANTAB),
of Middle Temple

W.V.H. ROGERS, M.A. (CANTAB),
Senior Fellow at the University of Leeds, Barrister of Gray's Inn

CONTRIBUTING EDITORS

GODWIN BUSUTTIL, M.A., M.PHIL. (CANTAB),
Barrister of Lincoln's Inn

RICHARD PARKES, Q.C., M.A. (CANTAB),
of Gray's Inn

CLIVE WALKER, LL.B. (LEEDS), PH.D. (MANCHESTER)
*Professor of Criminal Justice Studies at the
University of Leeds, Solicitor*

PRECEDENTS EDITOR

ADAM SPEKER, B.A.
Barrister of Middle Temple

HOW TO USE THIS SUPPLEMENT

This is the First Supplement to the Tenth Edition of *Gatley on Libel and Slander* and has been compiled according to the structure of the main volume.

At the beginning of each chapter of this Supplement the mini table of contents from the main volume has been included.
Where a heading in this table of contents has been marked with a square pointer (■), this indicates that there is material that is new to the work in the Supplement to which the reader should refer.

Within each chapter, updating information is referenced to the relevant paragraph in the main volume. New paragraphs which have been introduced in this Supplement have been identified as, *e.g.* 25.19A. This enables references contained within these paragraphs to be identified in the tables included in this Supplement.

PREFACE

When the publishers suggested a Supplement to the 10th edition within two years of that edition appearing on the bookstalls our reaction as editors was that defamation was such a small field in the legal landscape there simply would not be sufficient material to harvest to render the production of a Supplement worthwhile. We were wrong. The visible growth of case law in this period has been abundant, albeit fertilised by online reporting of virtually every High Court judgment. Perhaps only a limited number of these judgments contain fresh statements of principle or are the source of new developments in aspects of defamation law. But examples of the application of established tenets to new factual situations are often of assistance to the practitioner, although their citation is usually discouraged by judges. However, there are areas about which it can be said that the dynamic (if that is apt) of the law has been evident, notably in relation to *Reynolds* privilege, and the implications of levels of meaning arising from allegations which fall short of being accusations of guilt. We have given close study to the recent cases, such as *Jameel*, in which these topics have been discussed. From this the conclusion might be drawn that defamation law remains active but is (like life) not getting simpler. *Reynolds* in particular has thrown up many difficulties, and we must hope that some of them will be resolved when *Jameel* is heard by the House of Lords next year. More generally, our focus remains as before: English law as informed by the very strong light which continues to be shed on matters of general principle by other common law jurisdictions.

This Supplement attempts to bring the text of the 10th edition of *Gatley* up to date with material which was available to us at the end of August 2005. Each contributor prepared the sections for which he was responsible in the 10th edition but we have of course exchanged material and the general editors have read drafts of the whole text.

The multiplication of sources in which decisions can be accessed causes problems of consistency in nomenclature and citation. For example, one significant case is reported in the Weekly Law Reports on point A but not on point B, which appears only in the Entertainment and Media Law Reports. This is exacerbated where the litigation is ongoing and there are multiple interlocutory stages (for instance, the various claims being pursued by the Jameel family). We have been compelled to take a pragmatic approach to this problem, but at least there is the sheet anchor of the neutral citation.

We are grateful to friends who pointed us to material and to the editorial staff at Sweet & Maxwell, who, as always, maintained the faith that the horse would reach the starting gate on time.

Patrick Milmo
Horton Rogers

TABLE OF CASES

TABLE OF STATUTES

TABLE OF STATUTORY INSTRUMENTS

TABLE OF CIVIL PROCEDURE RULES

TABLE OF INTERNATIONAL LEGISLATION

TABLE OF EUROPEAN AND INTERNATIONAL CONVENTIONS

TABLE OF EUROPEAN DIRECTIVES

TABLE OF EUROPEAN REGULATIONS

CHAPTER 1

INTRODUCTION

SECTION 1. INTRODUCTORY

Foreign and international law. *The European Convention on Human Rights.* **1.2**
There has perhaps been a tendency in England to think of the right to the
protection of reputation in terms of a "negative" counterweight to the right to
freedom of expression under Art.10 of the European Convention on Human
Rights. However, it has been emphasised that reputation is accorded some
positive protection under Art.8 (see also this Supplement, para.23.10). In *Radio
France v France* (2005) 40 E.H.R.R. 29 the European Court of Human Rights
said at [31]:

> "La Cour souligne autant que de besoin que le droit à la réputation figure parmi les
> droits garantis par l'article 8 de la Convention, en tant qu'élément du droit au respect
> de la vie privée. [The Court emphasises that the right to reputation is included among
> the rights protected by Art.8 of the Convention in so far as it is an element of the right
> to respect for private life]."

The Court of Appeal has said that it is "content to assume" that this means that
"a person's right to protect his/her reputation is among the rights guaranteed
by... Article 8" (*Greene v Associated Newspapers Ltd* [2004] EWCA Civ
1462; [2005] 1 All E.R. 30) though it should be noted that the *Radio France* case
itself was a "traditional" Art.10 case, that is to say one which was concerned
with whether the civil and criminal sanctions imposed for statements that a civil
servant had been involved in wartime deportations of Jews constituted an
infringement of Art.10. Furthermore, in *Cumpana v Romania* (2004) Application
No.33348/96 the Grand Chamber referred to reputation of individuals as "a right
which, as an aspect of private life, is protected by Article 8 of the Convention"
(at [91]). While this may be a somewhat slender foundation on which to build a
free-standing claim based on injury to reputation, there may now be the possibility of an alternative claim against a public authority under the Human Rights Act,
with significant implications for the defences of truth and privilege as they apply
in libel: see this Supplement, para.21.12.
If there is now an overlap between Art.8 and libel law, how far do the matters
referred to have to be "private" (en tant qu'élément du droit au respect de la vie
privée) and what does that mean? Consider facts such as those in *Independent
Newspapers Holdings Ltd v Suliman* [2004] ZASCA 57, this Supplement,
para.1.5. C is arrested on suspicion of being involved in a bombing and this is

reported by D, a public official, to the newspapers. As long as the report is substantially accurate D has the defence of justification in the English law of libel. Conceivably, a court might hold that disclosure of an arrested person's identity at that stage of the investigation was disproportionate for the purposes of Art.8, thus engaging s.8 of the Human Rights Act 1998 for the purposes of a claim against D. Is the matter "private"? The Supreme Court of Appeal of South Africa held that the arrest was not a private matter for the purposes of the South African law of privacy since it took place in public. But is not his identity a private matter? Or is it of no consequence, as would be the case in the law of libel if it were untrue (subject to any defence of privilege)?

Add to note 25. It is said that damages for defamation are generally lower in Scotland than in England, since they are aimed at the affront caused rather than public vindication: *Lennon v Scottish Daily Record and Sunday Mail Ltd* [2004] EWHC 359, QBD; [2004] E.M.L.R. 18 at [22].

Malaysia: similarity to English defamation law. See *Lau v Life Publisher Bhd* [2004] 7 M.L.J. 7.

1.5   **What is defamatory.** *Note 51.* "The objective truth or falsity of the matter complained of is irrelevant to its defamatory nature. To say of a solicitor that he is dishonest is injurious to his reputation (and thus defamatory of him), and it does not become less injurious because the statement is true. To say of a member of the Bar (irony aside) that he is universally regarded as the best advocate in Sydney is not injurious to his reputation, and does not become injurious because the statement is false": *Ainsworth v Burden* [2005] NSWCA 174 at [88] *per* Hunt A.J.A. The difference between words being defamatory and being actionable is most obvious in a system which makes truth a defence only if there is some element of public benefit. In *Independent Newspapers Holdings Ltd v Suliman* [2004] ZASCA 57 the plaintiff was arrested in connection with a terrorist bombing. The defendants published this story, with the plaintiff's identity and photograph. This was held to be defamatory in that it imputed that the plaintiff was under suspicion and the majority of the court held that it was true in this sense. However, the disclosure of the plaintiff's identity at that stage was premature, notwithstanding the heinousness of the crime under investigation and therefore the other element of the defence was not made out.
See also *Adams v Guardian Newspapers Ltd* [2003] ScotCS 131, 2003 S.L.T. 1058 and *Hodgkinson v Economic Mutual Insurance Co.* (2003) 68 O.R. (3d) 587 at [33]; this Supplement, para.1.6.

1.6   **Malice, motive, intention and mistake.** The mental element in defamation was considered in a rather unusual context in *Hodgkinson v Economic Mutual Insurance Co.* (2003) 68 O.R. (3d) 587. The plaintiff posted statements on the internet which were sued on by the NF Corporation. The plaintiff contended that any liability was covered by the general legal liability provisions of his home owner's policy and that the insurers were therefore obliged to defend the claim under a clause undertaking to defend "any suit . . . alleging bodily injury or property damage and seeking compensatory damages". The policy excluded cover for "bodily injury or property damage caused by any intentional or criminal act". There was no appeal against the decision that "property damage" was in issue (seemingly because the corporate plaintiff in the libel action was complaining of injury to its goodwill, see *Blanchard v Halifax Insurance Co.* (1996) 184 N.B.R. (2d) 271) but the decision in favour of the insurers was upheld on the ground that that action fell within the exclusion. Although defamation fundamentally involved strict liability and the wording of the exclusion required that the intent went to the resultant injury (the lowering of the defamed person's reputation) and not merely the publication of the words, it was clear from the pleadings in the defamation action that the requisite intent was present.

> "[The plaintiff's] pleading that the statements were true is consistent only with the view that they were made with the intention of warning others of the [libel] plaintiffs' unethical behaviour and lack of financial viability. There is no room for concluding that it was not an essential part of this intention that the [libel] plaintiffs' reputation be lowered" (at [31]).

Nor would the truth, or the plaintiff's belief in the truth, of the allegations prevent the act being intentional. *Cf. Blanchard v Halifax Insurance Co.* (above) and *Wilkinson v Security National Insurance Co.* (1999), 81 Alta. L.R. (3d) 149, where the pleadings in the libel claims would not have justified the same conclusion.

Trial and remedies. The only proper purpose of a defamation action is to **1.8** enable the claimant to vindicate his reputation, to clear his name, and a genuine claim should therefore be brought and pursued with expedition: *Powell v Boladz* [2003] EWHC 2160, QBD (as to limitation in relation to defamation see Ch.18, section 4). However, if this is the claimant's purpose it is no objection that he also wishes to ruin the defendant, if that will be the outcome of successful proceedings: *Broxton v McLelland* [1995] E.M.L.R. 485 at [497], CA (but see *Steel and Morris v UK*, this Supplement, para.9.2).

It is not an abuse of process to bring proceedings against a person who will not be able to pay substantial damages where the claimant's purpose is to obtain vindication and prevent the dissemination of the libel: *Howe & Co. v Burden* [2004] EWHC 196, QBD. In *Rackham v Sandy* [2005] EWHC 1354, QBD, where an award of £2,000 damages was made against D1 but the claim failed against D2 and D3 on the basis of privilege, about two-thirds of the claimant's costs of £600,000 were attributable to D1. Gray J. awarded two-thirds of the claimant's costs against D1, saying:

> "libel actions are often not about money. Where an individual has been seriously defamed and the defamer refuses to apologize, that individual is not in my judgment to be criticized if, instead of abandoning his complaint, he institutes proceedings. That is what [the claimant] did. [D1] chose to contest the proceedings and, in the course of doing so, to ventilate in open court what were in my view exceedingly serious allegations of criminal dishonesty and other impropriety on the part of [the claimant] . . . I awarded him a small sum in damages in part because it appeared to me that a reasoned judgment would vindicate [the claimant's] reputation more efficaciously than a more substantial award of damages would do" (at [13]).

1.11   **Principle and precedent in defamation.** *Other legal systems*. The Supreme Court of Canada gave extended consideration to the basis of defamation law in Quebec in *Gilles E. Nérron Communication Marketing Inc. v Chambre des notaires du Québec* 2004 SCC 53; 241 D.L.R. (4th) 577 (see also *Prud'homme v Prud'homme* 2002 SCC 85; [2002] 4 S.C.R. 663; *Société Radio-Canada v Radio Sept Iles Inc.* [1994] R.J.Q. 1811). As in the case of French law, there is no special provision for defamation, liability resting on the general article (1457) of the Code Civil of Québec concerning injury to others by wrongful act. It has been said that it:

> "can be seen from the leading cases how often the Quebec courts have, when dealing with defamation and verbal abuse, borrowed from common law concepts (good faith and justification, qualified privilege), from decisions of English or Canadian courts or from common law commentators, such as Odgers. Borrowing from the common law in this manner is totally unnecessary and unwarranted . . . and it has the effect of greatly complicating a subject that, when examined in light of the Civil Code and the general principles of civil law, has the merit of being relatively straightforward" (*La responsabilité civile*, J.-L. Baudouin and P. Deslauriers (6th ed., 2003), p.193).

This sentiment was accepted by Le Bel J. in *Nérron* at [56]. At [61]–[62] he said:

> "In sum, the existence of a fault is the general and fundamental requirement in the law of defamation and fault is measured against professional journalistic standards. A journalist is not held to a standard of absolute perfection; he or she has an obligation of means. On the one hand, if a journalist disseminates erroneous information, this will not be determinative of fault. On the other hand, a journalist will not necessarily be exonerated simply because the information he or she disseminated is true and in the public interest. If, for other reasons, the journalist has fallen below the standard of the reasonable journalist, it is still open to the courts to find fault. Viewed this way, civil liability for defamation continues to fit nicely within the general framework of art. 1457 C.C.Q.
>
> As such, the conduct of the reasonable journalist becomes the all important guide-post. It is the tool which allows us to assess what conduct is reasonable within the context of art. 1457 C.C.Q. It is the ultimate standard against which fault is determined, and the framework through which other important considerations such as truth, falsity and the public interest are filtered."

Principle. It has been held in Australia that the various defences available to a defamation action under the common law are to be seen as a collection of matters which may be inconsistent one with another. Thus at common law there is a qualified privilege for a fair and accurate report of court proceedings; but a report which is not accurate may in certain circumstances shelter under the general qualified privilege based on duty and interest (see this Supplement, para.14.102).

> "The appellant's submissions appear to be founded on an assumption that the law of defamation has evolved through reference to a coherent legal policy which implicitly rejects the availability of two or more defences of privilege to a single defamatory imputation. Such an assumption in turn requires acceptance of the proposition that the

plurality of common law defences of privilege available in respect of a defamatory imputation exist within a framework which requires each defence to be developed with constant reference to each other defence. Neither that somewhat paradoxical proposition, nor the assumption upon which it is founded, should be accepted": *Bashford v Information Australia (Newsletters) Pty Ltd* [2004] HCA 5, 204 A.L.R. 193 at [124] *per* Gummow J.

Verbal torts and interests. In *PT Royal Bali Leisure v Hutchinson & Co. Trust* **1.17** *Co. Ltd* [2004] EWHC 1014 (Ch), a case of negligence, a claim for general loss of reputation was dismissed.

Note 89. See also *Disney v France Luxury Group S.A.* [2004] EWHC 2303, QBD (leave to appeal).

DEFAMATORY IMPUTATIONS

2.1   **The defamatory imputation.** *Note 12.* That it is the tendency, rather than the actual effect, of the words which is important where liability (as opposed to damages) is in issue is also supported by *Mthembi-Mahanyele v Mail & Guardian Ltd* [2004] ZASCA 67; 2004 (11) B.C.L.R 1182, Sup. Ct of Appeal of South Africa, at [32].

Add to note 2. For criticism of the NSW system see Kirby J. in *John Fairfax Pty Ltd v Rivkin* [2003] HCA 50; 201 A.L.R. 77 at [83].

Add to note 18. The matter is fully considered by the High Court of Australia in *John Fairfax Pty Ltd v Rivkin* (above). In *Saffron v John Fairfax Pty Ltd* [2004] NSWCA 254 the plaintiff, an applicant for a liquor licence, was described as having an unsavoury reputation. The court seems to have been of the view that, standing alone, that would almost inevitably be defamatory but refused to interfere with the verdict that in the context of the publication it was not. The jury might have regarded the imputation as meaning that the plaintiff had once had an unsavoury reputation but no longer had such a reputation. Furthermore, to the allegation of bad reputation were appended the words "all of it undeserved and completely the fault of the media". Many might have regarded that as a sarcastic comment on the argument of the plaintiff's counsel in the liquor licensing proceedings but presumably it was not possible to discount the fact that the jury might have taken it literally. See also *Pavy v John Fairfax Publications Pty Ltd* [2004] NSWCA 177 (verdict that plaintiff "had broken six ribs of his baby son, by doing a similar sort of act to shaking him" not defamatory was not perverse; but pleader had omitted original imputation that plaintiff "had directed physical violence towards his infant son thereby breaking six of his ribs").

SECTION 1. WHAT IS DEFAMATORY

2.6   **Words causing others to shun or avoid one.** *Note 60.* See also *Lau v Life Publisher Bhd* [2004] 7 M.L.J. 7.

SECTION 2. STANDARD OF OPINION

State of public opinion. In New South Wales, in considering whether an   **2.16**
imputation is defamatory, a jury is asked to apply general community standards.
In *Beran v John Fairfax Publications Pty Ltd* [2004] NSWCA 107 the jury's
decision that to say a doctor had been profiteering from drug trials was not
defamatory was upheld. "Its conclusion appears to . . . have meant that according to those standards a person's reputation was not lowered in the eyes of the
community if they earned a great deal, even an exorbitant amount, of money
from drug trials. Its conclusion is understandable in the materialistic atmosphere
of contemporary society" at [186].

SECTION 3. INSTANCES OF DEFAMATORY IMPUTATIONS

(a) *General*

Instances of defamatory words To describe a television actor as a "heartless,   **2.19**
rude bastard" is clearly defamatory: *Nail v News Group Newspapers Ltd* [2004]
EWCA Civ 1708; [2005] E.M.L.R. 12 at [21] (though the point was not in issue
since there had been an unqualified offer of amends). More particular allegations
were of indiscriminate sexual encounters, attempting to seduce the fiancée of a
friend, eating canned dogmeat when pressed for cash, being arrogant to col-
leagues, being mean, shunning his sick father, exploiting the death of a colleague
for financial advantage and illegally financing a property development business.

Sexual conduct. For an indication of what sort of allegations about the sexual   **2.20**
behaviour of a male actor might now be over the defamation threshold, see *Nail
v News Group Newspapers Ltd* [2004] EWCA Civ 1708; [2005] E.M.L.R. 12 at
[18] (though the point was not in issue since there had been an unqualified offer
of amends).

Note 26. In *John Fairfax Publications Pty Ltd v Rivkin* [2003] HCA 50, 201
A.L.R. 77 at [140] Kirby J. said:

"In most circumstances, it ought not to be the case in Australia that to publish a
statement that one adult was involved in consenting, private homosexual activity with
another adult involves a defamatory imputation. But whether it does or does not harm
a person's reputation to publish such an imputation is related to time, personality and
circumstance . . . The day may come when, to accuse an adult of consenting homosexual activity is likewise generally a matter of indifference. However, it would ignore
the reality of contemporary Australian society to say that that day has arrived for all
purposes and all people. At least for people who treat their sexuality as private or secret,
or people who have presented themselves as having a different sexual orientation, such
an imputation could, depending on the circumstances, still sometimes be defamatory."

(b) *Credit*

2.21   **Insolvency and credit.** *Unjustified demand.* It has been said that it is "fanciful" to suggest that in the absence of bad faith a person who gives a notice of acceleration of payment under a bond without legal justification would be exposed to substantial damages for defamation: *Concord Trust v Law Debenture Trust Corp. plc* [2004] EWCA Civ 1001; [2004] All E.R. (Comm) 737 at [83].

Where insurance is not required by law, a statement that a company is uninsured is not of itself capable of being defamatory, for it does not impute that it is unable to meet its obligations: *Lions Gate Marketing Co. v Used Car Dealers Assn of Ontario* [2005] BCCA 274.

(c) *Reputation in business, trade or profession*

2.27   **Insufficient that words damage claimant in business, etc.** In *John Fairfax Publications Pty Ltd v A.C.P. Publishing Pty Ltd* [2005] ACTCA 12 it was held that a story about a disastrous fall in circulation of a magazine could not reasonably be understood as imputing incompetence to the management. However, in *Ravnikar v Bogojavlensky* 782 N.E. 2d 508 (Mass. 2003) an oral statement that a physician was dying of cancer was held to be capable of being actionable per se because it might put off potential patients seeking long-term care without, seemingly, any imputation that the physician was misleading patients or was currently unfit to perform her duties. But did the court slide over the question of whether it was *defamatory*? All the illustrations to section 573 of the Restatement 2d, *Torts*, on which the court relied, involve imputations like drunkenness, incompetence, insolvency or insanity.

2.32   *The law. Note 40.* See also *Joceline Tan Poh Choo v Muthusamy* [2003] 4 M.L.J. 494, Mal CA.

2.33   *Politics.* In *Clark v Express Newspapers* [2004] EWHC 481, QBD, Tugendhat J. held that articles bearing the meaning that the claimant had been elected on a manifesto promise not to introduce top-up fees, that she had dishonoured that promise by voting against a motion opposing top-up fees and that she was likely to dishonour that promise in further votes in the future or would do so if not scared by newspaper exposure were defamatory of the claimant. The use of the word "ratted" precluded any suggestion that she had simply changed her opinion in the light of the circumstances. £5,000 damages under s.9 of the Defamation Act 1996 (summary disposal).

In *Galloway v Telegraph Group Ltd* [2004] EWHC 2786, QBD; [2005] E.M.L.R. 7 (this Supplement, para.14.91) the defendants published articles conveying that the claimant, a member of Parliament, had been in the pay of Saddam Hussein, that he had diverted "oil-for-food" money for his own enrichment and that his conduct was tantamount to treason. £150,000 damages.

2.34   *Doctors and other medical people.* Despite the considerable restraint shown by Australian courts in interfering with the verdict of a jury on whether words are or are not defamatory (*John Fairfax Publications Pty Ltd v Rivkin* [2003] HCA

50; 201 A.L.R. 77) the court in *Gorman v Barber* [2004] NSWCA 402 held that no reasonable jury could have come to the conclusion that an article in a medical magazine that a doctor's treatment of his patients was useless, dangerous and caused them harm was not defamatory.

Sport and stage. See *Armstrong v Times Newspapers Ltd* [2005] EWCA Civ   **2.35**
1007 (grounds for suspicion of taking performance-enhancing drugs).

Examples: disparagement of goods. See also *Charterhouse Clinical Research*   **2.39**
Unit Ltd v Richmond Pharmacology Ltd [2003] EWHC 1099, QBD and *Dorset Flint & Stone Blocks Ltd v Moir* [2004] EWHC 2173, QBD.

Examples: disparagement of newspapers. In *Chinese Herald Ltd v New Times*   **2.40**
Madia Ltd [2004] 2 N.Z.L.R. 749 the following meanings were found and were held to be defamatory: that the claimant newspaper "behaved in an underhand and devious manner, adopted a biased practice to reporting, was malicious and absurd in its reporting, was a sycophant and acted in an obscene manner, was evil and acted dishonourably, and was a less than upright newspaper". The statement that it opposed democracy was in the circumstances defamatory but if it had stood on its own without the other comments, it would not have led to more than nominal damages.

Chapter 3

THE FORM AND MEANING OF THE DEFAMATORY STATEMENT

Section 2. The Distinction between Libel and Slander

3.6 **The consequences of the distinction.** *Libel actionable per se. Text to note 41.* See *Jameel (Yousef) v Dow Jones & Co. Inc.* [2005] EWCA Civ 75; [2005] 2 W.L.R. 1614. Whether one says that damage is presumed from the publication of a libel or that the tort is complete upon publication without the need for damage would seem to make no difference in practice, since any presumption of damage is irrebuttable. Either way the rule makes pragmatic sense in avoiding having to call witnesses to testify what meaning they put upon the words and how the words affected the claimant's standing in their eyes and "English law has been well served by a principle under which liability turns on the objective question of whether the publication is one which tends to injure the claimant's reputation" (at [37]). This does not offend Art.10 of the European Convention on Human Rights because it does not mean that juries may award damages on a scale incommensurate with any damage likely in fact to have been suffered. Furthermore, where the claimant brings proceedings in circumstances where it is apparent that there has been no, or minimal, damage, it is open to the court to dismiss the action as an abuse of process or, where the defendant is based abroad and there has been minimal publication here, to refuse leave to serve process out of the jurisdiction on the ground that England is not an appropriate forum. An application to dismiss on the ground of an abuse of process is now more readily entertained in a libel action in view of the Civil Procedure Rules and Art.10 of the European Convention on Human Rights. See also this Supplement, paras 6.1, 32.7 and 32.45.

In New South Wales, where slander and libel are treated in the same way, s.13 of the Defamation Act 1974 provides that it is a defence to show that the circumstances of the publication were such that the person defamed was not likely to suffer harm. The meaning of this is examined in *Jones v Sutton* [2004] NSWCA 439.

3.9 **Broadcasting: statute.** Amendments to the definition of "programme service" (and many other matters) are made by the Communications Act 2003.

Note 91. In *Romano v D'Onofrio* [2004] O.J. No.4989 the Ontario legislation was held not to cover words spoken through a microphone in a hall.

The internet. In *Bahlieda v Santa* (2003) 68 O.R. (3d) 115, Ont. CA, the court   **3.11**
declined to deal with the applicability to the internet of the Ontario legislation on
broadcasting (see note 91) as a preliminary issue. See also *Weiss v Sawyer* (2002)
61 O.R. (3d) 526.

SECTION 3. INTERPRETATION

The meaning of words. *Note 28.* See also *Jameel v Wall Street Journal*   **3.12**
Europe Sprl [2003] EWCA Civ 1694; [2004] E.M.L.R. 6.

Add to second paragraph. The judge's function of ruling on possible meaning
may arise in the following contexts: in evaluating the defence of qualified
privilege; in relation to the defence of justification where the defendant proposes
to rely on a lesser defamatory meaning; for the purpose of assessing the degree
of injury to the claimant's reputation; in order to determine whether the words are
capable of having any defamatory meaning at all; or in order to determine
whether they are capable of having any non-defamatory meaning. "The judge's
function is no more and no less than to pre-empt perversity", that is to say, he is
deciding that no reader could reasonably understand the words to bear a meaning
outside the range he delimits (Simon Brown L.J. in *Jameel v Wall Street Journal*
Europe Sprl [2003] EWCA Civ 1694; [2004] E.M.L.R. 6 at [9]–[16]).

Intention and knowledge of the publisher. In *Klason v Australian Capital*   **3.13**
Territory [2003] ACTSC 104, 177 F.L.R. 216 Crispin J. held that a statement that
allegations of child abuse against the plaintiff had been "substantiated" could
only reasonably mean that the truth of the allegations had been established. It was
nothing to the point that some child care practitioners might treat the expression
as meaning only that there was a risk of abuse. "To suggest that the statement
might imply only that the child is at serious risk would be as absurd as suggesting
that a record of the substantiation of an allegation that a particular person had
robbed a bank implied only that security was lax and that, if a robbery had not
already occurred, it soon might" (at [88]).
    Surprising to English eyes is the decision of the majority in *Knievel v ESPN*
393 F.3d 1068 (CA9, 2005) that caption to photograph of stunt celebrity, wife and
unnamed woman, "[Plaintiff] proves that you're never too old to be a pimp" was
incapable of being defamatory because "pimp" is in some circles used as
meaning "cool" or "sharp dresser". But First Amendment attitudes may stray
over into "common law" issues.

Note 33. See this Supplement, para.7.6 (whether defendant may, for the
purposes of qualified privilege or fair comment, rely on facts relating to the
person he intended to refer to but not the claimant, who is held to be identified
by the words).

Reasonable understanding. *The single meaning.* "Of course, in reality, fair-   **3.14**
minded readers of a newspaper article may differ, on any day of the week, as to
the true implications or shades of meaning contained within it. Nevertheless, by
convention, English law operates on the principle that for determining most

[11]

issues in a libel action there is at least one definitive meaning in the light of which, for example, decisions have to be made on any defence of justification or on the level of compensation which is appropriate . . . On the other hand, I have never known a case in which a jury was asked to set out its definitive meaning or meanings. There may be examples where this has occurred, but it does seem to me that there are potentially serious problems about any such exercise. It is difficult to see how it would be possible to avoid asking the jurors to draft in committee, since they cannot generally be given a finite number of multiple option questions. They are not . . . bound by either side's contentions on meaning. It is open for them to come up with their own particular meaning or meanings. Also, where there is room for differences between ordinary readers as to the interpretation of a newspaper article, there is no reason to suppose that all 12 jurors are necessarily going to fit into one straitjacket. Any differences between them, which are likely to be relatively minor and limited to matters of shading or emphasis, would not normally have to be revealed. If they are asked to produce a carefully drafted set of meanings, however, which remove any ambiguity which has been left in the article ex hypothesi by the professional journalist or editor, there is much more scope for stalemate" (*Jameel v Wall Street Journal Europe Sprl (No.2)* [2004] EWHC 37, QBD; [2004] E.M.L.R. 11 at [6], *per* Eady J.).

3.16   **Ordinary meaning and implications.** Despite the current emphasis on proportionality in the resolution of disputes, the "information explosion" is a powerful counterweight. In *King v Lewis* [2004] EWCA Civ 1329; [2005] E.M.L.R. 4 there had been a web search of 900 dictionaries for the meaning of "shyster".

Galloway v Telegraph Group Ltd [2004] EWHC 2786, QBD; [2005] E.M.L.R. 7, this Supplement, para.14.91, a trial by judge alone, is unusual in providing detailed material as to why a particular conclusion was reached on meaning (as opposed to possible meaning). Thus:

"Here . . . I am concerned with the treatment of the denials as *attributed* to Mr Galloway in the articles. Mr Sparrow on p.3 describes how he asked him during his telephone conversation to '*explain away* the documents found in Baghdad' [emphasis added]. Mr Sparrow, in the witness box, described the introduction of the word 'away' as a 'figure of speech' or 'colloquialism'. Indeed it is. The question is what significance it would convey to the reader. It is most commonly used in the context of those placed in the predicament of having to explain evidence pointing to their guilt. It means, as everyone knows, that damning evidence has been produced, for which there is no plausible explanation consistent with innocence. Mr Rampton put it to Mr Sparrow that it simply meant that his client had been 'caught red handed': at [66].

The very first words on the front page of the April 23 issue were '*Telegraph* reveals damning new evidence on Labour MP'. The word 'damning' means that the 'evidence' condemns him; that it is conclusive of guilt. In the context, the publication of denials does not achieve balance or neutralise the charges. What it does is to show that the newspaper has decided that the denials were dishonest or unreliable, and thus to be discounted by the readers. The next bullet point heading, alongside the first, is 'Bluster, two homes and the unanswered questions'. Again the denials are portrayed as 'bluster'. What that means is that they are just hot air and lacking substance. The evidence is strong and, what is more, there is nothing but 'bluster' to put on the scales on the side of the defence. Therefore, the strong evidence prevails. It cannot be characterised as merely a *prima facie* case. Guilt has been established: at [67].

The same impression is confirmed by the coverage on pp.2 and 3, across the top of which appears the headline 'MP in Saddam's pay defends himself from £250,000 villa in the Algarve'. Underneath appears a very large colour photograph of the villa (or 'cottage' as Mr Galloway described it in evidence) with its swimming pool and another one of his house in Streatham. The *Telegraph* witnesses recognised that it would have been preferable to put the words 'in Saddam's pay' in inverted commas in the headline. But that shows how little significance they really attached to the distinction between direct assertions in this context and those merely reported as allegations. What matters, of course, is not what they intended but how the readers would understand the words and photographs. Yet they too would surely realise that the *Daily Telegraph* was not drawing any such fine distinction. The inference to be drawn from that headline and the photographs is inescapable. The huge colour photograph was not there to show readers the fortuitous and incidental fact of *where* Mr Galloway was expressing his denials, but rather to demonstrate the link between being 'in Saddam's pay' and the material rewards of those undeclared 'profits'. Readers can hardly have failed to get the message. Nor (in the context of *Bonnick v Morris*) can the journalists. To suggest otherwise is disingenuous or, at best, wishful thinking.

The references to two homes and expensive cars will only have relevance to the story as confirming the receipt of significant rewards over and above Mr Galloway's Parliamentary salary. The introductory paragraph said that Mr Galloway began his defence 'from the *comfort* of his holiday home in Portugal' [emphasis added]. These pointed references were not merely background 'lifestyle' colour, as was suggested at one stage in argument. It was not a lifestyle piece, such as one might find in (say) *Hello!* magazine. It was a gravely serious exposé of wrongdoing by a member of Parliament" (at [68]–[69]).

In *Hill v Cork Examiner Publications Ltd* [2001] IESC 95 the plaintiff was serving a sentence in Cork prison for actual bodily harm. The defendants published a feature about the prison and a photograph of the plaintiff in his cell appeared under the headline, "Isolation of Cork Jail's C Wing". In the article it was stated that C Wing prisoners were child molesters, sexual offenders or incarcerated there for their own protection. The Supreme Court held that a reasonable reader could have understood the article to have meant that the plaintiff was a prisoner in those categories and upheld an award of IR£60,000.

Notes 72–74 (inference upon an inference). In *John Fairfax Publications Pty Ltd v A.C.P. Publishing Pty Ltd* [2005] ACTCA 12 the Court said:

"[Counsel for the defendants] also relied upon a suggested principle that the ordinary reader will be presumed not to draw 'inference on inference'. Whilst this submission is frequently made in cases of this nature, such a formulation is potentially misleading. The legal test is simply whether the material in question was reasonably capable of conveying the relevant imputation and the significance of any distinction between primary and secondary inferences must be considered in the context of that test. There may be many circumstances ... in which a primary inference could fairly be drawn from the published material but a secondary inference said to arise from the first could not be regarded as an imputation reasonably drawn from that material. At the other extreme, there may be circumstances in which the second inference would be regarded an almost inevitable corollary of the first. In the latter event, there would be no rational reason to act upon some perceived truism that a reasonable reader would lack the intellectual acuity to draw it" (at [13]).

3.19 **True innuendo: extrinsic facts.** *Matters becoming known after publication.* See *Galloway v Telegraph Group Ltd* [2004] EWHC 2786, QBD; [2005] E.M.L.R. 7, this Supplement, para.3.31.

Add to note 2: Rivkin v John Fairfax Publications is reported on appeal to the HCA (sub nom. *John Fairfax Publications Pty Ltd v Rivkin*) in 201 A.L.R. 77.

3.22 **More than one meaning possible.** See also *Bonnick v Morris* [2002] UKPC 31; [2003] 1 A.C. 300 (considered at para.14.86) and *Jameel v Wall Street Journal Europe Sprl* [2003] EWCA Civ 1694; [2004] E.M.L.R. 6.

3.23 **Mere conjectures.** *Strained meanings. Note 17.* See also *Dorset Flint & Stone Blocks Ltd v Moir* [2004] EWHC 2173, QBD (statement of opinion about the suitability of a product dressed up by claimants to look like a reflection upon their honesty).

3.24 **The ordinary person: temperament.** The reasonable reader is not a person of "morbid or suspicious mind": *Byrnes v John Fairfax Publications Pty Ltd* [2004] NSWSC 635 at [11], citing Lord O'Brien C.J. in *Keogh v The Incorporated Dental Hospital of Ireland* [1910] 2 I.R. 577 at 586.

> "In any defamation suit the logical starting point is what the words complained of mean, more particularly, whether they convey the defamatory meaning which the plaintiff seeks to place upon them. In answering that question a court discards its judicial robes and the professional habit of analysing and interpreting statutes and contracts in accordance with long established principles. Instead it dons the garb and adopts the mindset of the reasonable lay citizen and interprets the words, and draws the inferences which they suggest, as such a person would do. It follows that meticulous attention to detail, an alertness to and awareness of the subtle nuances in meaning of words, a full appreciation of the influence of context, and a reluctance to draw inferences when they are not soundly based and fully justifiable and amount to no more than speculation, cannot be expected. The law reports are replete with reminders of the looseness of thought and low level of concentration with which even an eminently reasonable member of society may read newspaper reports.
>
> Yet there must be a limit to the allowances which a court should make in a claimant's favour when engaged in the notional exercise postulated. A defamatory meaning should not be attributed to an isolated part of a newspaper report if the rest of the report would show that it is not justified. A claimant should not be permitted to base his case upon the reaction of readers who do not bother to read the whole of the article even although a part of it has attracted their attention precisely because of its potential to lower the esteem in which society holds him. In saying this I am aware that judges have drawn attention to the propensity of readers to 'skim' reports in newspapers but I do not understand that to mean that they must be taken to have entirely ignored everything in a report which they skim, other than that part or those parts of it which, if viewed in isolation, would constitute defamatory material. Why should the writer or publisher of an article the whole of which is intended to be read and, if read, would plainly not be defamatory be held liable for defamation because there may have been lazy or careless readers who chose to focus only upon a particular sentence in it? I am also aware that

headlines are what attract readers to an article but that does not mean that one may ignore an accompanying headline ['material accompanying the headline' seems to be the correct sense—ed.]. However, 'those who print defamatory headlines are playing with fire' [referring to Lord Nicholls in *Charleston v News Group Newspapers Ltd* [1995] 2 AC 65 at 74]" (*Independent Newspapers Holdings Ltd v Suliman* [2004] ZASCA 57 at [19]–[20] *per* Marais J.A).

That some people will always be willing to take humorous or satirical material seriously is shown by the real life examples in *New Times Inc. v Isaacks* 146 S.W. 3d 144 (Tex. 2004) at 158, n.7 (cert. den. June 6, 2005).

Text to notes 41–44. See also *Somosi v John Fairfax Publications Pty Ltd* [2004] NSWCA 176.

The ordinary person: knowledge. It has been suggested that the ordinary **3.25** reader must now be credited with having achieved a level of education which was not widely accessible to earlier generations: *Lennon v Scottish Daily Record and Sunday Mail Ltd* [2004] EWHC 359, QBD; [2004] E.M.L.R. 18. See further this Supplement, para.30.5.

Illustrations: imputations of crime. The issue of the various level of defama- **3.26** tory meaning to be attributed to a statement has been considered in a number of cases. For further analysis see this Supplement paras 26.20, 27.7, 27.10 and 30.5.

In *Jameel v Wall Street Journal Europe Sprl* [2003] EWCA Civ 1694; [2004] E.M.L.R. 6 an article entitled "Saudi Officials Monitor Certain Bank Accounts. Focus Is On Those With Potential Terrorist Ties" was alleged to refer to the claimants and was said by them to mean that they "were reasonably suspected of having terrorist ties and of funnelling funds to terrorist organisations, and had therefore been included on a list of bank accounts which were required by the US law enforcement agencies to be closely monitored by the Saudi Arabian Monetary Authority", that is to say the meaning commonly known as "level 2" in contrast with "level 1", where guilt is directly imputed. The Court of Appeal allowed an appeal from a ruling of Eady J. ([2003] EWHC 2322) that the words were not capable of bearing the lesser ("level 3") meaning that there were merely grounds to investigate what the claimants had done. It might well be that the jury would find that the level 2 meaning was the natural and therefore the "right" one to place upon the words, but the lesser meaning was not strained or forced or utterly unreasonable. "Once it is recognised that the article may be asserting no more than that in one way or another the respondents may unwittingly have assisted terrorists in the past and may by introducing more controls be able to prevent that in future, the borderline between . . . 'level 2' meaning (reasonable grounds to suspect) and 'level 3' meaning (grounds merely for investigation) becomes somewhat blurred" (at [19]).

In *Jameel v Times Newspapers Ltd* [2004] EWCA Civ 983; [2004] E.M.L.R. 31 an article in another newspaper linked the same claimant with terrorism. The Court of Appeal, reversing Gray J., held that the article was capable of a level 2 meaning as well as (as the defendants conceded) one at level 3. In other words, the case was the converse of *Jameel v Wall Street Journal*, where the judge below had rejected the lesser meaning. See also this Suplement, para.3.29.

In *Armstrong v Times Newspapers Ltd* [2004] EWHC 2928, QBD) (on appeal, but not on this issue, [2005] EWCA Civ 1007) an article referred to and in part repeated a book published in France by another journalist on the same newspaper, which purported to raise "questions" about whether the claimant, a professional cyclist and five times winner of the Tour de France, had taken performance-enhancing drugs. Eady J. held that the article, taken as a whole, could not be read as imputing anything less than reasonable grounds to suspect the claimant of this. The article was not a general piece about drug-taking in cycling but about the claimant and it contained passages to the effect that "there are those who fear that" anyone who won five Tours in a row must have taken drugs and that experts were of the view that a for a "clean" cyclist to beat one who took drugs was "probably impossible". "The overall effect of the article is to leave readers with the impression that [the claimant's] denials of drug-taking beggar belief and are to be taken with a pinch of salt . . . I am quite satisfied that the words are not capable of conveying merely that a third party has alleged enough to warrant an investigation of the claimant's activities" (at [25]).

See also *Lennon v Scottish Daily Record and Sunday Mail Ltd* [2004] EWHC 359, QBD; [2004] E.M.L.R. 18.

Presumption of innocence. In South Africa it has been said that while it is an untenable proposition that reasonable people believe that the police only arrest on suspicion where there is evidence sufficient to warrant prosecution and conviction and there is a constitutionally entrenched presumption of innocence, yet:

"the harsh reality of the situation is that even mere suspicion, to put it at its lowest, raises doubts in the mind of those to whom it is communicated as to whether the hitherto unsullied reputation which the person enjoyed continues to be deserved or whether it should now be regarded as undeserved. To say that which imperils the continued existence of a person's good reputation and causes people generally to doubt the integrity of that person even though they may not be certain the doubt is justified, is to adversely affect to at least some degree his or her reputation. That the doubt may be temporary and ultimately transient because of the subsequently established innocence of the person concerned cannot cure the loss of esteem which that person endures pending the establishment of his or her innocence" (*Independent Newspapers Holdings Ltd v Suliman* [2004] ZASCA 57 at [24] and [32] *per* Marais J.A.).

3.28   **Context and circumstances of publication.** *Television broadcasts.* See *Australian Broadcasting Corp. v Reading* [2004] NSWCA 411, where the court was divided as to the likely impact of the programme on the viewer.

3.29   **Publication must be taken as a whole.** *Meaning: bane and antidote.* It has been said that there is a certain tension in the case law "between the principle that the feasible range of meanings is to be derived from the article as a whole, read through the eyes of a sensible person, and the principle that if the article contains a defamatory statement or imputation, that will define its meaning unless it is very plainly negatived in the same article": *Jameel v Times Newspapers Ltd* [2004] EWCA Civ 983; [2004] E.M.L.R. 31 at [16] *per* Sedley L.J. An article was headed "Car tycoon 'linked' to Bin Laden" and the caption to a photograph read, "Accused . . . Now [the claimant] is alleged to have helped fund training for the terrorists who carried out the September 11 attacks". However, the story was interwoven with passages which set out the claimant's denials. The Court of Appeal reversed Gray J. and held that the article was capable of conveying that there were reasonable grounds to suspect the claimant and not merely that there were grounds for investigation of the matter (see this Supplement, para.3.26), Sedley L.J. remarking that "the article contains significant material capable of dispelling both [meanings] but not so unequivocally presented as to constitute an incontestable antidote for whatever poison a jury may detect. It is . . . for a jury to say what the article as a whole means" (at [20]).

See also *Stanton v Metro Corp.* 357 F. Supp. 2d 369 (D. Mass. 2005) (juxtaposition of photograph and article potentially defamatory but not so because of modestly sized "disclaimer" denying any connexion between persons pictured and those in the story).

Qualifications. *Whether antidote sufficient.* In *Klason v Australian Capital Territory* [2003] ACTSC 104; 177 F.L.R. 216, a government agency had found that allegations of child abuse against the plaintiff had been substantiated. A judge of the Family Court then found that the allegations were not well-founded. A minute to a minister recorded: "In accordance with the legislation and policy and procedures of the day, Family Services conducted an investigation and substantiated the allegation of sexual abuse. At a later Family Court hearing the Judge subsequently found the allegations were not substantiated." Crispin J. held that, taking account of the fact that there was no further explanation of the background and did not make clear that the agency no longer regarded the plaintiff as an abuser, the minute left the reader with the impression that there were conflicting views on the matter and was defamatory. **3.30**

Add to note 6. In *John Fairfax Publications Pty Ltd v Rivkin* [2003] HCA 50; 201 A.L.R. 77 at [187–188] Callinan J. said:

"It is true that an article has to be read as a whole. But that does not mean that matters that have been emphasized should be treated as if they have only the same impact or significance as matters which are treated differently. A headline, for example, expressed pithily and necessarily incompletely, but designed to catch the eye and give the reader a predisposition about what follows may well assume more importance than the latter . . . The order in which matters are dealt with can be significant. The capacity of the first paragraph of an article, the 'intro', to excite the reader's attention is a matter upon which editors place store. The language employed is also of relevance. Here for example, the articles speak of 'new information', 'details of a secret investigation', 'Sydney has developed an obsession', 'high profile', 'long running . . . saga', 'black box', 'money trail', 'no negative aspersions were ever drawn', 'bonfire of speculation', 'celebrity stock broker', 'executive assistant (in quotation marks)', 'hangout for ex-drug dealers', 'closest cronies', 'a very serious crime', and 'how easy it is to make a murder look like a suicide'. The intrusion of irrelevant information may raise questions as to the meaning intended to be, and actually conveyed: for example: 'Rivkin had 18 cars ranging from . . . ' and ' . . . share price jump . . . after a fire on Christmas Eve . . . '. True it may be that readers may take an article or articles on impression, but the fact that they may do so is likely to have the consequence that ideas and meanings conveyed by graphic language will create the strongest impressions. Of course publishers are entitled to use colourful and seductive language, but in using it they may run the risk of seducing readers into believing only what is colourful and on occasions scandalous, rather than the facts conveyed by straight reportage.

An even moderately attentive and reasonable, but not unduly suspicious reader of one or more of the articles here, would be bound to ask himself what each or all of them is or are really about: why is a financial newspaper dwelling and speculating on the 'mysterious' death of a young model; what is the 'bad' as opposed perhaps to the 'sad' business of which the publisher is speaking; why was there so much secrecy; what did Mr Wood and the respondent wish or need to conceal; did the respondent have a motive to procure the death of Ms Byrne; and why are Mr Byrne's allegations given so much prominence? The repetition of one person's allegations by a newspaper, particularly if accompanied by other, balanced material may not always necessarily carry as an imputation the substance of the allegations, but the fact that an apparently responsible financial and broadsheet publisher has chosen to repeat them may well give them a meaning, credibility and impact that they might not otherwise possess."

3.31   **Meaning collected from other parts of same publication or from other publications.** *Context, series of articles.* In *Galloway v Telegraph Group Ltd* [2004] EWHC 2786, QBD; [2005] E.M.L.R. 7 (this Supplement, para.14.91) the claimant sued in respect of a number of articles extending over two days issues of a newspaper. Eady J. was of the view that the context included reproductions of documents upon which the articles were founded but in respect of which no complaint was made and that in determining the meaning of the material published on the second day one had to bear in mind the impression likely to be left by the first day's coverage. "The reverse is not the case, since it is not permitted when attributing a meaning or meanings to a published article to refer to subsequent material" (at [50]).

There is some danger of over-elaboration in attributing the meaning to be derived by the reasonable reader to passages many pages apart in a book: *Oduro v Time-Life Entertainment Group Ltd* [2003] EWHC 1787, QBD at [18].

See also *Beran v John Fairfax Publications Pty Ltd* [2004] NSWCA 107 (two pieces in same issue so interlinked that the ordinary reader would have read them as one publication).

3.32   **Context and circumstances: spoken words and words published in jest.**

"While a reader may initially approach the article [in this case] as providing straight news, [it] . . . contains such a procession of improbable quotes and unlikely events that a reasonable reader could only conclude that the article was satirical. On balance, the obvious clues in the article itself, the [journal's] general and intentionally irreverent tone, its semi-regular publication of satire, as well as the satire's timing and commentary on a then-existing controversy, lead us to conclude that [the article] could not reasonably be understood as stating actual facts about [the plaintiffs]" (*New Times Inc. v Isaacks* 146 S.W. 3d 144 at 161 (Tex. 2004), (cert. den. June 6, 2005), citing *San Francisco Bay Guardian v Superior Court* 21 Cal.Rptr.2d 464 at 466 (Cal. Ct App. 1993) ("The very nature of parody . . . is to catch the reader off guard at first glance, after which the 'victim' recognizes that the joke is on him to the extent that it caught him unaware.").

CHAPTER 4

SLANDERS ACTIONABLE *PER SE*

SECTION 4. WORDS CALCULATED TO DISPARAGE IN ANY OFFICE, PROFESSION, CALLING, TRADE OR BUSINESS

Callings. The Ontario legislation is in similar terms and in *Romano v D'Ono-* **4.18** *frio* [2004] O.J. No. 4989, Ont. Sup. Ct, it was held that the plaintiff, a law student, could not rely on it. Nor (*obiter*) was the position of "folklore group representative" of an Italian folk dancing club an "office" within the meaning of the legislation.

Offices of profit and honour. In *Maccaba v Lichtenstein* [2004] EWHC 1580, **4.19** QBD (ruling on need for special damage) Gray J. held, not following *Robinson v Ward*, that the words of the 1952 Act were too clear to permit any distinction now being drawn between offices of profit and offices of honour. It was not therefore necessary to deal with the defendant's alternative submission that at common law the special rule governing imputations of unfitness in the form of want of integrity, corruption or dishonesty (see note 9) was confined to "public" offices, but Gray J.'s view was that it was not (at [23]). In any event, a jury, properly directed, could have found the words actionable per se at common law on the ground that the imputation justified removal from office (see note 10) (at [25]). The law on offices of profit and honour appears to be the same under the Malaysian Defamation Act 1957: *Dato' Seri Tiong King Sing v Datuk Justine Jinggut* [2003] 6 M.L.J. 433.

SECTION 5. WORDS IMPUTING UNCHASTITY TO FEMALE

Slander of Women Act 1891. *Kerr v Kennedy* was followed in *Fotu v Loketi* **4.20** [2003] TOSC 26, the Tongan legislation being in the same terms.

Chapter 5

SLANDER ACTIONABLE ONLY ON PROOF OF SPECIAL DAMAGE

5.2 **What constitutes special damage.** *Note 14.* In *Romano v D'Onofrio* [2004] O.J. No.4989, Ont. Sup. Ct, the reason for the failure of the plaintiff's slander claim was that his loss of the use of the facilities of a club was caused by his own decision to withdraw.

CHAPTER 6

PUBLICATION

SECTION 1. GENERAL PRINCIPLES

General principles: publication. *Limited publication.* Although it remains **6.1**
the law that publication of a libel to one person will suffice to establish a cause
of action (damage being presumed), it is now more likely than formerly that
where there is a limited publication which is unlikely to have caused the claimant
any significant harm the claim will be struck out as an abuse of process (see
Jameel (Yousef) v Dow Jones & Co. Inc. [2005] EWCA Civ 75; [2005] 2 W.L.R.
1614 and this Supplement, paras 3.6, 32.7 and 32.45). However, it is submitted
that this case should not be pushed too far and that it does not mean that any sort
of mass publication is necessary for a successful suit, otherwise claims for
slander (which sometimes lead to substantial awards of general damages) would
largely disappear. It is not difficult to conceive of claims for slanders or libels
with limited circulation which would cause the claimant great embarrassment or
distress or which might blight his financial prospects. Thus in *Crossland v
Wilkinson Hardware Stores Ltd* [2005] EWHC 481, QBD (where the context was
CPR Pt 24 rather than abuse of process) Tugendhat J. said at [57] that the:

> "fact that a libel or slander has been communicated only to very few publishees within
> an organisation does not of itself give any indication of what is at stake. For example,
> if one employee makes an allegation of dishonesty or sexual harassment at work against
> a claimant, then the claimant may have very much at stake in bringing a libel action.
> Without vindication, that single accusation may seriously impair or destroy his or her
> prospects of obtaining employment in the future."

An early decision on the modern approach to this aspect of abuse of process is
Schellenberg v BBC (see Main Work, para.18.27), where Eady J. had spoken of
the game not being worth the candle. However, the same judge in *Howe & Co.
v Burden* [2004] EWHC 196, QBD (a slander case) said:

> "It will be remembered that [in *Schellenberg*] there had been a lengthy trial which the
> claimant had abandoned without a definitive result having been achieved. The essential

[21]

point was that he had the opportunity in those proceedings of having a determination on the merits of substantively the same issues as those in the later action which came before me. That was the context of the remarks. It would not be right to elevate that phrase into a general principle of some kind to be applied in other libel actions.

It is important to note [in this case] that the allegations complained of in the recorded telephone conversations . . . are very serious. It was said of the Claimant firm . . . that acts or omissions had regularly taken place with regard to public funding which were not only professionally improper but also tanatamount to criminal offences. By contrast with the *Schellenberg* case, the Claimants have not yet had any opportunity of having those matters determined on the merits. It is to be noted that there is no plea of justification and, accordingly, any outcome would be predicated upon the presumption that these serious allegations are false. Mr. Price's submissions, if successful on any of the grounds put forward, would have the consequence that the Claimants would be prevented from achieving vindication in respect of those allegations through the court process" (at [5]–[6]).

The claim in *Dow Jones* arose from a worldwide publication but the material had only been published to five subscribers in England and, though there had not been any trial on the facts, it was contended that three of the subscribers were associates of the claimant and therefore "in his camp" and two had never heard of the claimant. The Court said that if it had been faced with an application to refuse service outside the jurisdiction it would have done so (such a decision was made in respect of a minimal publication in England as long ago as 1937—*Kroch v Rossell* [1937] 1 All E.R. 725). Furthermore, any trial was likely to circle around qualified privilege rather than justification and if the claimant succeeded the only vindication he could be said to have obtained was for the very small injury to his reputation in this country and even that would be on the basis only of the presumption of falsity which the law attached to defamatory words, since the truth of the allegation would not have been explored at the trial. It is true that the Court also said that *Duke of Brunswick v Harmer* would not now survive an application to dismiss on the ground of abuse of process (see this Supplement, para.6.7) and that involved no foreign element but it was a case where the plaintiff procured his servant to buy a copy of the libel many years after its initial publication and if "his agent read the article he is unlikely to have thought the Duke much, if any, the worse for it and, to the extent that he did, the Duke brought this on his own head" (at [56]). *Jameel* was distinguished in *Steinberg v Pritchard Englefield* [2005] EWCA Civ 288. Nonetheless, it seems likely that attempts to have the case dismissed on the ground of abuse of process will now become more frequent.

6.2   **General principles: multiple publication.** In *Harris v 718932 Pty Ltd* [2003] NSWCA 38, 56 N.S.W.L.R. 276 the court applied the basic principle so as to allow further action in respect of reprints of a book.

"The substance of the matter is that each print gave rise to separate causes of action or groups of causes of action. They arose at different times, against different defendants, and caused different damage. There is no discernible reason why a judgment in respect of the first print should bar proceedings in respect of the reprints, and as already mentioned any other rule would allow defamatory material to be republished after judgment with impunity" (at [29]).

Two defendants were persons who had supplied information included in the first print as well as the later ones, but who had not been sued in respect of the first print.

The clear tendency of the Canadian authorities is in favour of the English and Australian position and not in favour of the American single publication rule: *Carter v B.C. Federation of Foster Parents Association* [2005] BCCA 398 at [18]. The single publication rule in New York was considered by the Court of Appeals in *Firth v State* 775 N.E. 2d 463 (2002) where it was held that the addition of unrelated material to a website after the initial publication of the defamatory matter could not be equated with, say, the publication of a new edition of a book.

SECTION 2. PUBLICATION

Acts amounting to publication. *Internet, common law.* In *Carter v B.C.* **6.5**
Federation of Foster Parents Association [2005] BCCA 398 the defendant: (a) allowed a defamatory comment about the plaintiff to remain in its "chat room" for two years; and (b) distributed a newsletter containing the address of a third party chat room which also contained defamatory comments about the plaintiff. The defendant was held to have published the first each time the material was accessed but not to have published the material at the second address. The defendant had no control over the second address and had taken no active steps to draw attention to any defamatory content. However, the court at [13] left open the question of whether the same would apply to a website link.

Husband and wife. *Wennhak v Morgan* was applied in *Markisic v Middletons* **6.6**
Lawyers [2005] NSWSC 258.

Communication to claimant's agent. *Duke of Brunswick v Harmer.* "We do **6.7**
not believe that *Brunswick v Harmer* could today have survived an application to strike out for abuse of process. The Duke himself procured the republication to his agent of an article published many years before for the sole purpose of bringing legal proceedings that would not be met by a plea of limitation. If his agent read the article he is unlikely to have thought the Duke much, if any, the worse for it and, to the extent that he did, the Duke brought this on his own head. He acquired a technical cause of action but we would today condemn the entire exercise as an abuse of process" (*Jameel (Yousef) v Dow Jones & Co. Inc.* [2005] EWCA Civ 75; [2005] 2 W.L.R. 1614 at [56] (see also this Supplement, para.3.6)).

Publication by claimant. *Text to note 94.* So also where D defames an **6.12**
unnamed person and C reveals to others that he is the person referred to. Clearly this cannot apply as a general rule where C's revelation of his identity takes place before the publication, for that would be inconsistent with the clear principle that words which do not defame or identify the claimant to the ordinary reader may yet do so if they are published to persons who have special knowledge which makes them defamatory or enable them to identify him. However, it has been said to be arguable that no claim would lie if the claimant provided the information

at a time when he knew damaging publicity to be imminent: *Craven v Hidding* [2004] TASSC 247.

Whether republication by claimant a likely consequence. In *Wen Yue He v Chinese Newspapers Pty Ltd* [2005] NSWSC 253, where the plaintiff told his wife about a newspaper story, Greg James J. held that:

> "it is capable of being the natural and immediate consequence of there being displayed to the community in a newspaper the name one has or at least shares, the birth date one has or at least shares, the suburb of residence one has, or at least shares, and a student visa status one has or at least shares, in the context of an allegation of serious criminal conduct, even if what the paper has said about the person might be untrue, that the person would naturally, immediately and in consequence of that publication inform their partner whose life is so inextricably, and whose associations are so inextricably bound up with theirs, of the matter that had been published" (at [6]).

SECTION 3. PARTICULAR PUBLISHERS AND DISTRIBUTORS

6.18   **Distributors: special defence at common law.** See this Supplement, para.6.26.

6.26   **Relationship of the Defamation Act 1996 and the common law.** The Legal Deposit Libraries Act 2003 adds another layer to the story concerning those who are not publishers in the popular sense as from February 1, 2004. Under s.10(2) of the Act, a legal deposit library is not liable in damages for defamation in relation to activities related to deposited material unless it knows, or knows of facts or circumstances from which it ought to know, that the material contains a defamatory statement and it has had a reasonable opportunity since obtaining that knowledge to prevent its use. Nor, under s.10(3), is the publisher (i.e. in the commercial sense) liable in damages for defamation in respect of the use of the material unless it has similar knowledge or means of knowledge that the material contains a defamatory statement and has had a reasonable opportunity to inform the library and has not done so. The Act empowers the Secretary of State to make regulations (none have been traced) governing the direct "harvesting" of publications from the Internet by the libraries. Where works are copied in this way no person other than the library can be liable in damages for defamation in relation to activities related to copied material and the library is liable on the same basis as for deposited material (s.10(6)). Section 10 also contains provisions restricting criminal liability.

SECTION 4. REPUBLICATION AND REPETITION

(a) Liability of republisher

6.34   **Belief in statement or expressions of doubt as to its truth.** *Text to note 52.* See also *John Fairfax Publications Pty Ltd v Obeid* [2005] NSWCA 60, referring to possible different senses of "adoption".

(b) *Liability of the original publisher*

General principle. *Harding v Essey* [2005] WASCA 30 turned on the distinc-   **6.35**
tion between a defendant's liability for initial publication and for republication
by another. A newsletter issued to school canteens defamed a company by name
but made no reference to those who ran it. This was read by one F, who knew of
the connexion between the plaintiff E and the company but F read it because it
had been left lying around in a canteen. This may have amounted to republication
by the person responsible for the canteen but the case had been conducted below
on the basis that no liability for republication was in issue in view of the nature
of the pleadings. Accordingly E's action failed.

See also *Sarayiah v Suren* [2004] EWHC 1981, QBD (defendant having
reasonable prospect of defeating the claim based on responsibility for republication).

However, as to further, separate publication by the original publisher see this
Supplement, para.9.13.

Authority to repeat. *Text to note 75.* See also *Richards v New South Wales*   **6.36**
[2004] VSC 198 at [20].

Text to note 77. See also *Dato' Seri Tiong King Sing v Datuk Justine Jinggut*
[2003] 6 M.L.J. 433 (speech at political meeting; reporters known to be present).

Examples where evidence that republication should have been within   **6.39**
contemplation of defendant. In *Hunter v Gerald Duckworth Ltd* [2000] I.R. 510
the second defendant was author of a book, copies of which were sold in Ireland.
He had expressed the wish that it should not be sold there, but there was no term
in the contract with the publisher to that effect and the publishers had pointed out
the difficulty of preventing all copies reaching Ireland. Kelly J. held that, for the
purposes of jurisdiction under the Brussels Convention, publication of copies in
Ireland was the natural and probable consequence of delivery of the manuscript
to the publisher.

See also *Wen Yue He v Chinese Newspapers Pty Ltd* [2005] NSWSC 253; this
Supplement, para.6.12.

Privileged occasion. *Repetition on privileged occasion.* This conundrum was   **6.41**
discussed in *Belbin v McLean* [2004] QCA 181. The defendants published
statements defamatory of the plaintiff to their common employer. The employer
then, as was his duty, passed the complaints on to the Criminal Justice Commission. The plaintiff sued in respect of the publication to the employer and relied
on the republication to the CJC as increasing the damages (i.e. she took the
second course described in Main Work, para.6.35). A statute provided that in
"proceedings for defamation there is a defence of absolute privilege in respect of
a publication to or by the commission or an officer of the commission made for
the purpose of the discharge of the functions and responsibilities of the commission or of any of the functions of an organisational unit of the commission". The
Court of Appeal refused an application to strike out a defence based on the
statutory provision on the ground that it was necessary to determine factual
matters at trial. However, Muir J. expressed the view that as a general rule the

original publisher could shelter behind the defence available to the republisher and that he could see no reason why the defence was not capable of operation so as to meet a claim for damages "in respect of a publication" under the statute even if the effect of the defence is only to reduce the quantum of damages. However, *Erglis v Buckley* [2004] QCA 223, [2004] Qd. R. 599 (republication in Parliament) seems to proceed upon a different assumption, though this point was not in issue there and in later proceedings it was held that the initial publication was protected by absolute privilege: this Supplement, para.13.30.

IDENTITY OF THE PERSON DEFAMED

SECTION 1. REFERENCE TO THE CLAIMANT

Statement capable of referring to the claimant. Where a common name is **7.3** included in an article, the name itself will not suffice to identify any individual who bears that name. The context in which the name appears, coupled with the name may, however, do so: *Jameel (Yousef) v Dow Jones & Co. Inc.* [2005] EWCA Civ 75, [2005] 2 W.L.R. 1614 at [45]. See also *Carter-Clark v Random House Inc.* 793 N.Y.S. 2d 394, affirming 768 N.Y.S. 2d 290 (librarian in work of fiction purportedly seduced by Presidential candidate; plaintiff employee of library visited by Presidential candidate).

Claimant not directly referred to. See *Harding v Essey* [2005] WASCA 30 (director of company which was named in libel).

SECTION 2. INTENTION TO REFER TO THE CLAIMANT

The common law rule: intention immaterial. In *Richards v New South Wales* **7.5** [2004] VSC 198 the defendant Minister told a journalist that a company was flouting the law in relation to betting and this was the basis of a story in *The Australian*. The plaintiff controlled the company but neither the defendant nor the journalist knew of him at the time of the conversation. There was evidence that some people instinctively associated the company with the plaintiff and had read the article as referring to him. The defendant was responsible for the publication of the story (this Supplement, para.6.36). Bongiorno J. held that the newspaper story was published "of and concerning" the plaintiff. While the story itself contained the plaintiff's name, the readers had identified the plaintiff quite independently of that. The judge declined to consider a further argument to the effect that in any event the publication of the name in the story was a probable result of the conversation, because the journalist would be prompted to do further research.

Same rule where statement true of X but false and defamatory of C. **7.6** Although rather different from the situation dealt with in this paragraph, *Bashford v Information Australia (Newsletters) Pty Ltd* [2004] HCA 5; 204 A.L.R.

193 illustrates how a claim may arise from the identification of an individual and a company which bears his name. The defendants reported a decision of the Federal Court of Australia in which they stated that the Court had ascribed to the plaintiff, R.A. Bashford, conduct contravening the Trade Practices Act 1974 (C'th), though in fact the Court had ascribed it to the company controlled by him, R.A. Bashford Consulting Pty Ltd. As Kirby J. remarked, "on the face of things, so much fuss about the failure of the publisher to add 'three little words' . . . to its report about the judgment might seem a trifle precious", but the defendants had rebuffed a demand for a correction and apology. The majority of the High Court of Australia held that the report was privileged.

Suppose the defendant uses words which are treated as sufficient to identify A but intended to use them of B. Suppose also that there are facts in relation to B which would have enabled the defendant to establish an occasion of qualified privilege or that the words were published as comment on those facts if B had brought the claim. In *Rogers v Allen* (1989) 154 LSJS 95 the Full Court of the Supreme Court of South Australia held that that the defendant was not entitled to rely on privilege. In *Peek v Channel Seven Adelaide Pty Ltd* [2003] SASC 346 the plea of fair comment was struck out since the particulars of facts on which the comment was based had insufficient connection with the plaintiff. However, it was held to be arguable that facts pleaded which did not relate to the plaintiff could be relied on to support the contentions that the broadcast consisted of the discussion of government and political matters and that the broadcast was reasonable, for the purpose of the extended "*Lange* form" of qualified privilege (see Main Work, para.14.96). Compare *Loveless v Earl* [1999] E.M.L.R. 530 (Main Work, para.3.13 where, however, the issue was malice) and *Bonnick v Morris* [2002] UKPC 31; [2003] 1 A.C. 300 (Main Work, para.14.86, where the issue was meaning—but whether the words referred to the claimant is an aspect of meaning).

SECTION 3. CLAIMANT MEMBER OF A CLASS

7.9   **Words referring to a class.** *Note 68.* For this case on appeal see this Supplement, para.7.12, though the proposition in the text is not doubted.

7.10   *Examples: sufficient reference.* The *Ortenburg* case (note 78) was taken considerably further under the law of Quebec in *Malhab v Metromedia CMR Montreal Inc.* (2003) 226 D.L.R. (4th) 772, Quebec CA (class action allowed on behalf of 1,000 Arab and Haitian taxi drivers). See also *Prud'homme v Prud'-homme* 2002 SCC 85, [2002] 4 S.C.R. 663 and compare, under the common law, *Kenora (Town) Police Services Board v Savino* (1997), 20 C.P.C. (4th) 13, Ont. CA.

7.11   *Examples: insufficient reference.* Thus a police officer has no claim in respect of an allegation that the force is infected with "systemic racism": *Gauthier v Toronto Star Daily Newspapers Ltd* (2004) 245 D.L.R. (4th) 169, Ont. CA. See also *Friends of Falun Gong v Pacific Cultural Enterprise Inc.* 288 F. Supp. 2d 273 (E.D.N.Y. 2003), affirmed 109 Fed. Appdx. 442.

Words incapable of referring to whole group. In *Cornwall v Rowan* [2004] **7.12**
SASC 384; 90 S.A.S.R. 269, a programme asserted that "some staff" at a shelter
had harassed inmates. The Full Court did not consider that this could be read as
referring to all staff and therefore could not impute this misconduct to the
plaintiff administrator. No doubt there may have been lesser imputations such as
that "she may have been guilty of such misconduct, or associated with persons
who were guilty of such misconduct, or as administrator . . . did not take
adequate and proper steps to detect and prevent such misconduct", but these were
not pleaded.

Reference by association. See also *Richards v New South Wales* [2004] VSC **7.13**
198; this Supplement, para.7.5.

PARTIES: WHO MAY SUE AND BE SUED

SECTION 1. GENERAL

(a) *Right to sue*

8.1   **General rule.** *Assignment.* But it has been held to be arguable in Canada that where there is a libel on a corporation, which can only affect its goodwill, then, "although the [claim is] . . . nominally personal, because [its] effect is a business effect only, an assignee can have the type of interest in the claim that can be assigned, if it is shown at trial that there is no champertous aspect or effect of the assignment": *P.S.C. Industrial Services Canada Inc. v Ontario (Ministry of the Environment)* [2005] CanLII 27657 (Ont. CA) at [11].

SECTION 9. CORPORATIONS AND GOVERNMENTAL BODIES

(a) *Right to sue*

8.16   **Trading corporations.** In *Steel and Morris v UK* (2005) Application No.68416/01; [2005] E.M.L.R. 15 the ECtHR said at [94]–[95]:

"The Court . . . does not consider that the fact that the plaintiff in the present case was a large multinational company should in principle deprive it of a right to defend itself against defamatory allegations or entail that the applicants should not have been required to prove the truth of the statements made. It is true that large public companies inevitably and knowingly lay themselves open to close scrutiny of their acts and, as in the case of the businessmen and women who manage them, the limits of acceptable criticism are wider in the case of such companies (see *Fayed v the United Kingdom*, judgment of 21 September 1994, Series A no. 294–B, § 75). However, in addition to the public interest in open debate about business practices, there is a competing interest in protecting the commercial success and viability of companies, for the benefit of shareholders and employees, but also for the wider economic good. The State therefore enjoys a margin of appreciation as to the means it provides under domestic law to enable a company to challenge the truth, and limit the damage, of allegations which risk harming its reputation (see *Markt Intern Verlag GmbH and Beerman v Germany*, judgment of 20 November 1989, Series A no.165, §§ 33–38).

If, however, a State decides to provide such a remedy to a corporate body, it is essential, in order to safeguard the countervailing interests in free expression and open debate, that a measure of procedural fairness and equality of arms is provided for. The Court has already found that the lack of legal aid rendered the defamation proceedings unfair, in breach of Article 6 § 1. The inequality of arms and the difficulties under which the applicants laboured are also significant in assessing the proportionality of the interference under Article 10. As a result of the law as it stood in England and Wales, the applicants had the choice either to withdraw the leaflet and apologise to McDonald's, or bear the burden of proving, without legal aid, the truth of the allegations contained in it. Given the enormity and complexity of that undertaking, the Court does not consider that the correct balance was struck between the need to protect the applicants' rights to freedom of expression and the need to protect McDonald's rights and reputation. The more general interest in promoting the free circulation of information and ideas about the activities of powerful commercial entities, and the possible 'chilling' effect on others are also important factors to be considered in this context, bearing in mind the legitimate and important role that campaign groups can play in stimulating public discussion (see, for example, *Lingens v. Austria*, judgment of 8 July 1986, Series A no.103, § 44, *Bladet Troms* § 64, *Thorgeir Thorgeirson* § 68). The lack of procedural fairness and equality therefore gave rise to a breach of Article 10 in the present case."

The Strasbourg Court also regarded the damages awarded as excessive in the light of the defendants' lack of means: see this Supplement, para.9.2.

In principle, therefore, the Strasbourg Court does not regard as objectionable the application to companies of the general rule of English libel law that damage is presumed from publication. The Court of Appeal has reaffirmed that position in *Jameel (Mohammed) v Wall Street Journal Europe Sprl (No.2)* [2005] EWCA Civ 74; [2005] 2 W.L.R. 1577 and it remains the law that a company does not need to prove special damage to found its case. The same applies to a foreign company which has a trading reputation here, though it is "likely in practice that a foreign corporation which trades outside this jurisdiction but does not trade within it will have greater difficulty in establishing that it has a trading reputation within this jurisdiction. If it succeeds, however, the interests of justice require that the same principles of law should apply to its claim for defamation" (at [117]).

Difficult issues may arise over the assessment of damages in a case where a company is defamed. In *Collins Stewart Ltd v Financial Times Ltd* [2004]

EWHC 2337, QBD; [2005] E.M.L.R. 5 a libel action was brought by CS Ltd ("Ltd") and by its parent, CST Plc ("Plc"), which owned all its shares. The loss alleged to have been caused by the libel fell primarily on the revenue of Ltd but this, it was contended, had produced a large fall in the market share price of Plc. The general principle of company law is that a shareholder may not claim damages for diminution in the value of his shareholding caused by a wrong actionable by the company, for that diminution is merely a reflection of the harm to the company, which is the proper claimant: *Johnson v Gore-Wood* [2002] 2 A.C. 1. However, it was contended in *Collins Stewart* that, on the assumption that the article was defamatory of Plc, the diminution in the value of Plc's shares in the market (those shares being the property of neither Plc nor of Ltd but of Plc's shareholders) was recoverable as representing the net present value, as assessed by the market, of Plc's future loss of revenue derived from Ltd. Striking out particulars of special damage framed on this basis, Tugendhat J. said that, whether or not this approach infringed the "reflective loss" principle, to base damages on the whole market capitalisation of the company in this way was too uncertain. Furthermore, the claimants' particulars assumed that the market price of Plc's shares did not already reflect the chance of a judgment being obtained.

> "If the market price is assumed to be so rational as to afford a reliable measure of damage, then it is inconsistent to assume that there is not also factored into the market price of Plc's shares a figure which represents the market's assessment of the value for the present claim. It is not reasonable to postulate a market which is both rational enough to provide a sound measure of damages, but which does not also take into account the prospects of the claimant recovering compensation for the damage in legal proceedings of which the market is aware."

Note 80. On s.6 of the NZ Act see also *Chinese Herald Ltd v New Times Madia Ltd* [2004] N.Z.L.R. 749, where there was no evidence of injury to revenue or goodwill.

8.17   **Defamatory statements against company's officers.** In *Jameel v Times Newspapers Ltd* [2004] EWCA Civ 983; [2004] E.M.L.R. 31, where the company's claim was struck out, Sedley L.J. echoed the sentiments in the *Elite Model Management* case (note 97) and said at [35]:

> "It has to be kept well in mind that a limited liability company is a distinct legal person, not an extension of its proprietor (if I may adopt an imprecise but useful term). To defame the proprietor, even in an article which identifies the business as his, is not to defame the company unless the article also suggests that the company is itself implicated in the wrongdoing or suspicion of wrongdoing attributed to the individual, or that it merits investigation for the same reasons as its proprietor. This article suggests none of these things. At most it suggests that the profits derived by Mr Jameel from his financial interest in Hartwell—in other words money which is his, not the company's—has found its way into terrorist hands. That is not a pleasant thing for any company to contemplate, but it implies no wrongdoing on its part, nor even grounds for investigation."

If, however, the allegation were to be that the natural claimant, being the controller of the company, had procured funds to be diverted directly from the company to the terrorists, the conclusion must be that the company, too, is defamed, for the diversion would be the company's act. Indeed, if the company suffered a serious loss of business as a result of the allegations, it is difficult to see how the natural claimant could recover damages for that (as opposed to the injury to his reputation stemming from the procurement) since the loss is the company's and the diminution in the value of the natural claimant's shareholding is merely a reflection of the loss suffered by the company (see this Supplement, para.8.16. *Johnson v Gore-Wood* [2002] 2 A.C. 1).

Provided that the words reflect on the company, a campaign of defamation against officers of the company may cause damage to the company as well as to them as individuals (*Barrick Gold Corp. v Lopehandia* (2004) 71 O.R. (3d) 416, Ont. CA).

Governmental bodies. *Indemnity to officer, notes 27 and 28.* The Local **8.20** Authorities (Indemnities for Members and Officers) Order 2004, SI 2004/3082, confers power to grant indemnities to local authority members and officers. Paragraph 6(3) provides that no indemnity may be provided under the Order in relation to the making by a member or officer of any claim in relation to an alleged defamation of him (but an indemnity may be provided in relation to the defence by him of any allegation of defamation made against him). However, these powers are in addition to, and not in substitution for, powers under s.111 of the Local Government Act 1972 (see the *Comninos* case, Main Work, this para., note 28).

Right of individuals to sue: South Africa. There is no principle in South African law barring a claim by a cabinet minister without proof of malice: *Mthembi-Mahanyele v Mail & Guardian Ltd* [2004] ZASCA 67; 2004 (11) B.C.L.R 1182, Sup. Ct of Appeal of South Africa.

Section 10. Trade Unions

(a) *Right to sue*

Generally. In New South Wales it was held in *Robertson v John Fairfax* **8.23** *Publications Pty Ltd* [2003] NSWSC 473, 58 N.S.W.L.R. 246 that a trade union could sue for libel and was not affected by the *Derbyshire* principle. However, it is said that a trade union in NSW is a corporation (at [23]) and now the matter might be affected by s.8A of the N.S.W. Defamation Act 1974 (see Main Work, para.8.16).

Section 13. Vicarious Liability

Vicarious liability: its scope. For a discussion of vicarious liability for agents **8.29** in the context of defamation see *Cornwall v Rowan* [2004] SASC 384; 90 S.A.S.R. 269 at [460] *et seq.* (where, however, the actor was held not to be an agent).

CHAPTER 9

REMEDIES

SECTION 1. COMPENSATORY (GENERAL) DAMAGES

9.1   **Damages the primary remedy.** *Text to notes 4 and 5.* See *Jameel (Yousef) v Dow Jones & Co. Inc.* [2005] EWCA Civ 75; [2005] 2 W.L.R. 1614 at [67]:

"English law and procedure does not permit the court to make a declaration of falsity at the end of a libel action. Where justification has been pleaded the verdict of the jury will determine whether the defendant has justified the defamation. Where there is no plea of justification, the jury is directed to proceed on the presumption that the defamatory allegation is untrue. The damages that they award will indicate their view of the injustice that has been done to the claimant by the allegation that is presumed to have been untrue. To this extent an award of substantial damages provides vindication to the plaintiff. The presumption of falsity does not however leave the judge in a position to make a declaration to all the world that the allegation was false. In the present case, where the matter will not even be explored at the trial, the judge could not possibly be expected to declare, with confidence, that the claimant never [did the acts alleged]."

In *Chin Bay Ching v Merchant Ventures Pte. Ltd* [2005] SGCA 29; [2005] 3 S.L.R. 142 at [24] the Singapore CA expressed the view that "the fact that the courts have, to date, refrained from issuing mandatory injunctions does not mean that this remedy was not available in a defamation action". And see *TV3 Network Ltd v Eveready New Zealand Ltd* [1993] 3 N.Z.L.R. 435, NZCA.

However, it has been suggested that, in so far as Art.8 of the European Convention on Human Rights now gives protection to a person's reputation, it might be that the court, in an action against a public authority, could grant a declaration of falsity under s.7 of the Human Rights Act 1998, even if a claim for damages were defeated by absolute or qualified privilege (*W v Westminster City Council* [2004] EWHC 2866, QBD at [103]; this Supplement, para.21.12). Tugendhat J. summarised the common law position at [102]:

"Privilege is available as a defence in cases where the words complained of are, or may be, false. Of course, the claimant benefits from the presumption of falsity. But if he wishes to clear his name, and obtain public vindication, that is difficult to achieve. Even if he succeeds in defeating the defence of privilege, the court will not have investigated the truth or falsity of the words complained of, and his reputation will be vindicated only on the presumption of falsity. If he fails to defeat the plea of privilege, he gets nothing by way of damages. In either case he can point to the absence of a plea of justification, and to the presumption of falsity."

See also *Rackham v Sandy* [2005] EWHC 1354, QBD, this Supplement, para.1.8 (reasoned judgment in claimant's favour after trial by judge alone may justify lower award of damages).

Summary procedure: financial cap. In *Mahfouz v Ehrenfeld* [2005] EWHC 1156, QBD the allegation was of funding terrorism. Nothing had been done to mitigate the effect of the publication and on the claimants' application Eady J. made the maximum award of £10,000 and a declaration of falsity. Under s.9(1)(c) of the Defamation Act 1996 the Lord Chancellor has power to vary the figure of £10,000. By s.9(2A) inserted by Pt I of the Schedule to the Constitutional Reform Act 2005 (not yet in force) he is required to consult the Lord Chief Justice (or the Lord Chief Justice of Northern Ireland in relation to that jurisdiction) before doing so.

General damages compensatory. In *Steel and Morris v UK* (2005) Applica- **9.2** tion No.68416/01; [2005] E.M.L.R. 15 the primary ground of the applicants' success was that the denial of legal aid to them as defendants constituted a violation of Art.6 of the Convention. However, the ECtHR also held that there had been a violation of Art.10 by reason of the size of the awards of damages.

"Under the Convention, an award of damages for defamation must bear a reasonable relationship of proportionality to the injury to reputation suffered (see *Tolstoy Miloslavsky v. the United Kingdom*, judgment of 13 July 1995, Series A, No. 316-B, § 49). The Court notes on the one hand that the sums eventually awarded in the present case (£36,000 in the case of the first applicant and £40,000 in the case of the second applicant) although relatively moderate by contemporary standards in defamation cases in England and Wales, were very substantial when compared to the modest incomes and resources of the two applicants. While accepting, on the other hand, that the statements in the leaflet which were found to be untrue contained serious allegations, the Court observes that not only were the plaintiffs large and powerful corporate entities but that, in accordance with the principles of English law, they were not required to, and did not, establish that they had in fact suffered any financial loss as a result of the publication of the 'several thousand' copies of the leaflets found to have been distributed by the trial judge (see paragraph 45 above and compare, for example, *Hertel v. Switzerland*, cited above, § 49).
While it is true that no steps have to date been taken to enforce the damages award against either applicant, the fact remains that the substantial sums awarded against them have remained enforceable since the decision of the Court of Appeal. In these circumstances, the Court finds that the award of damages in the present case was disproportionate to the legitimate aim served" (at [96]–[97]).

The applicants were unwaged or in low-paid part-time work. No indication is given of what might have been a suitable figure in the circumstances. Given that it is extraordinarily difficult to prove consequential pecuniary loss in such cases, that there was no question in the original proceedings of exemplary damages and that a corporate claimant cannot suffer worry or distress (though the applicants did recover €20,000 and €15,000 as "non-pecuniary damage" for breach of the Convention) one could not have stigmatised as perverse a jury which awarded one-tenth of the sums which were in fact awarded. However, the damages were set by the Court of Appeal, which reduced Bell J.'s award somewhat in view of the applicants' success on some aspects of their substantive appeal. The libels were undoubtedly serious and the Court of Appeal's award could not possibly be regarded as extravagant. Furthermore, there is no indication that the ECtHR would have objected to the awards if they had been made against, say, a national newspaper. The case was, of course, a very untypical libel action but it seems clear that the ECtHR's reasoning is entirely inconsistent with English law's approach to general damages. These are compensatory and are based on the claimant's loss (difficult as it may be to assess what that is) and have nothing to do with whether the defendant can afford to pay them. Some European legal systems have provisions—apparently very rarely used—allowing a court to reduce tort damages if they would have a disproportionately damaging effect on the defendant (see, e.g. Art.6:109 of the Dutch Civil Code). See further this Supplement, para.33.28.

Causation and damages. The fact that it is generally difficult to show a direct causal link between the libel and loss of any particular earnings or other financial loss is adverted to in *The Gleaner Co. Ltd v Abrahams* [2003] UKPC 55 (which is now reported [2004] 1 A.C. 628) at [56]). "Nevertheless it is clear law that the jury are entitled to take these matters into account in the award of general damages. The strict requirements of proving causation are relaxed in return for moderation in the overall figure awarded." Subject to this, "factual causation" of damage is no doubt a necessary part of establishing a claim for substantial damages for libel and that involves a hypothetical question of what would have happened if the defendant had not published the defamatory words, but a claimant is not to be deprived of the substance of his remedy merely because the words might have been published by others or in circumstances in which there would have been a defence to a claim. If a Member of Parliament defames the claimant in an interview, he cannot contend that the damages should be nominal because he might have published the words in a speech in the House: *Galloway v Telegraph Group Ltd* [2004] EWHC 2786, QBD; [2005] E.M.L.R. 7 at [216]. The defendants (see this Supplement, para.14.91) published articles which accused the claimant of seeking to profit from dealings with the Saddam Hussein regime and the origins of the articles were documents found in Baghdad. However, the articles went beyond anything contained in the documents (of the publication of which no complaint was made). The defendants contended unsuccessfully that the documents would probably have come into the public domain eventually by some other route, that this would have damaged the claimant's reputation to some extent and that damages should be discounted accordingly. Permission to appeal on this point: [2005] EWCA Civ 435.

The internet. "It is true that in the modern era defamatory material may be communicated broadly and rapidly via other media as well. The international distribution of newspapers, syndicated wire services, facsimile transmissions, radio and satellite television broadcasting are but some examples. Nevertheless, internet defamation is distinguished from its less pervasive cousins, in terms of its potential to damage the reputation of individuals and corporations, by the features described above, especially its interactive nature, its potential for being taken at face value, and its absolute and immediate worldwide ubiquity and accessibility. The mode and extent of publication is therefore a particularly significant consideration in assessing damages in Internet defamation cases" (*Barrick Gold Corp. v Lopehandia* (2004) 71 O.R. (3d) 416 at [34], Ont. CA). Increasing the award of general damages from $15,000 to $75,000 and adding an exemplary award of $50,000, the majority of the Court observed that the "style" of the internet was not that of a traditional medium of communication and readers of bulletin boards might well take seriously attacks which might appear exaggerated or ludicrous in a newspaper.

Emails. "[T]he present case is concerned with emails which, given their content and ease of communication, may remain in circulation for the indefinite future. It is thus even more important for the plaintiff to be able to point to the sum awarded to 'convince a bystander of the baseness of the charge' in case 'the libel, driven underground, emerges from its lurking place at some future date' (see Hailsham L.C. in *Broome v Cassell*)" (Levine J. in *Markovic v White* [2004] NSWSC 37 at [21]).

Companies: effect of libel on share price. See *Collins Stewart Ltd v Financial Times Ltd* [2004] EWHC 2337, QBD; [2005] E.M.L.R. 5; this Supplement, para.8.16.

Text to note 19. While the level of damages should not be so high as unduly to curtail freedom of expression, "the court should be careful not to drive down damages in libel cases to a level which publishers might with equanimity be tempted to risk having to pay" (*Nail v News Group Newspapers Ltd* [2004] EWCA Civ 1708; [2005] E.M.L.R. 12 at [39]). The issue of deterrence is most often associated with conduct that would attract aggravated or exemplary damages (*ibid. Cf. Steel and Morris v UK*, above).

Text to note 22. See *Downtex plc v Flatley* [2004] EWHC 333. Similar libel on a corporation, so that distress was irrelevant. Proper figure would have been not less than £30,000 had the summary procedure cap not applied.

Text to notes 26–28. See *Campbell-James v Guardian Media Group plc* [2005] EWHC, QBD 893 at [10].

Text to notes 29–31. "Vindication includes the ability at some future date, if the libel resurfaces, to show by reference to a substantial award that it has been decisively rejected by the court" (*Downtex plc v Flatley* [2004] EWHC 333 at [27], *per* Tugendhat J.). However, in that case the claimant company had, before the trial, been restructured, changed its name and no longer traded in the same line. It was accepted that this would have been relevant to reduce the damages had the £10,000 cap under the summary procedure not been applicable.

Note 36. New South Wales. See also *Rogers v Nationwide News Pty Ltd* [2003] HCA 52; 201 A.L.R. 184; *Markovic v White* [2004] NSWSC 37. *Cf.* in Western Australia, *Cullen v White* [2003] WASC 153, much smaller sum in what seems a much worse case than *Markovic* (though there had been a default judgment against the defendant, who was resident in the United States and had never appeared).

Singapore. See also *Ei-Nets Ltd v Yeo Nai Meng* [2003] SGCA 48; [2004] 1 SLR 153 (imputation of fraud but with very limited circulation).

9.3 **Role of Court of Appeal.** The Irish practice on reviewing jury awards has been considered by the ECtHR in *Independent News and Media plc v Ireland* (2005) Application No.55120/00. The defendants published a story which imputed to the plaintiff, de R, a politician, involvement in or toleration of serious crime and support for anti-Semitism and violent Communist oppression. The jury awarded IR£300,000 and this was upheld by the Supreme Court. This was not the highest award ever made by an Irish libel jury but it was three times the amount in any case which had been appealed to and upheld by the Supreme Court. The Irish Supreme Court has rejected the *Rantzen/John* developments as an undue interference with the sanctity of the jury verdict (nor, where it does interfere, does it substitute its own figure rather than order a retrial). Nevertheless, the ECtHR dismissed the defendants' application. The direction to the jury had been marginally more specific than that in *Tolstoy Miloslavsky* and in the ECtHR's opinion the Irish Supreme Court more clearly enunciated the requirement of "proportionality" than the English courts did in the past.

Text to note 57. For Ontario see *Barrick Gold Corp. v Lopehandia* (2004) 71 O.R. (3d) 416, Ont. CA.

9.5 **Relevance of personal injury damages.** *Note 73.* The effect of s.46A(2) of the NSW Act was explained by Hayne J. in *Rogers v Nationwide News Pty Ltd* [2003] HCA 52, 201 A.L.R. 184 as follows:

"[74] In the end, what s 46A draws to attention is that damages awarded for defamation must take their proper place in the administration of justice. In particular, they must stand in a proper relationship with awards for the non-economic consequences of personal injury. The relationship which s 46A (2) identifies is not, however, some precise or mathematical relationship between particular cases of defamation and personal injury or between particular classes of such cases. To do that would compare the incomparable. Nonetheless, s 46A (2) should be understood as having two particular consequences of relevance to the present appeal.

[75] First, it invites attention to the nature of the injury done by defamation compared with the consequences of physical injury. The injury done by defamation, even if serious, is often evanescent. By contrast, some personal injuries are permanent and devastatingly disabling. One of the principal purposes of an award of damages for defamation is to vindicate the wrong that was done. By contrast, damages for personal injury can compensate, but cannot right the wrong that was done. Yet, in neither defamation nor in personal injuries is there any measure by which the compensation for the non-pecuniary loss which the particular plaintiff has suffered can be assessed except what is 'reasonable'.

[76] The second effect of s 46A (2) flows from both the reference to the 'general range' of damages allowed in personal injury cases and the inclusion, within the class of personal injury cases to be considered, of cases where the damages to be allowed are regulated by statute. Treating cases where the damages allowable are capped by statute as included within the 'general range' to be considered shows that those statutory limits

imposed in cases of motor or workplace accident are not to be taken as being indirectly imposed as limits on the amount to be allowed in defamation. But the reference to the general range of damages does identify the highest sums awarded for the non-economic consequences of personal injury as what might be called a presumptive outer limit to awards for defamation. So much follows from the fact that rarely, if ever, will the harm done by a defamation be greater than the most serious form of physical injury which leads to permanent and serious disabilities. And if that represents the presumptive outer limit to awards for defamation, each particular award that is made must find a place within a range which is marked out in that way."

See also Heydon J. at [188] *et seq.* There is now a statutory cap on non-economic damages for personal injury in NSW of A$384,000 (Civil Liability Act 2002). This is lower than the previous de facto ceiling under the common law and illustrates a problem of comparing personal injury and libel damages. As Heydon J. points out, statutory restrictions on personal injury damages are

"not to be explained by reason of a different perception of 'value'. [They are] . . . to be explained as resulting from a perception by the legislature that some classes of compensation have become too substantial and have gone beyond the capacity of those bodies which have to fund them to do so . . . The motivations are financially based, not value based" (at [191]).

Text to note 79. Modern considerations of the relevance of personal injury damages to libel have been in the context of the defamation of natural persons. In *Collins Stewart Ltd v Financial Times Ltd* [2004] EWHC 2337, QBD; [2005] E.M.L.R. 5 (this Supplement, para.8.16) it was conceded that a decline in the share price of a claimant company can be relevant to general damages on the footing that it is evidence of damage to the goodwill of the company but it was contended that the ceiling of about £200,000 would still apply. No decision was necessary on this point (at [31]).

Jury to deal with damages on the evidence. *Note 97, multiple publications* **9.8** *to similar effect.* See also *Cornwall v Rowan* [2004] SASC 384, 90 S.A.S.R. 269 at [790] *et seq.*

SECTION 2. AGGRAVATED DAMAGES

Aggravated damages. *Repetition of the libel.* But see now the remarks of **9.13** Gray J. in *Collins Stewart Ltd v Financial Times Ltd* [2005] EWHC 262, QBD (see further this Supplement, para.32.51).

"[26] . . . What is the position where a claimant is the subject of a series of articles? There are various possibilities. Assume that the defendant publishes three defamatory articles referring to the claimant, articles A, B and C. If articles B and C add to the damage caused by the publication of the original article A and are not defensible, then I think that articles B and C should in principle generally be made the subject of separate complaint as separate causes of action. To do so would make matters simpler and clearer for the jury (or judge) if and when it comes to assessing damages. If on the other hand articles B and C, whilst defamatory of and damaging to the claimant, do not repeat the libel which was contained in article A, it appears to me to be objectionable in principle to allow the claimant to rely on articles B and C in connection with damages recoverable for the publication of article A. Articles B and C would be separate torts giving rise to separate claims for damages. If on the other hand articles B and C consist in part of the repetition of the libel contained in article A and in part of other distinct libels on the claimant, formidable problems will in my opinion arise in disentangling the recoverable and the irrecoverable damage in respect of article A.

[27]. My starting point is therefore that there are sound reasons both of principle and of practice why a claimant, whether an individual or a corporation, should not be permitted to seek to recover increased damages in respect of the publication by the defendant of article A by reason of the publication by that defendant of subsequent articles B and C which are not themselves the subject of complaint."

It is, on the other hand, clearly established that where the gist of an article published by D is repeated by another person in circumstances for which D is responsible, the claimant may recover further damages in respect of the later publications without asserting separate claims against either D or the other publishers (though it is open to him to take that course: see Main Work, para.6.35).

Note 17. Despite *Carson*'s case, the current effect of failure to apologise in New South Wales seems to be as follows: first, it may be the basis of aggravated damages if it is part of a course of improper and unjustified conduct on the part of the defendant; secondly, it may affect the amount of hurt suffered by the plaintiff in relation to ordinary general damages (*Cotter v John Fairfax Publications Pty Ltd* [2003] NSWSC 503; *Markovic v White* [2004] NSWSC 37). In Malaysia, an unsuccessful plea of absolute privilege and a failure to apologise was not a basis for aggravated damages (*Joceline Tan Poh Choo v Muthusamy* [2003] 4 M.L.J. 494, Mal CA).

9.14   **Relationship of aggravated and other damages.** *Aggravated damages based on post-publication conduct. Rogacki v Belz* (2004) 243 D.L.R. (4th) 585, Ont. CA:

"[52] [W]e see no difficulty conceptually with the notion that a defendant can act without malice at the time of publication and with malice thereafter. That holds true regardless of the fact that the disparate findings may (and often will) rest upon the same evidence. Illogical though that may seem, it makes sense once it is understood that the focus of the inquiry into malice at the liability stage (the time of publication) is much narrower than the focus of the inquiry at the damages stage (pre-publication to the conclusion of the trial).

[53] The logic becomes especially apparent in those cases where the evidence of malice consists largely of post-publication conduct. For liability purposes, such conduct is treated as circumstantial evidence which the trier of fact may take into account in assessing the defendant's state of mind at the time of publication. Powerful though such evidence may be in establishing malice after the fact, it may fall short of establishing malice at the time of publication. In these circumstances, the disparate findings cannot be said to be inconsistent. On the contrary, both can exist."

Note 30. It has now been confirmed that aggravated damages are not available to a corporate claimant (*Collins Stewart Ltd v Financial Times Ltd* [2005] EWHC 262, QBD).

SECTION 3. EXEMPLARY DAMAGES

Nature of exemplary damages. *Note 45.* For Canada see also *Barrick Gold*   **9.15**
Corp. v Lopehandia (2004) 71 O.R. (3d) 416 at [34], Ont. CA.

SECTION 4. MULTIPLE PARTIES

Co-defendants: general. There is a detailed account of the history of con-   **9.22**
tribution between co-defamers in the English and Australian contexts in *Belan v*
Casey [2003] NSWSC 159, 57 N.S.W.L.R. 670.

Co-defendants: exemplary and aggravated damages. There is a valuable   **9.24**
discussion of the problems involved in awards of exemplary and aggravated
damages against joint tortfeasors in *De Reus v Gray* [2003] VSCA 84; 9 V.R. 432
(not a defamation case).

In *Konstantinidis v Foreign Media Pty Ltd* [2004] NSWSC 835 (earlier
proceedings [2003] NSWSC 1135) an award of $200,000 had been made against
one defendant but an award of only $100,000 was made against another because
his conduct did not exhibit the same aggravating factors.

CHAPTER 11

JUSTIFICATION (TRUTH)

11.1 **Terminology and policy.** *Note 1.* The basic test of liability in media cases in South Africa is whether the defendants behaved reasonably in publishing (see Main Work, para.14.99). In *Mthembi-Mahanyele v Mail & Guardian Ltd* [2004] ZASCA 67; 2004 (11) B.C.L.R 1182, Sup. Ct of Appeal of South Africa (this Supplement, para.14.99) Lewis J.A. preferred to frame this as whether the publication was "justifiable", which seems closer to ordinary usage than the technical meaning of that term in English law.

Note 9 and text. In a system which makes truth *simpliciter* a defence defamation and invasion of privacy are, logically, mutually exclusive. But once introduce an element of public benefit or interest and a potential overlap appears.

"Invasion of privacy can take many forms. Some may involve no publication of defamatory statements or material, such as, for instance, 'peeping Tom' cases. Others may be part and parcel of a defamatory publication as, for example, a statement that a person has blackmailed a medical practitioner because he failed to diagnose timeously that the person was suffering from cancer. The allegation of blackmail is destructive of *fama*; the allegation that the person suffers from cancer is not but it is an intrusion upon the right of privacy. In this example, there is no overlapping of the two *injuriae*. But where a published statement accuses a person of being addicted to pornography (a defamatory statement) the invasion of privacy is so inextricably enmeshed with the assault upon *fama* that the assessment of compensation for the assault upon *fama* will necessarily entail an evaluation of the impact upon both the public and the plaintiff of the publication of the fact (if it is true) that the person is addicted to pornography. To treat the invasion of privacy as a separately actionable delict in such a situation is akin to what would be an impermissible splitting of charges in the criminal law.

It is not necessary to decide whether the very institution of a separate claim for damages for invasion of privacy in circumstances such as those in the last-mentioned example is permissible. It is sufficient to say that where such a situation arises, it will seldom, if ever, be possible to quantify separately from the damages which ought to be awarded for the defamation, the damages which ought to be awarded for the concomitant invasion of privacy and, generally speaking, no such attempt should be made. Just as in the case of a concomitant affront to dignity, the damages (if any) should be merged into one globular amount" (*Independent Newspapers Holdings Ltd v Suliman* [2004] ZASCA 57 at [56]–[57] *per* Marais J.A.).

11.3 **The burden of proof.** In *Jameel (Mohammed) v Wall Street Journal Europe Sprl (No.2)* [2005] EWCA Civ 74; [2005] 2 W.L.R. 1577 the defendants contended that "the common law presumption that defamatory words are false is irrational and unnecessary and gravely prejudicial, and in breach of Article 10 and Article 6 of the European Convention on Human Rights". Permission to advance this ground of appeal was refused since the parties had conducted the case on the premise that any defamatory imputation was presumed to be untrue unless the defendants pleaded and proved justification. However, the Court of Appeal remarked that it was a far-reaching submission which would require a major change in the law of defamation (at [55]). An appeal to the House of Lords in this case is pending. In *Steel and Morris v UK* (2005) Application No.68416/01; [2005] E.M.L.R. 15 at [93] the ECtHR referred to the fact that in its *McVicar* judgment (Main Work, para.11.3) it "had held that it was not in principle incompatible with Article 10 to place on a defendant in libel proceedings the onus of proving to the civil standard the truth of defamatory statements." With regard to the presumption of falsity and *Reynolds* privilege, see this Supplement, para.14.88.

Repetition and rumour. *Text to notes 31 and 32.* In *Hamilton v Clifford* **11.4** [2004] EWHC 1542, QBD a statement "All I would say is that when it comes to judging who's telling the truth I totally believe what the young lady told me" was regarded as a clear endorsement or adoption of her allegation of criminality against the claimants. Other statements, however, were regarded as potentially capable of meaning only that there were reasonable grounds to suspect the claimants (see this Supplement, para.11.6).

Scope and application of the repetition rule. *Summary of the repetition rule.* **11.6** In *Musa King v Telegraph Group* [2004] EWCA Civ 613; [2004] E.M.L.R. 23 the court upheld the decision of Eady J., who had accepted the following formulation of counsel:

"(1) There is a rule of general application in defamation (dubbed the 'repetition rule' by Hirst LJ in *Shah*) whereby a defendant who has repeated an allegation of a defamatory nature about the claimant can only succeed in justifying it by proving the truth of the underlying allegation—not merely the fact that the allegation has been made;

(2) More specifically, where the nature of the plea is one of 'reasonable grounds to suspect', it is necessary to plead (and ultimately prove) the primary facts and matters giving rise to reasonable grounds of suspicion objectively judged;

(3) It is impermissible to plead as a primary fact the proposition that some person or persons (eg law enforcement authorities) announced, suspected or believed the claimant to be guilty;

(4) A defendant may (for example, in reliance upon the Civil Evidence Act 1995) adduce hearsay evidence to establish a primary fact—but this in no way undermines the rule that the statements (still less beliefs) of any individual cannot themselves serve as primary facts;

(5) Generally, it is necessary to plead allegations of fact tending to show that it was some conduct on the claimant's part that gave rise to the grounds of suspicion (the so-called 'conduct rule').

(6) It was held by [the CA] in *Chase* at [50]–[51] that this is not an absolute rule, and that for example 'strong circumstantial evidence' can itself contribute to reasonable grounds for suspicion.

(7) It is not permitted to rely upon post-publication events in order to establish the existence of reasonable grounds, since (by way of analogy with fair comment) the issue has to be judged as at the time of publication.

(8) A defendant may not confine the issue of reasonable grounds to particular facts of his own choosing, since the issue has to be determined against the overall factual position as it stood at the material time (including any true explanation the claimant

may have given for the apparently suspicious circumstances pleaded by the defendant).

(9) Unlike the rule applying in fair comment cases, the defendant may rely upon facts subsisting at the time of publication even if he was unaware of them at that time.

(10) A defendant may not plead particulars in such a way as to have the effect of transferring the burden to the claimant of having to disprove them."

On the application of the principles in the case, see this Supplement, para.27.10.

The repetition rule and conduct of the claimant. In *Hamilton v Clifford* [2004] EWHC 1542, QBD, M had alleged that the claimants had been involved in her rape but after an investigation it emerged that this was untrue and M was sentenced to three years' gaol. The defendant was a publicist who had taken charge of M's affairs and made statements about the matter in the media. A plea of justification was advanced in relation to that part of the claim which asserted that the statements bore the meaning that there were reasonable grounds for suspicion that the claimants were guilty of what M charged. However, neither the persistence of M's complaints nor the long drawn out police investigation could be relied on in support of the plea: they did not amount to evidence of conduct by the claimants nor circumstantial evidence implicating them.

It may be, however, that the proper meaning of the imputation is not that there are reasonable grounds to suspect the claimant of crime, a so-called "level 2" imputation, but the lesser (though still defamatory) meaning that there are sufficient grounds for investigation, a so-called "level 3" imputation (see para.3.26, see also *Miller v Associated Newspapers Ltd* [2005] EWHC 21, QBD; [2004] E.M.L.R. 33). The latter grounds may exist independently of the conduct of the claimant, indeed they may be based on pure hearsay, as in the case of a complaint which a police officer investigates. In *Jameel v Times Newspapers Ltd* [2003] EWHC 2609, QBD Gray J. held therefore that in such a case the plea of justification need not be based upon conduct by the claimant unless the basis asserted for the need for investigation was such conduct. The matter was not argued on appeal ([2004] EWCA Civ 983; [2004] E.M.L.R. 31) where it was held that the words were also capable of meaning that there were reasonable grounds to suspect the claimant's guilt. Sedley L.J. said:

"[29] The repetition rule, in essence, prevents a defendant from hiding behind the fact that he is only repeating what others have alleged. He can accordingly not justify the libel by proving that the allegations have been made, but only by proving that they are true. But if a level (iii) libel is to have any legal existence distinct from the first two levels, it has to be because it asserts something less than either guilt or conduct founding reasonable suspicion. If so, it ought to be possible in principle to justify it by pleading and proving no more than that a third party has alleged enough to warrant an investigation of the claimant's activities.

[30] This much, at least, might suggest that Gray J was right to hold that the repetition rule does not, or not always, apply to a level (iii) libel. But the consequences of so holding are disquieting. It means that, so long as a slur on an individual's reputation is cast in level (iii) terms, it can be justified by reliance on the bare fact of assertions made by others, without any need to make them good. The court which decided *Bennett* [*v News Group Newspapers Ltd* [2002] E.M.L.R. 860] was not asked to address this problem. Faced with it in the course of preparing to hear this appeal, it

seemed to me, first of all, that there was no prior reason why the repetition rule should apply to this third and novel class of libel; secondly, that there were defensible theoretical reasons why it should not; but thirdly that there were strong practical reasons why it should—among them that disapplying the rule will place a premium upon formulating slurs as level (iii) allegations and defending them unembarrassed by the otherwise general restraint on repeating the allegations of others."

This disquiet was shared by Eady J. in *Armstrong v Times Newspapers Ltd* [2004] EWHC 2928, QBD where the article referred to and summarised a book (written by another journalist on the same newspaper) raising "questions" about whether the claimant, a professional cyclist, had taken performance-enhancing drugs. The judge said (at [28]):

"The scattering throughout the article of the 'questions' formula suggests that this may have been the very strategy anticipated by Sedley L.J. Be that as it may, whenever a defendant seeks to rely on 'neutral reportage', whether for purposes of setting up a case of *Reynolds* privilege or to justify by reference to a 'level (iii)' libel, it is important to determine whether the public policy considerations which have led to the need for reportage to be protected are truly engaged, or whether it is simply a situation where the journalist is seeking to by-pass the constraints of the repetition rule and the well-established principles in English defamation law relating to the burden of proof. These rules are equally defensible in terms of public policy considerations which should be given their proper weight."

In the event, it was held that, taken as a whole, the article could only convey the higher, level 2, meaning that there were reasonable grounds to suspect that the claimant had used drugs (see this Supplement, para.3.26). The striking out of the plea of *Reynolds* privilege was reversed but not on this basis ([2005] EWCA Civ 1007; this Supplement, para.14.90).

Justification required of and limited to the imputation. Section 13 of the   **11.8** Civil Evidence Act 1968 (Main Work, para.33.16) provides that where the question whether the claimant did or did not commit a criminal offence is relevant to an issue arising in an action for libel or slander, proof that, at the time when that issue falls to be determined, he stands convicted of that offence shall be conclusive evidence that he committed that offence. A person stands convicted of an offence for this purpose even though there is an appeal pending against conviction: *Sarayiah v Suren* [2004] EWHC 1981, QBD. However, the issue there related only to the question of whether the third defendant had a real prospect of making out the defence of justification; it seems unlikely that a court would allow the claim to proceed to verdict if an appeal was pending. The case raised another issue on justification. Although the claimant's case lacked clarity, he appears to have contended that the third defendant was responsible for a publication by the second defendant to S, which included the imputation that the claimant was a stalker (though the express statement that the claimant had been stalking appears to have been made by the first defendant to the third defendant). The claimant's conviction under the Protection from Harassment Act 1997 was based on events between September 2002 and February 2003, whereas the claim was based upon a republication by the second defendant in 2001. Tugendhat J. held that the defendant had a real prospect of success on his plea of justification. That does not of course mean that he considered that the defence would succeed.

On the face of it, there is a certain tension between the prospect of such a defence succeeding and what is said in *Chase*. However, a criminal prosecution for such an offence, likely to be committed over a long period of time, will commonly be based on a "sample" of incidents which are most easily provable and it would seem unrealistic not to allow the defendant to rely on justification in such a case. In any event, the fact of the conviction under s.13 must be relevant on damages as "directly relevant background context" under *Burstein v Times Newspapers Ltd* (Main Work, para.11.16).

11.9　　　**Substantial justification sufficient.** When considering substantial truth it is important to "isolate the essential core of the libel and not to be distracted by inaccuracies around the edge—however substantial" (*Turcu v News Group Newspapers Ltd* [2005] EWHC 799, QBD at [105]). Journalists "need to be permitted a degree of exaggeration even in the context of factual assertions" (*ibid.* at [108]) and "one needs to consider whether the sting of a libel has been established having regard to its overall gravity and the relative significance of any elements of inaccuracy or exaggeration. Provided these criteria are applied, and the defence would otherwise succeed, it is no part of the court's function to penalise a defendant for sloppy journalism—still less for tastelessness of style" (*ibid.* at [111]).

11.11　　　**Specific and general meanings.** See also *Eastwood v Harper Collins Publishers Ltd* [2002] NICA 46 (allegation of untrustworthiness by one person in a deal with another cannot reasonably be taken to mean that the former is generally untrustworthy).

11.14　　　**Justification and the case advanced by the claimant: scope and effect of plea.** *McKeith v News Group Newspapers Ltd* [2005] EWHC 1162, QBD emphasises that, where there are distinct charges and the claimant sues only in respect of some of them, the practice of allowing the defendant to plead justification only in respect of those charges is founded upon the need to keep the scope of a libel action under control. The claimant was an author and broadcaster on nutrition and the defendants published an article which the claimant contended meant she was a charlatan because she had deceived the public about the nature of her qualifications. The defendants proposed to justify a pleaded meaning that the claimant made claims about food and nutrition which have no scientific basis. Eady J. struck out this plea:

> "The Claimant is entitled to confine the dispute to whether she has made false claims about her qualifications. That is an important and serious charge. She should not be saddled with having also to enter into an expensive open-ended inquiry about the merits of various nutritional theories. I apprehend that if the Defendant's allegations in the newspaper had been addressed solely to those the Claimant would not be litigating on the subject. If such an inquiry were permitted, the wealthy Defendant with all its resources will be placed in a position of unacceptable tactical and financial advantage over an individual litigant. In any event, these scientific issues may not all be capable of a definitive resolution through the judicial process" (at [21]).

An attempted amendment pleading that the claimant made claims which she knew to have no scientific basis and which she was not qualified to make was rejected: it was an attempt to provide a hook on which to hang the wide-ranging scientific investigation, it had never been raised earlier and was wholly lacking in particulars about the claimant's state of mind. As to qualified privilege, see this Supplement, para.14.87.

Note 20. The relationship between the meaning pleaded by the plaintiff and the scope of justification continues to give rise to difficulty in New Zealand, notwithstanding the recasting of the defence of truth in the Act of 1992. Section 8 provides:

> "(2) In proceedings for defamation based on only some of the matter contained in a publication, the defendant may allege and prove any facts contained in the whole of the publication.
> (3) In proceedings for defamation, a defence of truth shall succeed if—
>
> > (a) The defendant proves that the imputations contained in the matter that is the subject of the proceedings were true, or not materially different from the truth; or
> > (b) Where the proceedings are based on all or any of the matter contained in a publication, the defendant proves that the publication taken as a whole was in substance true, or was in substance not materially different from the truth."

This has been considered on several occasions but the fullest consideration is in *Haines v Television New Zealand Ltd* [2004] NZAR 513 (which refers to the earlier cases). In summary, Venning J. held:

(1) s.8(2) enables the defendant to refer to and prove any part of the publication, notwithstanding that the plaintiff complains only of part of it and overrules *Templeton v Jones* in that respect;
(2) the "imputations" referred to in s.8(3)(a) were those pleaded by the plaintiff and the paragraph did not allow the defendant to plead alternative meanings, so that *Crush*'s case remains the law;
(3) s.8(3)(b) did not allow the defendant to plead some lesser meaning encapsulated within the general imputation pleaded by the plaintiff, though he might seek to show that the proved facts alleged in the publication as a whole showed that imputation to be true.

Section 5 of the Defamation Act 1952. *Distinct charges.* Where a statement **11.15** is capable of bearing the meaning that the claimant is guilty of an offence or that there are reasonable grounds for suspecting him, those are not distinct charges for the purposes of s.5: *Armstrong v Times Newspapers Ltd* [2004] EWHC 2928, QBD (on appeal, but not on this point [2005] EWCA Civ 1007).

Justification and damages. There is no doubt that the claimant's bad reputa- **11.16** tion may be relevant to damages which are awarded for a libel which is not proved to be true. But may a defendant say "Your reputation is so bad that there is nothing left of it worthy to be compensated and the claim should be struck out altogether"? This argument was advanced in *Magee v MGN Ltd* [2003] IEHC 27, where the plaintiff, a person convicted and imprisoned for terrorist offences, was alleged to be planning to undermine the Northern Ireland peace process and commit various further offences. McKechnie J. said that while the plaintiff's reputation had been gravely and perhaps terminally damaged, yet the special circumstance of the Good Friday Agreement made it arguable that a jury could find in his favour:

> "[34] . . . I believe that society in general and as a whole, including its many classes and sections cognisable by law, has been acutely conscious of this historical process and has displayed, quite legitimately, an openness of reconciliation and a level of tolerance, if not acceptance, which heretofore would have been unimaginable. This society has shown a degree of forbearance toward people to whom previously it would not have countenanced. Amongst those people are individuals like the Plaintiff, to whom such tolerance is afforded I believe largely if not exclusively on account of their acceptance of, support for and participation in the process.
>
> [35] If this should be correct, in any substantial way it seems to me that I cannot say at this stage of the . . . proceedings that the Plaintiff's claim must fail. In other words, that it cannot possibly succeed. In other words, that before a properly representative jury he could not even argue that the imputations as alleged were defamatory of him. I cannot agree that this is necessarily so. In such altered circumstances I believe that the existence or not, as the case may be, of damage to reputation, is at least capable of argument."

The scope of *Burstein* was considered in *Turner v News Group Newspapers Ltd.* [2005] EWHC 892, QBD, a case on the offer of amends procedure (see this Supplement, para.18.6). Eady J. said that since the clause in the Defamation Bill to reverse the rule in *Scott v Sampson* (see note 41) had been rejected "it is reasonable to assume that [the concept of background context under *Burstein*] must be narrower than the proposed statutory wording (i.e. 'all facts affecting or liable to affect his reputation . . . in relation to the sector of his life to which the defamatory statement relates')" (at [19]). The allegations concerned the circumstances in which the claimant and his wife attended a BDSM club and the supposed pressure on her to indulge in sexual activities with other people, so the history of their attendance at the club and the wife's career as a model for explicit publications were held to be part of the background context. Eady J. said that he was "not persuaded that a defendant need always establish a direct causal link between the 'background context' and the fact of publication: that would be likely to lead to over-elaborate analysis in some cases, and detract from the flexibility which the Court of Appeal in the *Burstein* case clearly intended" (at [25]). The claimant's "self-invited exposure in the tabloid newspapers" was relevant to the extent to which he valued his privacy and "would, or would not, suffer hurt feelings by tabloid exposure on the subject of his marital relations". See also this Supplement, para.33.43.

CHAPTER 12

FAIR COMMENT

SECTION 2. COMMENT

(a) *Comment and fact*

The distinction. On the distinction between fact and opinion see also *Haines* **12.6**
v Television New Zealand Ltd [2004] NZAR 513. See this case at [74] for many
illustrative examples of the distinction from the pleadings (though the conclusions are no doubt all matters of opinion). See also this Supplement, paras 12.8
and 12.10.

> "If one says, 'If Mr Justice X took a bribe, he is not fit to hold office', that is not of itself
> defamatory of Mr Justice X. It would be true as a moral proposition whichever name
> appeared. It would equally be true of Mr Justice Y and Mr Justice Z. The function of
> a plea of fair comment is to defend a defamatory comment about the relevant claimant.
> I have never encountered a plea of fair comment in this conditional form previously and
> the reason is not far to seek. A statement in that form is not defamatory. Of course it
> may be, depending upon a particular context, that the words do give the impression that
> the claimant actually did the reprehensible act in question. If so, the appropriate defence
> would be one of justification, either on the basis of 'guilt' or perhaps 'reasonable
> grounds to suspect'" (*Galloway v Telegraph Group Ltd* [2004] EWHC 2786, QBD;
> [2005] E.M.L.R. 7 at [178] *per* Eady J.).

Fact and comment: the significance of supporting facts. *Note 40.* So in **12.7**
Buffery v Guardian Newspapers Ltd [2004] EWHC 1514, QBD no difficulty
seems to have arisen from the fact that it was a television programme aired once
that was the subject of the comment.

Construction. *Headlines. Galloway v Telegraph Group Ltd* [2004] EWHC **12.8**
2786, QBD; [2005] E.M.L.R. 7 illustrates the dangers of punchy headlines. A
leader about the claimant was headed "Saddam's Little Helper". If it had read,
"If Mr Galloway were Saddam's little helper, this would be a very serious matter
and should therefore be fully investigated" it would not, at least on a literal

reading, have been defamatory at all (see this Supplement, para.12.6). But the "eye-catching imperative" turned it into an assertion that the claimant was Saddam's little helper (at [181]). The following paragraphs contain other illustrations of assertions of fact in the leader unsuccessfully pleaded as comment. Thus:

> "The third paragraph contains the sentence that 'David Blair uncovered strong *prima facie* evidence that a British MP had been in the pay of a foreign dictator with whom this country had just been at war'. That is not comment. It is a classic example of a defamatory assertion that is susceptible to a defence of justification (along the lines of 'strong grounds to suspect')" (at [185]).
>
> "Lower down the question is asked, 'Where did the money go?' As Mr Rampton submits, that necessarily asserts that there was money paid to Mr Galloway and that it has 'gone' somewhere" (at [186]).

Overall, the "sting" was "factual rather than comment. It is the difference between tentative comment and a rush to judgment" (at [188]).

See also *John Fairfax Publications Pty Ltd v O'Shane* [2005] NSWCA 164, where the fact that the piece appeared in an "Opinion" section and was couched in "judgmental" language played a role in the decision.

12.10   **Inferences of fact as comment.** In *Hamilton v Clifford* [2004] EWHC 1542, QBD (as to which in relation to justification, see this Supplement, para.11.6) the defendant, having made statements which were held capable of bearing the meaning that there were reasonable grounds to suspect the claimants of criminality, based a plea of fair comment upon an opinion held by him that there were reasonable grounds for suspicion in view of the fact of the police investigation into the claimants. Eady J. struck out the defence. The allegation made by the defendant had to be treated as one of fact and the case of *Branson v Bower* was distinguishable because what was in issue was the nature of the claimant's motive for his actions, something which, although a question of fact, was unverifiable as an objective matter. The suggestion in the text that fair comment might cover an imputation that the claimant acted as he did because he had been bribed would therefore seem to go too far. In refusing leave to appeal, Pill L.J. said that it was not arguable that Eady J. had been wrong on this issue ([2004] EWCA Civ 1407 at [22]). There is no doubt that a liberal application of the proposition that a conclusion of fact may amount to a comment would go a long way to subvert the repetition rule (see Main Work, paras 11.4 *et seq.*) where the allegation was carefully framed. However, the line suggested is a difficult one to draw. In *Hamilton* the whole affair upon which the allegation of suspicion of criminality was based was a figment of the "victim's" imagination. In other cases, however, the question of whether the claimant committed a criminal offence may turn solely on whether he had the requisite *mens rea* and that is difficult to distinguish from the bad motive alleged in *Branson*.

For a case in which an allegation about the claimant's "lack of conscience" was arguably the subject of fair comment, see *Buffery v Guardian Newspapers Ltd* [2004] EWHC 1514, QBD. In *Oliver v C.C. Northumbria* [2003] EWHC 2417, QBD Gray J., though he did not decide the issue, was inclined to regard the assertion that what the claimant had said in a report was "unfounded" was fact but that the report was "discredited" was comment.

What is sufficient reference to supporting facts: context. In *Oliver v C.C.*   **12.12**
Northumbria [2003] EWHC 2417, QBD the claim was in respect of allegations that a report by the claimant had been shown to be "unfounded" and "discredited" as a result of an investigation by his superiors. No detail of the investigation was given. In rejecting the defence of fair comment Gray J. said at [30]:

> "[Counsel for the defendant] may be right in saying that the trend of modern authority is to adopt a more liberal approach to the availability of the defence of fair comment, but I do not think that the cases entitle the court effectively to dispense with the requirement that the publishee must be provided with sufficient information to judge for himself how far the opinion of the current commentator is well-founded."

See also *Buffery v Guardian Newspapers Ltd* [2004] EWHC 1514, QBD.

(b) *Facts sufficiently true*

Facts upon which comment is based must be true. In *Galloway v Telegraph*   **12.14**
Group Ltd [2004] EWHC 2786, QBD; [2005] E.M.L.R. 7 the defendants published articles alleging that the claimant had corrupt relations with the Saddam Hussein regime. Their main defence was qualified privilege (this Supplement, para.14.91) but they also relied on fair comment. The origin of the articles was documents found in Baghdad after the occupation. Eady J. held that, by analogy with the repetition rule in justification, one could not rely on the documents as facts upon which to base comment about the claimant (see [45]). If A makes a defamatory allegation of fact about C and B then comments adversely on C on the basis of that, B has to show that what A said was true (or was said under protection of privilege).

Note 86. See also *Rogacki v Belz* (2004) 243 D.L.R. (4th) 585, Ont. CA.

Comment on privileged statement. In *Galloway v Telegraph Group Ltd*   **12.20**
[2004] EWHC 2786, QBD; [2005] E.M.L.R. 7 one of the defendants' pleas of fair comment was that leader articles and headlines were fair comment upon their own articles alleging that the claimant was in the pay of Saddam Hussein. But since those allegations were held not to be protected by privilege (this Supplement, para.14.91; no attempt was made to plead justification) the fair comment defence fell with the privilege defence.

(c) *Words capable of being comment*

The domain of comment. *Note 33.* See also *Buffery v Guardian Newspapers*   **12.22**
Ltd [2004] EWHC 1514, QBD.

SECTION 3. A MATTER OF PUBLIC INTEREST

12.28 **Private lives and public interest.** *Text to note 71.* The context of *Millane v Nationwide News Pty Ltd* [2004] NSWSC 853 is "substantial truth" under s.15 of the NSW Defamation Act 1974 but that contains a requirement of public interest. The behaviour of the plaintiffs, real estate agents, towards tenants in a flat above their premises of which the plaintiffs wished to obtain vacant possession (but which was not being managed by them) was held to be a matter of public interest, though the matter was "not without doubt". The matter was not a mere private dispute between neighbours as it would have been if, say, the plaintiffs had been running a travel agency or a newsagent's shop. The interest of the public:

"would not be one of mere curiosity relating to a dispute between neighbours, but would be founded in a proper concern for how these real estate agents conducted themselves in circumstances where there was a dispute affecting their business and the dispute was of such a kind as to involve matters with which real estate agents had a particular interest—tenancies and the disputed occupation of property" (at [123]).

See also *Star Hotel Holdings Ltd v Newcastle Newspapers Pty Ltd* [2001] NSWSC 53.

In *Anderson v Ah Kit* [2004] WASC 94 the plaintiff sued on a report that animals at a private animal sanctuary had been caused suffering. A plea of fair comment was struck out: the animals were kept on private premises, there was no evidence that the plaintiff had opened the premises to the public or in any other way invited comment on his activities and "the fact a person's activities have excited the interest of others, including the media, does not of itself make those activities a matter of public interest in the sense that that concept is used in the defence of fair comment" (at [27]). Nor was the fact that an activity was governed by legislation enough to make it a matter of public interest for this purpose. Compare the *South Hetton* case, Main Work, para.12.32.

12.39 **Public performances and performers.** A "television programme transmitted on national television at prime time is plainly a matter of public interest, as is the nature of the programme, what it portrays, the calibre of the performance of the actors and the decision of the actors to participate in the programme" (Gray J. in *Buffery v Guardian Newspapers Ltd* [2004] EWHC 1514, QBD at [14]).

12.40 **Anything which may fairly be said to "invite comment" or "challenge public attention".** *Quality of products.* In *Delta Motor Corp. (Pty) Ltd v van der Merwe* [2004] ZASCA 61 the legend "Worst 4 × 4 × Far" inscribed by the owner on a broken-down truck was held within the scope of fair comment.

"The comment 'swakste 4 × 4 ver' is a skit on a well-known advertisement of another product, which calls itself the best 4 × 4 far. The respondent's adaptation of it is, of course, an exaggeration. But this does not make the comment malicious or change its nature to something other than a genuine expression of opinion. There is no factual basis for concluding that the respondent was actuated by malice. In the circumstances the description of the vehicle as the worst 4 × 4 by far because its chassis bent on a gravel road is a fair comment . . . Furthermore, and in so far as the comment is understood to extend to the product and not merely to the respondent's vehicle, the inference that other vehicles of the same make may present with similar problems on gravel roads arises as a logical and natural inference and cannot be regarded as unfair. It is part of the same fair comment" (at [15]).

CHAPTER 13

ABSOLUTE PRIVILEGE

SECTION 1. INTRODUCTION

13.1 **General principles.** In *W v Westminster City Council* [2004] EWHC 2866, QBD Tugendhat J., applied *S v Newham* to a publication in connection with a child protection case conference under the Children Act 1989 which imputed grounds to suspect the claimant of "grooming" a child for sexual abuse, the balance between the public interest in the welfare of children and the a claimant's interest in vindicating his reputation being comparable in both cases. Although in such a case no duty of care would be owed to the claimant for the purposes of a claim for negligence (*JD v East Berkshire Community Health NHS Trust* [2005] UKHL 23; [2005] 2 W.L.R. 993) that did not justify a defence of absolute privilege for defamation purposes, the burden of rebutting qualified privilege (which was clearly applicable) being a more substantial hurdle for the claimant to overcome than establishing negligence. See further, this Supplement, para.21.12.

SECTION 2. STATEMENTS MADE IN OR IN CONNECTION WITH JUDICIAL
PROCEEDINGS

13.5 **General rule.** *Foreign proceedings.* The question of whether the absolute privilege of those participating in judicial proceedings applies to foreign proceedings was considered in *Bell Group Ltd v Westpac Banking Corp. Ltd* [2004] WASC 162; 208 A.L.R. 491 in the context of an application, in Western Australian proceedings, to take the evidence of 80 persons in London, either before the judge sitting as a commissioner or by video link between London and

Western Australia. Owen J. held that it was unclear whether in such circumstances an English court would extend the scope of absolute privilege to words spoken in England for the purposes of the Australian proceedings, despite *Anderson v Gorrie* [1895] 1 Q.B. 668 (which involved proceedings for acts done by the judges of a colonial court). His Honour said (at [119]):

> "I would be surprised if the courts of the United Kingdom failed to extend immunity to this court in the circumstances envisaged in this application. But I cannot convert that surprise into a conclusion that the risk of the courts not doing so is either unreal or at an acceptable level. And in relation to the administration of justice generally, the comfort that might be gained from the shared heritage with the United Kingdom would not apply to other foreign jurisdictions."

However, he thought (though the point was not argued) that if the High Court in England were to issue a commission pursuant to a letter of request from the Australian court absolute privilege would attach by virtue of the commission.

Text to notes 42 et seq. That the absolute immunity for things done in judicial proceedings is not confined to claims for defamation is reaffirmed in *Heath v Metropolitan Police Commissioner* [2004] EWCA Civ 943 (members of police disciplinary board immune from suit in respect of allegation of sex discrimination in conduct of proceedings).

> "[It] attaches to anything said or done by anybody in the course of judicial proceedings whatever the nature of the claim made in respect of such behaviour or statement, except for suits for malicious prosecution and prosecution for perjury and proceedings for contempt of court. That is because the rule is there, not to protect the person whose conduct in court might prompt such a claim, but to protect the integrity of the judicial process and hence the public interest. Given that rationale for the rule, there can be no logical basis for differentiating between different types of claim in its application" (at [17] *per* Auld L.J.).

The immunity is well-established for judicial proceedings in general and the consideration of its "necessity" in cases such as *Taylor v Director of the Serious Fraud Office* (Main Work, para.13.12) proceeds:

> "on the basis that the necessity for the core immunity and its wide application to claims of all sorts is established. Necessity as a consideration arose in those cases in relation to more peripheral issues, in the main as to outer limits of the judicial process giving rise to the protection of the rule, for example in the investigation of and preparation for trial" (at [53]).

Nor is the immunity removed by the European Convention on Human Rights or the Equal Treatment Directive (EC Council Directive 76/207).

Categories of privilege. *Initiation of complaint.* See also *Murtough v Betham*   **13.6**
[2004] NSWSC 753; this Supplement, para.13.23.

(a) *Privilege of Judges and Jurors*

Privilege of judges. *Note 59. Rogers v Nationwide News Pty Ltd* is reported   **13.7**
at 201 A.L.R. 184. Gleeson C.J. and Gummow J. said (citations omitted) at [21]

in relation to the fair protected report defence under s.24 of the Defamation Act 1974 (NSW):

> "The delivery by a court of its reasons for judgment is part of the proceedings of the court. The reasons for judgment do not constitute a report of the proceedings to which the judgment relates; they constitute part of those proceedings. The court itself is not a 'person' within [the section]. Court officials who, in accordance with the practice of the court, undertake administrative acts involved in the publication of reasons for judgment are not persons engaged in the publication of reports of the court's proceedings; they are participating in those very proceedings. The legislative purpose of s 24(3) is to provide a defence to a person who publishes matter in reliance upon a protected report previously published by someone else, where that person does not have grounds for knowing the report to be unfair. It is not the purpose of the provision to treat court officials who administer that part of the business of the court which involves making available its reasons for judgment as publishers of reports of court proceedings."

(b) Privilege of Witnesses

13.12 **Extent of privilege.** *Note 1.* The question whether *Hall v Simons* (Main Work, para.13.14) has any effect on the immunity of expert witnesses in respect of *negligence* is considered in *Karling v Purdue* [2004] ScotCS 221; [2005] P.N.L.R. 13, OH (where the point is made that although *Hall* and *Darker* were decided within seven days of each other and there were common elements in the panels, neither case appears to refer to the other). However, if, as is submitted in para.13.14, *Hall v Simons* does not affect an advocate's liability for defamation, nor should it affect that liability of any sort of witness.

(c) Privilege of Lawyers

13.14 **Privilege of advocates.** *Former immunity from suit for negligence of advocates.* The HCA has declined to follow the lead of the HL in *Hall v Simons* and the immunity for negligence of advocates in Australia remains: *D'Orta-Ekenaike v Victoria Legal Aid* (2005) HCA 12; 214 A.L.R. 92.

13.15 **Extent of privilege.** *Note 28.* See also *Big Pond Communications 2000 Inc. v Kennedy* (2004) 236 D.L.R. (4th) 727 (statement of claim in action for breach of confidence against plaintiff; identifying file pathname at foot of page referred to plaintiff and "theft"; pathname part of statement of claim for purposes of absolute privilege).

SECTION 3. STATEMENTS MADE BEFORE OTHER TRIBUNALS HAVING FUNCTIONS OF A JUDICIAL NATURE

13.17 **General.** *Inquiries.* The Inquiries Act 2005 sets up a framework for inquiries set up by Ministers to look into matters of public concern. Such inquiries are not courts, their findings do not have legal effect and they have no power to determine civil or criminal liability. Their proceedings are not necessarily public.

However, s.37(3) of the Act provides that for the purposes of the law of defamation, the same privilege attaches to:

(a) any statement made in or for the purposes of proceedings before the inquiry (including the report and any interim report of the inquiry; and
(b) reports of proceedings before the inquiry as would be the case if those proceedings were proceedings before a court in the relevant part of the United Kingdom.

In other words, the privilege for the proceedings, the conclusions and press reports of the proceedings is absolute. Does (b) cover reports of the conclusions? In *Tsikata v Newspaper Publishing Ltd* [1997] 1 All E.R. 655 (Main Work, para.15.9) under different legislation, the conclusions were held to be "proceedings in public of the [public] inquiry". Furthermore, although the wording may leave something to be desired, no one ever seems to have doubted that a report of a court judgment is a "report of proceedings . . . before a court" for the purposes of s.14 of the Defamation Act 1996.

Immunity from any civil liability is granted to a member of the inquiry panel, assessors, counsel and solicitors to the inquiry and persons engaged to provide assistance to the inquiry in respect of any act done or omissions made during the course of the inquiry in the execution of their duties as such, or any act done or omission made in good faith in the purported execution of their duties as such (s.37(1), (2)). As to the relationship between the absolute privilege in defamation and the general judicial immunity, see Main Work, para.13.9.

As to ad hoc local authority inquiries, see this Supplement, para.15.23.

Examples: tribunals of a judicial nature. *Police disciplinary tribunal.* A   **13.23**
police disciplinary tribunal established by Regulations made under the Police Act 1964 was held to be a tribunal in respect of the proceedings of which there was absolute immunity from suit in *Heath v Metropolitan Police Commissioner* [2004] EWCA Civ 943. The essential features of the disciplinary hearing rendered it closely analogous to a judicial proceeding before a court of justice.

Office for the Supervision of Solicitors. In *Murtough v Betham* [2004] NSWSC 753 Buddin J. had to consider, for the purpose of a claim for malicious falsehood, the status of a complaint made by the defendants to the OSS in respect of alleged professional misconduct by the plaintiff in connection with his practice in England. It was common ground that the relevant law was that of England. His Honour said:

"[23] [Referring to *Lincoln v Daniels*, where a complaint to the Bar Council was held not to be the subject of absolute privilege] The Bar Council performs, it would appear, a substantially similar role to the OSS in that it does not ultimately hear and determine complaints against barristers. That is a matter for the Benchers of the Inns of Court and those proceedings are, as I have said, the subject of absolute privilege.

[24] *Lincoln v Daniels* has the advantage of being a decision of the Court of Appeal. Moreover, given its significance, it is somewhat surprising that it received no attention in *Gray v Avadis* [Main Work, para. 13.23]. It may be, in any event, that there is a material difference between the contents of a spontaneous voluntary complaint such as the one which was made in the present case and the contents of a response, such as the

one made in *Gray v Avadis*, to the OSS which has power to compel a response from a solicitor. That is not something however which falls to me to decide.

[25] I am not persuaded, upon that analysis of the authorities that the law on this issue in England and Wales can be said to have been finally determined. That being so, it cannot in my view be realistically contended that the plaintiff's proposition that absolute privilege does not provide a defence in the present case, is unarguable."

Text to notes 92 and 93. In *Hung v Gardiner* [2003] BCCA 257; 227 D.L.R. (4th) 282 the BCCA held that letters to the Law Society of British Columbia and the Certified General Accountants Association of British Columbia informing them of disciplinary action against the plaintiff were protected by absolute privilege even though neither body elected to take any further action. It was not contested that the two professional bodies, established by statute, had judicial functions for this purpose. See also *Hamouth v Edwards & Angell* [2005] BCCA 172 (Securities and Exchange Commission inquiry); *D v Kong* [2003] SGHC 165; [2003] 3 S.L.R. 146 (Complaints and Disciplinary Committees of Singapore Medical Council).

Section 5. Proceedings in Parliament

13.29   **The Bill of Rights.** For a review of the basis, background and justification of absolute privilege for statements in Parliament see *Buchanan v Jennings* [2004] UKPC 36; [2005] 1 A.C. 115 at [6]–[9] (this Supplement, para.13.30).

Note 34. In *Adams v Guardian Newspapers Ltd* [2003] ScotCS 131; 2003 S.L.T. 1058 Lord Reed, in concluding that the substantive law of Parliamentary privilege was the same on both sides of the border, said at [13] that no:

"difficulty arises . . . from the fact that the Bill of Rights was passed by the Convention Parliament in England and had its Scottish equivalent in the Claim of Right (the latter being less specific on the issue of freedom of speech). As Mitchell [*Constitutional Law,* 2nd ed.] explains (at page 125), doctrines of Parliamentary privilege were more fully developed in 1707 in England than in Scotland, and it was therefore natural that the greater should be accepted as the basis of the privileges of the Union Parliament (quite apart from the natural tendency of that Parliament to refer to precedents which were familiar to the majority of its members). The assignment of a particular local origin is in any event unlikely to be important, since the current scope of Parliamentary privilege depends on wider considerations."

Notes 37 and 38. *A v UK* is reported, (2003) 36 E.H.R.R. 51. In that case, it had been said by an MP in Parliament that the applicant was a "neighbour from hell". Her name and address had been given. The Applicant complained of interference with her rights under Art.6 and Art.8. The Court rejected her complaint, in spite of agreeing with her that the words complained of were entirely unnecessary. The Court said:

"[77] The Court concludes that the parliamentary immunity enjoyed by the MP in the present case pursued the legitimate aims of protecting free speech in Parliament and maintaining the separation of powers between the legislature and the judiciary."

And:

"[88] The Court agrees with the applicant's submissions to the effect that the allegations made about her in the MP's speech were extremely serious and clearly unnecessary in the context of a debate about municipal housing policy. The MP's repeated reference to the applicant's name and address was particularly regrettable. The Court considers that the unfortunate consequences of the MP's comments for the lives of the applicant and her children were entirely foreseeable. However, these factors cannot alter the Court's conclusion as to the proportionality of the parliamentary immunity at issue, since the creation of exceptions to that immunity, the application of which depended upon the individual facts of any particular case, would seriously undermine the legitimate aims pursued."

Extent of the privilege. *Statements repeated outside Parliament. Notes* **13.30** *53–57.* The Privy Council upheld the decision of the majority of the NZCA in *Buchanan v Jennings* ([2004] UKPC 36; [2005] 1 A.C. 115). The plaintiff was suing on the repetition and confirmation by reference in the newspaper story of what the defendant had said in the House of Representatives and that was not protected by absolute privilege. Nor did the adjudication of the claim offend Art.9 of the Bill of Rights by intruding into the proper sphere of the House.

"[I]f, as may happen, the absolute privilege of Parliament is abused, procedures exist both in New Zealand (Standing Orders of the House of Representatives, Orders 160–163) and in the United Kingdom (see *A v United Kingdom* 36 EHRR 917, 925, 938, paras 27, 86) to afford a remedy to a person defamed, and it is not the function of the court to provide one. In a case such as the present, however, reference is made to the parliamentary record only to prove the historical fact that certain words were uttered. The claim is founded on the later extra-parliamentary statement. The propriety of the member's behaviour as a parliamentarian will not be in issue. Nor will his state of mind, motive or intention when saying what he did in Parliament. The situation is analogous with that where a member repeats outside the House, in extenso, a statement previously made in the House. The claim will be directed solely to the extra-parliamentary republication, for which the parliamentary record will supply only the text" (at [18]).

Note that at [17] it is said that if a member chooses to repeat his statement outside Parliament, it "may very well be that in such circumstances the member may have the protection of qualified privilege". Presumably this is likely to be on the basis of *Reynolds v Times Newspapers*.

Statement in Parliament originating with defendant who is not a member. A member tables and/or reads in Parliament a document defamatory of C prepared by D, who is not a member. There is a publication to the member (but see below) but the member cannot be sued in respect of the "publication" in Parliament. Can C, notwithstanding the Bill of Rights, rely on the introduction of the document in Parliament and its dissemination thereby as a matter going to the damages recoverable (see Main Work, para.6.35)? Alternatively, can D rely on absolute privilege in respect of the whole affair on the ground that the submission of the document is a proceeding in Parliament?

The first question was considered by the Queensland CA in *Erglis v Buckley* [2004] QCA 223; [2004] Qd. R. 599. The plaintiff alleged that the defendants had made defamatory statements about her in a document which they had sent to a

Minister, at the Minister's invitation, and which was tabled and read in the Queensland Legislative Assembly. The plaintiff did not, of course, sue the Minister, nor did she contend that the defendants were liable for a further publication in the Assembly; rather she argued that that publication was a matter relevant to the assessment of damages in relation to the initial publication to the Minister. Philippides J. struck out this element of the claim ((2003) QSC 440).

> "[26] The plaintiff does not seek to question the motives or intention of the Minister in republishing the imputations. However, it is apparent on the pleadings as they presently stand, that the plaintiff intends to rely on what was said and done in the Assembly, in order to ask that inferences be drawn and to make submissions concerning the adverse consequences for the plaintiff flowing from the Minister's conduct. The plaintiff thus seeks to prove inferences which reflect on the propriety of the Minister's conduct in that it is sought to be asserted that the plaintiff was adversely affected by that conduct because it exacerbated the damage to her reputation (albeit that compensation for such damage is sought against the defendants, rather than the Minister). The plaintiff's intended use of the evidence is thus not merely confined to proof of the republication as a matter of historical record. Furthermore, what the plaintiff seeks to do is no less a 'questioning' of the Minister's conduct in the Assembly because the plaintiff seeks to sheet home liability for that conduct to the defendants as the original publishers, being precluded from suing the Minister.
> [27] Moreover, in relying on the republication as a matter which it is argued ought to be reflected in greater damages against the defendants, the plaintiff seeks to impeach the freedom of speech and debates or proceedings in the Assembly. A Member must not be inhibited from speaking freely in the Assembly and taking part in proceedings in the Assembly because of the risk that such conduct may result in an increased award of damages against another. The freedom of speech, debate and proceedings in the Assembly would be hindered, impeded and impaired and detrimentally or prejudicially affected if such considerations influenced what was said and done in Parliament. [. . .]
> [29] I conclude that the plaintiff seeks to rely on the republication in the Assembly not as a historical fact, but in order to question and impeach what was said and done by the Minister. In those circumstances, I am of the view that the plaintiff is seeking to rely on the republication in a manner contrary to s 8 of the Parliament of Queensland Act 2001."

A majority of the Court of Appeal allowed an appeal against the striking out, Jerrard J.A. dissenting. McPherson J.A. was of the opinion that the Minister would not:

> "have been inhibited in any way by the risk, if she had contemplated it, that, by doing so, the defendants might, if the plaintiff later brought these proceedings for defamation, be likely to incur liability for larger damages by reason of the potential for greater publicity following the Minister's action. Parliamentary democracy in Australia is, in my opinion, sufficiently vigorous not to be threatened by considerations like those . . . " (at [11]).

Fryberg J. was more doubtful about the effect on the Minister's behaviour and thought the issue could not be determined in isolation from the other question above, whether the publication *to* the Minister was protected as a proceeding in Parliament.

The other issue was addressed at the trial of the action (*Erglis v Buckley* [2005] QSC 25). Section 8 of the Parliament of Queensland Act 2001 (Qd.) is the equivalent of Art.9 of the Bill of Rights and s.9(2) of the Act is a partial definition of "proceedings in the Assembly" which is similar (but not identical) to s.13 of the Defamation Act 1996. Such proceedings are stated to include:

"(a) giving evidence before the Assembly, a committee or an inquiry; and
(b) evidence given before the Assembly, a committee or an inquiry; and
(c) presenting or submitting a document to the Assembly, a committee or an inquiry; and
(d) a document tabled in, or presented or submitted to, the Assembly, a committee or an inquiry; and
(e) preparing a document for the purposes of, or incidental to, transacting business mentioned in paragraph (a) or (c); and
(f) preparing, making or publishing a document (including a report) under the authority of the Assembly or a committee; and
(g) a document (including a report) prepared, made or published under the authority of the Assembly or a committee."

Helman J. held that the submission of the document to the Minister was protected under s.9(2). There had in fact been an ongoing debate in the Assembly on the matter to which the document related, but this was not necessary: the result would have been the same even if the matter had been first raised in the Assembly as a result of the tabling of the document. What was crucial was that the Minister, by agreeing to present the document, had "appropriated" it to the business of Parliament (at [37]).

"There could be no doubt that had [the Minister] herself written out a document at the meeting recording the views of the nurses so that she could present or submit it to the Assembly, her act of preparing the document would have been a proceeding in the Assembly . . . Similarly, had [the Minister] had a member of her staff write out such a document for that purpose the staff member's preparing the document would also have fallen within the expression 'proceedings in the Assembly'. There is, I think, no distinction of substance between, on the one hand, [the Minister's] preparing such a document herself or a staff member's doing it at her behest and, on the other hand, the defendants' doing it at her invitation when [the Minister] had made it clear that provided it was as had been discussed at the meeting she would present or submit it to the Assembly."

The contrary view expressed in *Rowley v Armstrong* [2000] QSC 88 was rejected. The position would, however, have been different if the defendants had merely sent an unsolicited letter to the Minister (*R. v Grassby* (1991) 55 A. Crim. R. 419 on the NSW legislation) or even if they had approached her and she had said she would consider the document (at [41]).

See also this Supplement, para.6.41.

In *Adams v Guardian Newspapers Ltd* [2003] ScotCS 131; 2003 S.L.T. 1058 an article accused an M.P. of leaking the confidential suicide note of another M.P. The note was not a "proceeding in Parliament" even though it was addressed to some other M.P.s.

Extent of privilege. Notes 47–48. Where a document is prepared otherwise than with a view to submission to Parliament, parliamentary privilege does not attach to all copies of the document under the Australian Act merely because a member proposes to table it in Parliament.

"It is for this reason that the tabling or retention of copy of a newspaper can not prevent the continued circulation of the paper or the receipt in evidence of another copy. Similarly, whilst . . . a document containing allegedly defamatory statements retained by a Member for a relevant purpose can not be obtained on discovery and used to prove such possession, the Member's possession for that purpose would not give rise to a wholesale application of privilege to other copies. If copies had also been supplied to newspapers for publication, the fact that the Member had decided to keep the copy in his or her possession for a relevant purpose would not prevent the copies supplied to the newspapers from being tendered in defamation proceedings against others" (*Szwarcbord v Gallop* (2002) 167 F.L.R. 262 at [22] *per* Crispin J.).

Similarly, "a Member of Parliament sued for defamation in respect of the publication of a letter for purposes unrelated to Parliamentary business could not effectively prevent the maintenance of the proceedings against him by the simple expedient of tabling the only copy of the offending letter" (at [23]). See also *Szuty v Smyth* [2004] ACTSC 77.

In note 48, *Thompson v Bradley* should read *Thomson v Broadley*.

SECTION 7. REPORTS OF JUDICIAL PROCEEDINGS

13.35   **Defamation Act 1996.** Although the case has nothing to do with defamation privilege for reports of court proceedings, the importance of the freedom of the press to report criminal trials has been emphasised by the House of Lords in *Re S (A Child) (Identification: Restrictions on Publication)* [2004] UKHL 47; [2005] 1 A.C. 593. It was held that it was correct to refuse an injunction prohibiting the publication of any material which might lead to the identification of a child of X, who was charged with the murder of another child, for that would have had the effect of prohibiting newspaper identification of X. Given the numerous statutory reporting restrictions (none of which was applicable) the courts should be reluctant to create another, potentially open-ended exception to the principle of open justice.

Prohibited reports. In *Nicol v Caledonian Newspapers Ltd* [2002] ScotCS 106; 2003 S.L.T. 109 libel proceedings were brought in respect of a report of a divorce case which was alleged to contravene the Judicial Proceedings (Regulation of Reports) Act 1926. The events took place before the coming into force of s.14 of the Defamation Act 1996, the former (probably absolute) privilege under the Law of Libel Amendment Act 1888 did not apply to Scotland so *qualified* privilege under Scots common law was relied on. Lady Paton held that contravention of the 1926 Act did not affect the privilege in defamation proceedings: the Act was directed at regulation of the press and the protection of public morals, not the alteration of private rights under the law of defamation. Nor was the matter altered by Art.8 of the European Convention on Human Rights.

Contents of documents not read in court. Note 91. The clear assumption in *Stern v Piper* [1997] Q.B. 123, CA that the reporting privilege does not cover documents which have not been read in open court would seem to require reconsideration. Under CPR, r.5.4(5) any non-party may obtain from the records of the court a copy of the claim form or (if the court gives permission) a copy of "any other document filed by a party, or communication between the court and a party or another person". Nowadays much evidence-in-chief is taken in the form of witness statements rather than being elicited by oral question and answer in court and there appears to be a presumption in favour of granting permission for access to such material. The press and public should not be deprived of access to material which in former times would have been available via a transcript (to which there is an absolute right on payment of the relevant charges) because of changes in court practice and a party opposing disclosure will not succeed with a bald, unparticularised assertion of confidentiality. See *Chan U Seek v Alvis Vehicles* [2004] EWHC 3092 (Ch); [2005] 3 All E.R. 155, sub nom. *Re Guardian Newspapers Ltd.* In that case the newspaper was allowed to have copies of pleadings and witness statements even though the judge was satisfied that its purpose was not to prepare a full report of the case but to follow up a newsworthy "spin-off" story from the proceedings. Although CPR, r.5.4 says nothing about privilege, it would seem odd, on the basis of the reasoning in *Chan U Seek*, if a newspaper which relied on a witness statement to prepare a report were to be deprived of the protection of privilege. *Chan U Seek* was a case which was part heard and then settled and it was held that CPR, r.5.4 was not limited to the time when the proceedings were on foot.

Furthermore, as is pointed out in the Main Work, para.15.11, a report of the contents of the claim form (which may include the particulars of claim) would seem to fall under para.5 of Pt I of Sch.1 to the Defamation Act 1996 (qualified privilege) but since access to other documents requires the court's permission, it may be difficult to say that they "are required by law to be open to public inspection". In *Jameel v Times Newspapers Ltd* [2005] EWHC 1219, QBD it was accepted that the particulars of claim in an American civil action and the "proffer" in a criminal prosecution fell within both para.2 (reports of court proceedings) and para.5 of Sch.1, but not a sealed appendix to the proffer which was not available to the public.

Meaning of "contemporaneously". Report on following day held contem-   **13.36**
poraneous under the similar Malaysian legislation: *Joceline Tan Poh Choo v Muthusamy* [2003] 4 M.L.J. 494, Mal. CA.

Abridged reports. *Report of part of proceedings.* See *Nationwide News Pty*   **13.40**
Ltd v Moodie [2003] WASCA 273 (parliamentary inquiry; this Supplement, para.14.104).

Publication of contents of documents not brought up in open court. See   **13.47**
this Supplement, para.13.35 on the effect of CPR, r.5.4.
See also *Joceline Tan Poh Choo v Muthusamy* [2003] 4 M.L.J. 494, Mal. CA.

SECTION 8. MISCELLANEOUS STATUTORY HEADS OF ABSOLUTE PRIVILEGE

The following additional instances of statutory absolute privilege have been   **13.49**
found:

Public Services Ombudsman (Wales) Act 2005, s.32.
Inquiries Act 2005, s.37 (see this Supplement, para.13.7).
Higher Education Act 2004, s.17.
Children Act 2004, Sch.1.
Housing Act 2004, Sch.12 (new Sch.2A to Housing Act 1996).
Pensions Act 2004, s.216.
Communications Act 2003, Sch.11.
Water Act 2003, s.55, Sch.4.
Scottish Public Services Ombudsman Act 2002 (asp), s.18.
Scottish Parliamentary Standards Commissioner Act 2002 (asp), s.17.
Transport Act 2000, s.18, Sch.10 (substituted by Enterprise Act 2002, s.278(1), Sch.25).
Ethical Standards in Public Life etc (Scotland) Act 2000 (asp) s.27.
Local Government (Scotland) Act 1973, s.103H, inserted by Ethical Standards in Public Life etc (Scotland) Act 2000 (asp), s.33.

CHAPTER 14

QUALIFIED PRIVILEGE AT COMMON LAW

SECTION 1. INTRODUCTION

Introduction. For the possibility that a claim under the Human Rights Act 1998 may outflank the protection of qualified privilege in some cases see *W v Westminster City Council* [2004] EWHC 2866, QBD; [2005] 1 F.L.R. 816 and [2005] EWHC 102, QBD; this Supplement, para.21.12. **14.1**

Nature of qualified privilege. Downtex plc v Flatley [2003] EWCA Civ 1282 is a difficult case. The defendant, who was in dispute with the claimants about the sale of a business, sent letters to suppliers of the claimants casting doubt upon the claimants' solvency and suggesting the calling of a creditors' meeting. Elias J. refused to strike out a plea of qualified privilege based on the community of interest among creditors since in the absence of the detailed examination of the facts which would occur at trial he could not say that it had no reasonable prospect of success. This was reversed by the Court of Appeal, which granted the claimants judgment for damages to be assessed. The only extended judgment is that of Potter L.J., who said at [47]:

"Summarising the position, therefore, it does not appear to me that, objectively, any imputation of insolvency or near insolvency could be objectively justified from the material which the defendants themselves relied upon as founding the plea of qualified privilege. With respect to the judge, it seems to me that, having rightly identified the necessity for the statement to be 'fairly warranted by the occasion', and having indicated that he understood the strength of the arguments of the claimants to the effect that it was not so warranted, he should have gone further. For the defendants, simply to express subjective 'concern' that the company was insolvent was insufficient. It appears clear from her skeleton argument below, and from para.16 of the judgment, that Miss

[65]

> Addy was effectively accepting that references in the letters went further than simply to suggest that Downtex was in poor financial health and imputed insolvency or imminent danger of insolvency. In those circumstances, it seems to me that the judge should have grasped the nettle and dealt with the question of whether or not Mr Flatley's concerns were objectively justified by the material on which he relied."

The difficulty with this is that it seems to strike at the root of the defence of qualified privilege by introducing an objective element into the defendant's perception of the facts upon which he acts by asking whether what he did was "fairly warranted" by the evidence available to him. On this basis, even though persons who are "careless, impulsive or irrational" are protected from a finding of malice (see [16.17]) they might yet find their defence defeated at an earlier stage (and without the benefit of a jury) by a ruling that there was no privileged occasion to begin with. In holding that unreasonable belief or carelessness was not malice, Lord Diplock in *Horrocks v Lowe* ([1975] A.C. at 150) said:

> "In greater or in less degree according to their temperaments, their training, their intelligence, they are swayed by prejudice, rely on intuition instead of reasoning, leap to conclusions on inadequate evidence and fail to recognise the cogency of material which might cast doubt on the validity of the conclusions they reach. But despite the imperfection of the mental process by which the belief is arrived at it may still be 'honest,' that is, a positive belief that the conclusions they have reached are true. The law demands no more."

On the basis of *Downtex*, it is difficult to see how one can ever reach that stage, because a leap to a conclusion on inadequate evidence will destroy the defence at the outset. Compare *Oliver v C.C. Northumbria* [2003] EWHC 2417, QBD; this Supplement, para.14.9, and *McCormack v Olsthoorn* [2004] IEHC 431, where a requirement of reasonable cause on an accusation of theft was specifically rejected.

This is not, of course, to say that automatically and in all circumstances a communication by one creditor to others will be protected by privilege (*cf.* Main Work, para.14.9, n.57) but on the facts of *Downtex* one would have thought that on the facts as the defendant must be taken to have believed them to be it was at least arguable (*cf. Aspro Travel v Owners Abroad Group*, Main Work, para.14.44).

In *Wood v C.C. West Midlands* [2004] EWCA Civ 1638; [2005] E.M.L.R. 20; this Supplement, para.14.35, qualified privilege was rejected at common law for the voluntary disclosure by the police of information about an arrest. May L.J. remarked at [64]:

> "In so far as the requisite duty needed to measure up to human rights considerations, [the] publications . . . were not in the circumstances proportionate to the legitimate aim [the publisher] was pursuing. But I think that that is really saying the same thing in a different language."

Section 2. Existing Relationships: Duty and Interest, General Principles

14.7   **Imprecision and overlap of duty and interest.** The principles of duty and interest "are stated at a very high level of abstraction and generality" (*Bashford*

v Information Australia (Newsletters) Pty Ltd [2004] HCA 5; 204 A.L.R. 193 at [10]).

Voluntary statements. Although the statement in the case was not "volun- **14.9** teered", *Oliver v C.C. Northumbria* [2003] EWHC 2417, QBD considers how far, even where there appears to be a privileged occasion in a well-established category, its requirements may be modified by "the circumstances of the case". The statement sued upon was made at a press conference called to respond to journalistic enquiries about a leaked report into allegations made about a murder investigation. It was incontrovertible that there was a legitimate public interest in the quality of the investigation, that the police force as a public body needed to respond to the enquiries and that it had a proper interest in defending the professionalism and competence of its officers. Rejecting the claimant's argument that the occasion would not be privileged if it could be shown that the report was not reasonable or objectively justifiable in view of alleged deficiencies in the way it had been prepared, Gray J. said, that the incontrovertible facts set out above:

> "and those facts alone, suffice to establish that the occasion of the publication of the press release was privileged. In my view, the factors listed by Mr. Suttle in his skeleton argument [i.e. the alleged deficiencies] . . . are relevant to the issue of malice and not to the question whether the occasion of the publication was privileged" (at [39]).

What is a duty. In *Maccaba v Lichtenstein* [2004] EWHC 1577, QBD; [2005] **14.10** E.M.L.R. 9 (ruling on qualified privilege) it was contended (though not clearly established) that the defendant, a Rabbi and an officer of the Beth Din of the Federation of Synagogues, was forbidden by Jewish law to use the words alleged and that therefore he could not be regarded as being under a duty to use them for the purposes of qualified privilege in the law of defamation. Gray J. rejected the view that Jewish law would operate as a trump card in this way.

> "In a secular English court . . . [the question of privilege] is ultimately one of public policy and public interest as identified in the English authorities. The answer to that question may be affected by some other system of law but it cannot and in my view should not be determined by a system of law other than English law" (at [17]).

Reciprocity of duty and interest. *Reciprocity dependent on particular facts.* **14.13** Although given in a dissenting judgment, the general thesis of McHugh J. in *Bashford v Information Australia (Newsletters) Pty Ltd* [2004] HCA 5; 204 A.L.R. 193 must, it is submitted, be correct, provided that one guards against taking an unreasonably narrow view of what information is germane to the inquiry made:

> "[63] The correct approach in determining the issue of qualified privilege is [that] . . . the court must consider all the circumstances and ask whether *this* publisher had a duty to publish or an interest in publishing *this* defamatory communication to *this* recipient. It does not ask whether the communication is for the common convenience and welfare of society. It does not, for example, ask whether it is for the common convenience and welfare of society to report that an employee has a criminal conviction. Instead, it asks whether this publisher had a duty to inform this recipient that the latter's employee had been convicted of a particular offence and whether this recipient had an interest in

receiving this information. That will depend on all the circumstances of the case. Depending on those circumstances, for example, there may be no corresponding duty and interest where the conviction occurred many years ago or where it could not possibly affect the employment."

Or, in fashionable terminology, the question of qualified privilege is "fact-sensitive". In *Howe & Co. v Burden* [2004] EWHC 196, QBD, a case of communication between co-employees about their employer's conduct, Eady J. held that it was not inevitable that qualified privilege would apply without investigation of the facts in all "off the peg" categories. See also, in the context of *Reynolds* privilege, *McKeith v News Group Newspapers Ltd* [2005] EWHC 1162, QBD, this Supplement, para.14.87.

SECTION 3. DUTY AND INTEREST: PARTICULAR SITUATIONS

(a) *Communications made in discharge of a duty*

14.23   **Subsequent communications.** In *Adoko v Pal* [2004] EWHC 25, QBD, D recommended C's professional services to X. D then discovered information to C's discredit and told X. Hooper J. held it to be beyond dispute that this was a privileged occasion.

14.28   **Credit agencies.** *Note 54.* In *Bashford v Information Australia (Newsletters) Pty Ltd* [2004] HCA 5; 204 A.L.R. 193 the majority of the High Court of Australia dismissed an appeal by the defendants. The defendants published a subscription newsletter on occupational health and safety. This contained a report of Federal Court of Australia proceedings involving a company called ACOHS in which it had been said that it was in the public interest that the circulation of "material safety data sheets" should not be too closely constrained by copyright. However, the report added erroneously (see this Supplement, para.7.6) that the plaintiff had been found by the Court to have engaged in a deceptive trade practice contrary to the Trade Practices Act 1974 (C'th). A majority of the High Court upheld the decision of the NSWCA in favour of the publication being on an occasion of qualified privilege. There is unanimity of view that *Macintosh v Dun* should not be taken as authority for the proposition that a profit motive on the part of the publisher should automatically take the case outside the protection of privilege. In the majority judgments there is much emphasis on the importance of occupational health and safety to society and on the fact that the defendants were in the business of informing those responsible for health and safety about risks rather than "trading in the characters of others". *Cf.* the dissent of McHugh J. (with which Callinan J. agreed):

"[62] By regarding the interest of the bulletin's recipients as simply an interest in receiving information concerning occupational health and safety matters, the Court of Appeal appears to have concluded that Information Australia's contractual promise to publish the bulletin to each subscriber constituted the required reciprocal duty. If the Court of Appeal had attempted to define the interest of each recipient more concretely and precisely, it would have seen that each recipient had no interest that created a reciprocal duty in Information Australia to publish the defamatory matter concerning Mr Bashford."

And:

> "[91] . . . Unlike the recipients of the communication in *Howe* [*v Lees*], the recipients of the bulletin had no direct interest in being informed that Mr Bashford had engaged in false and misleading conduct by publishing seriously misleading statements that had caused harm to the repute and goodwill of ACOHS. No evidence was led that the recipients, or any of them, had any imminent or even potential dealings with Mr Bashford that made it imperative that they be told of his misconduct. Because that is so, it is impossible to hold that Information Australia had any legal, moral or social duty to publish this communication containing defamatory material to the recipients. And as I have indicated, the recipients did not have 'a real and direct personal, trade, business or social concern' in information concerning Mr Bashford . . .
> [92] Nor did Information Australia make the communication in answer to a request for information concerning Mr Bashford or such people as the subscribers were likely to deal with in the future. Nor did it make the communication to protect its own interests . . .
> [93] Thus, for the purpose of the law of qualified privilege, Information Australia was a volunteer. It was in no different position to an ordinary citizen who informed the safety officers of a number of companies that Mr Bashford had published a false and misleading report that caused damage to ACOHS. A claim for qualified privilege by such a citizen would be hopeless. Information Australia's position is in fact worse than the claim of the hypothetical citizen: it has published the defamation to at least 900 persons. The extent of a publication is always a relevant matter in determining whether the occasion was privileged."

Cf. Gutnick v Dow Jones & Co. Inc. (No.4) [2004] VSC 138; 9 V.R. 369, where there was held to be no reciprocity of interest between the financial journal *Barron's* (and its online version) and its subscribers. It was said that *Bashford* turned on the narrow focus of the publication both in respect of its readership and its subject matter. In *Gutnick* the audience was anyone interested in business who was able to pay the subscription and the subject matter was anything connected with business: essentially the journal was not distinguishable from a serious newspaper with a financial section.

Volunteered statements in performance of a duty. There may be circum- **14.32** stances in which A will be able to claim privilege in respect of defamatory words about C published to B where that is necessary to enable A to communicate with C (e.g. by using B as an intermediary) (*Maccaba v Lichtenstein* [2004] EWHC 1577, QBD; [2005] E.M.L.R. 9 (ruling on qualified privilege) at [25]).

Volunteered statements in aid of justice. "A report, made to the appropriate **14.35** authorities, that a person has or may have committed a crime attracts qualified privilege" (*JD v East Berkshire Community Health NHS Trust* [2005] UKHL 23; [2005] 2 W.L.R. 993 at [77] *per* Lord Nicholls).

In *Wood v C.C. West Midlands* [2004] EWCA Civ 1638; [2005] E.M.L.R. 20, H had been arrested in connection with handling stolen vehicles found at his home (though in the event he was not convicted). The police communicated the fact of the arrest to various persons connected with vehicle salvage and added that H had been working for a company known as VSG, of which the claimant was a director. The Court of Appeal rejected an appeal based on the argument that the communications were privileged. There were circumstances in which it was legitimate for the police to disclose pre-conviction information for the purpose of preventing crime (see, e.g. *R. v C.C. North Wales, ex p. Thorpe* [1999] Q.B. 396) but this disclosure was in contravention of official guidelines and police regulations.

> "The police had no business, let alone duty, to make statements anticipating that [H] would be convicted . . . Nor did the police have secure information sufficient to justify statements that VSG were complicit with [H's] alleged criminality. Factual statements about [H's] arrest were one thing. But defamatory statements about VSG and, as it turned out, [the claimant] were quite another. These statements were . . . ill-considered and indiscriminate. They did not, as the judge held, sufficiently contribute to the prevention of crime or the protection of victims of crime to sustain a duty of disclosure" (at [64]).

14.40   **Relationships of trust and reliance.** See also *Maccaba v Lichtenstein* [2004] EWHC 1577, QB; [2005] E.M.L.R. 9 (ruling on qualified privilege) at [19] *et seq.*

(b) *Communications in pursuance of an interest*

14.44   **Business and commercial interests.** *Communications with creditors.* See *Downtex plc v Flatley* [2003] EWCA Civ 1282, this Supplement, para.14.1. See also *Alexander v Clegg* [2004] NZCA 91; [2004] 3 N.Z.L.R. 586 (network of distributors of products; those who shared a common interest in the functioning of the network had a duty to advise of perceived risks both to those who remained in the network and those who shifted allegiance).

14.49   **Reply to attack.** See also *Hamilton v Clifford* [2004] EWHC 1542, QBD; this Supplement, para.14.55.

14.50   **Reply to retort.** *Note 85 and text thereto.* In *Oliver v C.C. Northumbria* [2003] EWHC 2417, QBD Gray J. was of the opinion that knowledge of the validity of the criticism went to malice rather than the existence of privilege and pointed out that Staughton L.J. in *Fraser-Armstrong* spoke only in terms of malice.

14.55   **Defence of principal's interests.** A attacks the character of B. B responds by way of defence in a manner which is defamatory of A, but B knows the charge against him is well-founded. B is not protected by privilege: see Main Work, para.14.49. But suppose B's response is delivered via his agent C, who is unaware of the truth. The "correct analysis would almost certainly be" that C would be protected by privilege: *Richardson v Scwharzenegger* [2004] EWHC 2422, QBD.

> "Take the following scenario. If the first Defendant [B in the notation above] had issued a denial of the Claimant's story either directly or through agents acting on his behalf, *and* it were held that he knew that the Claimant's story was actually true, then he would lose the protection of privilege. If, however, he issued such a denial through agents and the agents themselves were not malicious, then they, if sued separately, might still claim the protection of privilege" (*per* Eady J. at [14]).

In *Hamilton v Clifford* [2004] EWHC 1542, QBD, the defendant acted as M's publicist in connection with her allegations against the claimants (subsequently shown to be unfounded) of complicity in rape and made statements which were capable of being defamatory of them. Although a defence of qualified privilege based on response to an attack by the claimants on his own character was allowed to go forward, an alternative plea of privilege on the basis that he was defending M's reputation was struck out. His own pleading had denied that he was M's agent and it was not possible to regard his position as analogous to that of the legal representative in *Regan v Taylor* (see [2004] EWCA Civ 1407 (permission to appeal refused)).

(c) *Complaints about public officers, persons in authority or with responsibilities towards the public*

Complaints and redress. In *Wong Sui Fung v Yip Siu Keung* [2003] HKEC **14.57** 1711, Ct of First Instance, the defendant was a neighbour of the plaintiff, a civil servant, and wrote letters to the head of the plaintiff's Section and to the Financial Secretary accusing the plaintiff of threatening and unneighbourly behaviour and non-payment of estate management fees and asking for an investigation. It was held that both letters were privileged, the first on the ground that, although it did not concern the plaintiff's performance of her public functions, her employer's disciplinary powers extended to conduct outside that area so long as the conduct related to her character, temperament, ethics and personal integrity; the second on the ground that the Financial Secretary, having a charge over the property, had sufficient interest in hearing of non-payment of management fees, even though his security would not be affected by any action taken to enforce them. It seems unlikely that such a case would go the same way here, but as with many aspects of defamation, the application of broad principles must be affected by local conditions and culture.

Public responsibilities. *Add to note 41.* In *Meade v Pugh* [2004] EWHC 408, **14.60** QBD at [11], it was said to be clear beyond argument that a report on the progress of a student under training was made on an occasion of qualified privilege.

(d) *Relevance*

Irrelevant statements not privileged: general principle. *Irrelevance: out-* **14.61** *side privilege or evidence of malice?* In *Maccaba v Lichtenstein* [2004] EWHC 1577, QBD; [2005] E.M.L.R. 9 (ruling on qualified privilege) at [12] Gray J. said, citing Lord Loreburn in *Adam v Ward*, that to lose the protection of privilege without malice the words had to be "not in any reasonable sense germane to the occasion of privilege". Eady J. in *Hamilton v Clifford* [2004] EWHC 1542, QBD at [77] inclined to the view that "in so far as there may be any inconsistency between Lord Diplock's approach [in *Horrocks v Lowe*] and that of their Lordships in *Adam v Ward*, it would appear to be appropriate to lean towards the later interpretation, which is the more generous in favour of free speech". However, he accepted that "there may be circumstances in which it would be possible for the judge to rule, on uncontroversial facts, that the allegations against the claimant were in no sense germane to the subject matter and thus exclude privilege ... But the irrelevance would need to be plain and obvious" (at [74]). In *W v Westminster City Council* [2004] EWHC 2866, QBD Tugendhat J. said that he agreed with Eady J.'s approach in *Lillie v Newcastle CC* of treating irrelevance as evidence of malice. *Cf. Wood v C.C. West Midlands* [2004] EWCA Civ 1638; [2004] E.M.L.R. 17 at [61].

In *Alexander v Clegg* [2004] NZCA 91; [2004] 3 N.Z.L.R. 586 the NZCA found it unnecessary "to attempt to resolve the conflicting views that, on the one hand, the relevant defamatory matter incorporated into a statement made on a privileged occasion will not be actionable outside the privilege but may be relevant to malice, and on the other hand that such irrelevancy removes the defamatory words beyond the pale of the privileged occasion and leaves them unprotected by it." However, had it been the first, notice and particulars of ill-will (i.e. malice) from the claimant would have been required under s.41 of the NZ Defamation Act 1992.

Note 52. The High Court of Australia, by a majority, dismissed the appeal in *Bashford v Information Australia (Newsletters) Pty Ltd* [2004] HCA 5; 204 A.L.R. 193. There is little discussion of the impact of relevance. However, the appellants' case was framed in terms that the "part of the matter which defamed the appellant was not sufficiently connected to the occasion to attract the defence" (at [7]) and the dismissal of the appeal may be taken to be consistent with the view argued in the text. Callinan J., who dissented on the issue of whether the material complained of *was* relevant, suggests at [236] that where there is material which is relevant and irrelevant to the privilege, the inclusion of the irrelevant part in the communication affords evidence of malice and can destroy the privilege attaching to the relevant part. Whether one regards relevance as going to the scope of the privilege or as to malice may be particularly significant where it is sought to rely on qualified privilege at common law in respect of media publication, given the general reluctance to apply the "pure" form of privilege to such publications (see Main Work, paras 14.81 *et seq.*). In *El Azzi v Nationwide News Pty Ltd* [2005] NSWSC 247 the police issued an appeal for information on a gangland killing. In publishing this, the defendants added further material implicating the plaintiff in criminality. Levine J. was prepared to accept that the publication of the appeal was privileged, but not the additional material.

14.62   **Excess and exaggeration not irrelevance.** *Note 67. Bashford* case, appeal dismissed ([2004] HCA 5; 204 A.L.R. 193), the High Court being similarly divided.

14.65   **Answers to attacks.** See also *Hamilton v Clifford* [2004] EWHC 1542, QBD at [63] *et seq.*

14.66   **Counter-attack on credibility.** See also *Alexander v Clegg* [2004] NZCA 91; [2004] 3 N.Z.L.R. 586, NZCA: the judge "was wrong to find, in effect, that the [defendants] had to keep one hand behind their backs and were permitted to retaliate to only some of the appellants' blows" (at [63]).

(e) *Excessive publication*

14.68   **Unnecessary publication.** See, however, *Hewitt v Grunwald* [2004] EWHC 2959, QBD, where Eady J. declined to strike out a plea relating to a website publication aimed at British Jews on the ground that it might come to the attention of "uninterested" persons. "If one tries to think of an alternative method of communicating information to British Jews about terrorism, and the sources of funds for that purpose, it is not easy to arrive at a solution. It could hardly be suggested that the Board [of Deputies] should address their information by individual letters to each and every Jew in the country" (at [74]). He referred to the words of Brett L.J. in *Williamson v Freer* quoted in para.14.68 as sounding "a little quaint in the context of the internet and Article 10 of the European Convention on Human Rights" (at [73]). However, in fairness to Brett L.J. the telegrams in that case contained accusations of theft by the plaintiff from her employer, not international terrorism.

Reasonable to take risk of publication to uninterested persons. *Publication*   **14.75**
to uninterested persons: reply to attack. In *Harding v Essey* [2005] WASCA 30 a newsletter addressed to 178 school canteens in Western Australia defamed the plaintiff company. The plaintiffs, not knowing to which it had been sent, circulated a response to all 1,000 school canteens. The majority of the court held on a counterclaim in respect of the response that the plea of qualified privilege based on reply to attack failed: the company should have first sought information from those who issued the newsletter about its distribution.

SECTION 4. PUBLICATION IN THE MEDIA: *REYNOLDS V TIMES NEWSPAPERS LTD*

Background. In *Hewitt v Grunwald* [2004] EWHC 2959, QBD the defendants   **14.81**
published statements on the Internet to the effect that the claimants' organisation was involved in the support of terrorism. The plea of qualified privilege (which Eady J. declined to strike out) was:

"based upon a more traditional form of common law qualified privilege, uncomplicated by the refinements of their Lordships in [*Reynolds*]. In other words, the case is expressed in terms of a duty, owed to the Jewish community to inform them of developments, and/or upon a common and corresponding interest between the Jewish community and the Defendants in the subject matter of the website postings."

Lord Nicholls' 10 factors in *Reynolds* are not to be approached "artificially as   **14.83**
though they occupied separate compartments" and the gravity of the allegation "permeates through and affects most, if not all," of the other matters (*Jameel v Wall Street Journal Europe Sprl (No.2)* [2004] EWHC 37, QBD; [2004] E.M.L.R. 11 at [39]; this Supplement, paras 14.87, 14.91). In particular:

"a failure to put allegations to a claimant is not necessarily determinative (as the judge himself recognised). After all, in *Reynolds* no effort was made to contact Mr Reynolds before publication, and his defence, as given in the Dail, did not feature at all in the article complained of. Nevertheless, following a full trial of the action, the House of Lords was split 3–2 on the question whether this was fatal to the defence of qualified privilege. In *GKR Karate v Yorkshire Post (No.2)* [2000] E.M.L.R. 410 Popplewell J., at the end of the trial of the action, upheld a defence of *Reynolds* privilege, notwithstanding the fact that the journalist had made only one inadequate attempt to put damaging allegations to the claimant. After referring to Lord Nicholls's seventh factor in *Reynolds* Popplewell J simply said that this criticism of the journalist was a matter to be put in the balance on the claimant's behalf" (*Armstrong v Times Newspapers Ltd* [2005] EWCA Civ 1007 at [82]; this Supplement, para.14.90).

14.84   The impact of the European Convention on Human Rights.

"The reasoning and guidance given in the appellate courts in England over recent years, including that in *Reynolds* itself, is supposed to be Convention compliant . . . it is not, therefore, for individual judges in any case which comes along to apply and interpret the Convention afresh. If one applies the English law of defamation properly, there should be no reason to think that the principles underlying the Convention are infringed . . . This is more particularly so with the regard to appellate decisions which expressly advert to the Convention and its compatibility with English law" (*Galloway v Telegraph Ltd* [2004] EWHC 2786, QBD; [2005] E.M.L.R. 7 at [132]).

Nevertheless, it may be necessary to examine recent decisions from Strasbourg. Thus in *Galloway* Eady J. considered *Selistö v Finland* (2004) Application No.56767/00; [2005] E.M.L.R. 8, the judgment in which had been delivered on the second day of the *Galloway* trial (see this Supplement, para.14.91).

14.86   The application of the factors referred to in *Reynolds*: the test of responsible journalism. There can be no doubt that in English law the court is the final arbiter of what is "responsible journalism". *Cf.* the (to us, startling) assertion of the European Court of Human Rights in *Selistö v Finland* (2004) Application No.56767/00; [2005] E.M.L.R. 8 at [59]: "The methods of objective and balanced reporting may vary considerably, depending among other things on the medium in question; *it is not for the Court, any more than it is for the national courts, to substitute its own views for those of the press as to what techniques of reporting should be adopted by journalists*" (emphasis added). See this Supplement, para.23.18.

Publisher's belief. The relevance of the publisher's belief to the *Reynolds* privilege was considered in *Jameel (Mohammed) v Wall Street Journal Europe Sprl* [2005] EWCA Civ 74; [2005] 2 W.L.R. 1577 (an appeal to the House of Lords in this case is pending), which arose from an article to the effect that the claimant's group of companies was on the list of those the accounts of which were being monitored by US authorities in connection with inquiries into terrorism (see this Supplement, para.14.91). Although matters of subjective belief have traditionally been in issue in qualified privilege cases over malice, which will not be relevant in a *Reynolds* case (see Main Work, para.16.21) yet:

"in seeking to demonstrate that a publication accords with the requirements of responsible journalism, a publisher will almost certainly wish to adduce evidence of the subjective belief of those responsible for the publication. To demonstrate that it was reasonable to believe that a defamatory article was true, the writer is likely to be called to give evidence of why he thought that it was true. To demonstrate that it was reasonable to believe that a third party was conducting an investigation, or inquiry, or monitoring, the writer is likely to be called to explain why he believed this to be the case. To demonstrate that it was reasonable not to appreciate that an article bore a defamatory meaning [see *Bonnick v Morris*, below] the writer is likely to be called to say that he did not appreciate this" (at [27]).

It may, therefore, be "necessary or at least admissible for a defendant to allege and prove subjective belief in order to establish a defence of *Reynolds* privilege" (at [29]). However, as *Al Fagih* (Main Work, para.14.90) shows, this does not mean that the publisher necessarily and in all cases need have a belief that allegations he reports are true. Where belief is in issue, all of Lord Nicholls' criteria in *Reynolds* are predicated on the assumption that the defendant is not allowed to pray in aid matters which came to his attention after publication (*McKeith v News Group Newspapers Ltd* [2005] EWHC 1162, QBD at [36]).

Reynolds privilege and meaning. Bonnick v Morris was also considered in *Jameel (Mohammed) v Wall Street Journal Europe Sprl.* Eady J. below ([2004] EWHC 37, QBD; [2004] E.M.L.R. 11) said that it was not wholly clear whether the "alternative" meaning that the Court was contemplating in *Bonnick* would necessarily be a defamatory meaning or whether it might also be non-defamatory. He thought it was unlikely that it could be the latter if the context was the basic question of whether there was a duty to publish for otherwise:

> "judges would find themselves in the position sometimes of recognising, in the light of a jury's decision, that the offending article was defamatory but holding that it was nevertheless privileged because some people (including perhaps the author) thought it had a non-defamatory meaning. The matter could not surely be judged on the basis of a duty to publish a non-defamatory imputation" (at [72]).
> "On the other hand, [if] the objective is not so much to answer directly the primary question of duty, but rather to assess one of the subsidiary tests along the way, ... [then in] determining whether it was reasonable or responsible not to have made further pre-publication checks, it might well be relevant to consider how the journalist understood the allegations he was making and, if he genuinely thought the words bore no defamatory imputation at all, it would be difficult to criticise him for not addressing such a meaning for the purpose of checks or (say) giving an opportunity to comment upon it" (at [73]).

Furthermore, *Bonnick* was not a jury case and where there was a jury it "is important not to give jurors the impression that the judge is by sleight of hand, in his ruling on qualified privilege, side-stepping their conclusions and giving weight to some different meaning" (at [74]). However, on the facts *Bonnick* was of no relevance. Here, on any view, there was an express statement about the claimant which bore the meaning either that his conduct gave grounds for suspicion or that there were grounds for investigation. Whatever the defendants may have intended the statement to mean, no responsible journalist could conceivably disregard the first and more serious meaning. The Court of Appeal was of the view that the facts of *Bonnick* showed that it was applicable where the "alternative" meaning was a non-defamatory one. However, they held that Eady J. was entitled to find that no responsible journalist could have failed to realise that the article was capable of a defamatory meaning. Accordingly, it was not necessary to "consider whether the Privy Council's decision represents the law of England and Wales" ([2005] EWCA Civ 74; [2005] 2 W.L.R. 1577 at [97]). Eady J. was also right to refuse to ask the jury to find "the meaning" of the article, since for the purposes of *Bonnick* "the issue was not what the article meant. The issue was whether those responsible for the publication may reasonably have believed that the article was not defamatory" (at [94]). Despite the caution expressed in *Jameel*, the Court of Appeal clearly assumed that *Bonnick* represented English law in *Armstrong v Times Newspapers Ltd* [2005] EWCA Civ 1007 at [77].

See also *Galloway v Telegraph Group Ltd* [2004] EWHC 2786, QBD; [2005] E.M.L.R. 7 where the more serious defamatory meaning, imputing venality and greed, was regarded as obvious.

Reynolds privilege and justification. Where there are a number of distinct allegations and the claimant sues only in respect of some of them, then the defendant may only seek to justify those, unless there is some "common sting" (see Main Work, para.11.14). However, where *Reynolds* privilege is pleaded it would not be right to shut out the defendant's belief as to some wider meaning which the words are reasonably capable of bearing. Such questions as whether there was a duty to publish, and a right on the part of readers to be informed, need to be assessed in the light of the words complained of as a whole, rather than artificially confining the court's attention to one particular meaning (*McKeith v News Group Newspapers Ltd* [2005] EWHC 1162, QBD at [33]). There may be difficulties in shutting out evidence on the issue of justification while admitting it for the purpose of establishing one of the *Reynolds* factors (for example the status of the information upon which the defendant relied). However, in determining whether a privilege defence has a reasonable prospect of success the judge should proceed on the basis that the factual assertions pleaded in support are correct, unless they have been convincingly demonstrated to be unfounded (at [34]). In pleading particulars in support of privilege it is necessary to take guard against what has been described (*Armstrong v Times Newspapers* [2004] EWHC 2928, QBD at [94], on appeal but not on this point, [2005] EWCA Civ 1007) as a "sloppy . . . cross-over technique" whereby particulars of in support of privilege are treated as simply interchangeable with particulars of justification. Not only may privilege cover a wider ground than justification (see above) but:

> "one can often legitimately plead facts subsequent to publication in support of a plea of justification (in particular, to justify a defamatory allegation about general character traits); also, facts relied upon to support a plea of *Reynolds* privilege need to have been known to the relevant defendant or journalist prior to publication—which is not the case with a plea of justification" (*McKeith* at [53]).

14.87   **Duty and interest.** *The general approach.* The Court of Appeal in *Jameel (Mohammed) v Wall Street Journal Europe Sprl* [2005] EWCA Civ 74; [2005] 2 W.L.R. 1577, this Supplement, para.14.91 (appeal to House of Lords pending), held that "responsible journalism" is too imprecise to constitute the sole test for *Reynolds* privilege. That must be shown before the privilege can be established but it is also necessary that the subject matter is of such a nature that it is in the public interest that it should be published. "That is a more stringent test than that the public should be interested in receiving the information" (at [87]). It is worth noting what Eady J. below said on this issue ([2004] EWHC 37, QBD; [2004] E.M.L.R. 11). There has been a tendency (of which Main Work, para.14.87 is guilty) to exaggerate the degree to which *Reynolds* gives rise to uncertainty. The correct view is that although the standard of "responsible journalism" is a matter to be addressed en route to the decision whether there is a moral or social duty to publish the matter complained of, the latter remains the ultimate test (at [23]). While it is true that we live in a more open society in which people feel entitled to more information about matters of genuine public interest than in the past, it is necessary to bear in mind the warning by Lord Cooke in *McCartan Turkington Breen v Times Newspaper Ltd* [2001] 2 A.C. 277 at 301 that *Reynolds* was less a "breakthrough" than "a reminder of the width of the basic common law principles, although it was much more encouraging of their invocation than previous English decisions" (*Jameel* at [27]). The defence "exists ultimately not to afford journalists a special privilege, or a degree of protection which is not available to other citizens, but to protect the public itself in respect of allegations of which it would be wrong to deprive us" (at [33]). Furthermore, while there is nowadays a tendency to refuse to strike out a plea where the law is in a state of development, it has been said that issues on *Reynolds* privilege do not generally fall into this category (though *cf. Armstrong v Times Newspapers Ltd* [2005] EWCA Civ 1007 at [76]): it is one thing to say that the principles in that case have to be applied in a flexible way to an infinite variety of facts, always bearing in mind the values of the Human Rights Convention, but that is not the same as saying that the law is in a state of flux. If "this distinction is not borne in mind, there is a danger that any plea citing a few generalities about the duty of the media to be a public watchdog will be allowed to pass muster and thus to prolong and complicate unnecessarily a significant number of libel actions in which qualified privilege has no legitimate role to play" (*Miller v Associated Newspapers Ltd* [2003] EWHC 2799, QBD; [2004] E.M.L.R. 33 at [33]). The warning about generalities is repeated in *McKeith v News Group Newspapers Ltd* [2005] EWHC 1162, QBD. It is not the law that "one may publish anything under the cloak of privilege provided only that it is relevant to public health or that the subject matter is of interest to the public in general terms. The question needs always to be more focussed" (at [55]). Nevertheless, while *Reynolds* defences require close scrutiny, the judge must be on his guard that the underlying issues of fact may make them unsuitable for summary disposal without the benefit of witness statements and evidence (*Armstrong v Times Newspapers Ltd* [2005] EWCA Civ 1007; this Supplement, para.14.90). See also this Supplement, para.27.19A.

Neutral reportage. As stated in para.14.90, the defendants in *Al-Fagih* eschewed reliance on a *general* doctrine of neutral reportage (or reporting) in the sense that there was a defence for *any* attributed but unadopted statement in the media. Indeed, a doctrine of such width would effectively render the media immune from the repetition rule applicable to justification. However, provided the other relevant elements of the *Reynolds* privilege are made out, the fact that a newspaper is merely reporting rather than publishing the results of its own investigations may be a factor which points in favour of privilege and the expression "neutral reportage" is now being used in this context (see *Galloway v Telegraph Group Ltd* [2004] EWHC 2786, QBD; [2005] E.M.L.R. 7; this Supplement, para.14.91). However, the claim to privilege failed. *Al-Fagih* was a case which involved the reporting of accusation and counter-accusation by two sides in a political dispute in which the public had a legitimate interest; in *Galloway*, on the other hand, the gravamen of the complaint went to the conclusions which the defendants themselves had drawn from documents concerning the claimant. Permission to appeal on qualified privilege and in particular on neutral reportage ([2005] EWCA Civ 435). The concept of neutral reportage is touched on by the Court of Appeal in *Jameel (Mohammed) v Wall Street Journal Europe Sprl* [2005] EWCA Civ 74; [2005] 2 W.L.R. 1577; this Supplement, para.14.91, appeal to House of Lords pending. It was only at a late stage before the Court of Appeal that the defendants relied explicitly on such a doctrine and the Court remarked:

> "That had not been clear to us and we doubt whether it was clear to the judge. Had it been it would have been necessary to consider whether such a doctrine exists under English law. It would also have been necessary to consider a further question. The defence of 'reportage' normally requires the 'report' to be 'fair and accurate'. If qualified privilege can attach to neutral reporting, does the report have to be accurate, or is it enough that the publisher believes that the report is accurate? These questions are particularly important in a case such as the present where the report is of an investigation or of an inquiry, or of monitoring of a nature that carries with it defamatory implications relating to the claimant" (at [22]).

However, the Court was prepared to accept that the ninth of Lord Nicholls' factors in *Reynolds* suggests "the possibility that *Reynolds* privilege may attach to the neutral reporting of allegations made by a third party, notwithstanding that the publisher does not believe that the allegations are true" and that *Al Fagih* "would seem to have been such a case" (at [19]–[20]). In any event, however, the Court was of the view that even if the matter had been specifically raised, Eady J. would have rejected it in view of his general conclusions under *Reynolds* that the circumstances were not such as to create a duty to publish.

This is clearly an area that requires further elucidation. At the moment it seems reasonable to conclude that:

(1) a form of neutral reportage defence does exist in English law;
(2) it is an aspect of the general *Reynolds* principle rather than a separate doctrine;
(3) it extends at least to the attributed and neutral reporting of allegations and counter-allegations by parties to a political dispute in which the public has a legitimate interest.

14.88   **Reliability of sources.** For admissible evidence on *Reynolds* issues, see further this Supplement, para.32.57.

Judge and jury. "The division between the role of the judge and that of the jury when *Reynolds* privilege is in issue is not an easy one; indeed it is open to question whether jury trial is desirable at all in such a case" (*Jameel (Mohammed) v Wall Street Journal Europe Sprl* [2005] EWCA Civ 74; [2005] 2 W.L.R. 1577 at [70]). Much difficulty has arisen in the *Jameel* litigation over the relationship of this form of privilege and the presumption of falsity. In the "classical" common law qualified privilege case there may be disputed facts going to the existence of the privileged occasion but the jury's role is likely to be mainly concerned with determining the issue of malice and on this they are likely to be required (if they are required to do more than return a general verdict) to simply say "yes" or "no". However, under *Reynolds* issues of fact are at the heart of the very existence of the privilege, questions like What was the nature and background of the source of the story? What did the newspaper do to verify it? What did the newspaper do to enable the claimant to respond? A not unlikely scenario nowadays, therefore, is that at the end of the trial the jury will be presented with a series of questions going first to meaning and reference (if those are in dispute) then to the *Reynolds* factors and then to damages, the *Reynolds* issue then being reserved for ultimate determination by the judge, who has to "evaluate" the effect of the jury's answers to determine whether there was the requisite duty to publish. *Cf. Jameel v Times Newspapers Ltd* [2005] EWHC 1219, QBD where it was agreed that all issues of privilege were to be determined by the judge as a preliminary issue.

As with other, more traditional forms of qualified privilege, the ultimate issue is not whether the defamatory imputation is true but whether, upon an objective consideration of the information possessed by the publisher at the time, there is a duty to publish even if it may be untrue (as it will be presumed to be unless there is a successful plea of justification). However, the proposition that the truth of the allegation is irrelevant to privilege (*G.K.R. Karate (UK) Ltd v Yorkshire Post Newspapers Ltd* [2001] 1 W.L.R. 2571) has to be read subject to the qualification that it may be relevant to an issue of fact necessary to establish a successful *Reynolds* defence. Thus suppose D publishes a story to the effect that there are grounds for suspicion (or at least investigation) as to C's involvement in criminality. D says that he received this information from X and Y, described as impeccable sources. Although C cannot compel D to reveal who X and Y are, C may seek to introduce evidence from A and B to the effect that what X and Y are alleged to have said is not true. In doing so he is not introducing irrelevant material, nor embarking on a pointless exercise in proving untrue what is already presumed to be untrue. Rather, he is using the evidence of A and B to rebut the evidence of D that what X and Y told him was a basis for a legitimate duty to publish: the evidence of A and B may show that D's understanding or recollection of what X and Y told him is incorrect or, of course, that D's evidence is fabrication. See *Jameel v Wall Street Journal Europe Sprl* [2003] EWCA Civ 1694; [2004] E.M.L.R. 6. Eady J. below, referring to the difficulty which the claimant faces in a *Reynolds* case in going behind the journalist's assertions as to his sources, said:

> "There is always a risk that anonymous sources will acquire, in the eyes of a jury, an aura of saintliness, wisdom, or infallibility when they are not permitted to take on human form, especially having regard to the natural tendency of journalists to buff up the quality of their character or experience—for example, by using the standard description for anonymous sources, which is 'impeccable'. In such circumstances there is room, potentially, for injustice if the claimant is not permitted to introduce evidence capable of casting doubt on the accuracy of the journalist's evidence, or the reliability of his source of information" ([2003] EWHC 2322, QBD at [19]).

In *Jameel (Mohammed) v Wall Street Journal Europe Sprl* [2005] EWCA Civ 74; [2005] 2 W.L.R. 1577 the defendants published an article to the effect that the claimants' accounts were on a list of those being monitored to ensure that they did not, wittingly or unwittingly, become methods of channelling funds to terrorists. This was capable of the defamatory meaning that there were reasonable grounds to suspect the claimants of funding terrorism or at least that there are grounds for investigation of their conduct (see this Supplement, para.3.26). The defendants did not attempt to prove that either meaning was true but relied on *Reynolds* privilege. Eady J. had directed the jury that "you and I . . . proceed on the basis that neither claimant was being monitored nor suspected nor on any list of suspects provided to the Saudis by the United States Government or anyone else" (see [2005] EWCA Civ 74 at [41]). It was argued that this was a misdirection because the presumption of falsity related only to the defamatory imputation or sting and not the existence of the monitoring list. The plea of *Reynolds* privilege was founded upon the defendants' belief in the existence of the list from information received from their five sources and, while evidence had been introduced on this (indeed the *claimants* had been allowed to adduce evidence that there was no list for the purpose, *inter alia*, of showing that the defendants' account of what they had been told by their sources could not be correct (at [35])) and the jury had found that none of the sources B to E had confirmed the suggestion of the "lead" source A that the list existed, it was argued that the direction could be taken as an instruction that the jury *could not* find that the defendants had proved that the other sources had confirmed the information. The Court described this submission based on a distinction between the existence of the list and the defamatory sting as having "force" (at [59]), even though throughout the proceedings below both judge and counsel seem to have treated the existence of the monitoring list as largely synonymous with the sting of the libel and in the Court of Appeal in earlier proceedings which dealt with the admissibility of the claimant's evidence with regard to the list (see above), Simon Brown L.J. had referred to its existence as "the article's central assertion" (*Jameel v Wall Street Journal Europe Sprl* [2003] EWCA Civ 1694; [2004] E.M.L.R. 6 at [29]). Furthermore, although the ground of appeal was that "by directing the jury to apply the presumption to the information given by the sources, the judge effectively foreclosed them from finding that D *had proved on the balance of probabilities* that the journalist . . . had received confirmation from them of the information that he published" (at [58], emphasis added), the detailed *Reynolds* questions left to the jury directed them to determine whether the defendants had proved confirmation by sources B to E on a balance of probabilities (at [40]).

However, for the actual decision on misdirection the Court referred to "a more general ground" for criticising the judge's approach, namely that "we do not consider that it was appropriate for the jury to apply the presumption of falsity when considering the issues of fact that were relevant to *Reynolds* privilege". And later:

> "Where, as in this case, an issue is raised as to whether those responsible for the publication of an article have accurately described the information supplied to them by their sources, the question of whether the information allegedly supplied was true or false will have obvious relevance. In that context it does not seem to us right that the jury should apply a presumption that the article was false. It follows that the jury are required to perform some mental gymnastics. They must presume that the defamatory allegation is false when considering liability and damages, but must not apply this presumption when resolving issues of fact that are relevant to the claim of *Reynolds* privilege. The judge should give a careful direction to this effect" (at [61]).

With respect, there is a risk that any direction along these lines may leave the jury confused, for, putting aside the complication in the case about the difference (if any) between the existence of the list and the defamatory sting, an instruction not to apply the presumption of falsity to the "issues of fact that relevant to *Reynolds* privilege" might give them the impression that everything the defendant says about verification is to be presumed to be true unless the claimant proves the contrary. That can hardly be the law, as is implicitly admitted by the ground of appeal (though that is the position where the judge is performing the different task of determining whether a privilege defence has a reasonable prospect of success). To say that "what D says is presumed to be untrue" is only another way of saying that the burden is on D to prove that it is true and reflects the general principle that he who asserts must prove.

On the facts, however, the Court held that it was far from plain that the misdirection had resulted in a miscarriage of justice: the jury's answers on sources B to E were not determinative of the judge's ruling rejecting qualified privilege and he would have reached the same conclusion simply on the basis of the other respects in which the defendants' case failed to come up to the *Reynolds* criteria.

Scope of publication of material supplied by reliable source. Even if a source is completely reliable, it does not follow that there is necessarily a duty to publish everything that he says on a matter of general public interest: the question remains whether *this* publication was necessary at *this* time to protect a legitimate interest of the public (see *Miller v Associated Newspapers Ltd* [2003] EWHC 2799, QBD; [2004] E.M.L.R. 33 at [18]; *Jameel v Wall Street Journal Europe Sprl (No.2)* [2004] EWHC 37, QBD; [2004] E.M.L.R. 11 at [66]). This is all the more so in respect of speculation or opinions expressed by the source (*Miller*, above).

Cases where privilege has been found or found to be arguable. The **14.90** claimant's name in the case described as *Al-Faghi* is *Al-Fagih*. On neutral reportage see further this Supplement, para.14.87.

In *Armstrong v Times Newspapers Ltd* [2005] EWCA Civ 1007 a newspaper article carried the meaning that at least there were reasonable grounds to suspect the claimant (a cyclist) of taking performance-enhancing drugs (see this Supplement, para.3.26). The article was based on a book published in France by another journalist on the same newspaper. Eady J. ([2004] EWHC 2928, QBD) struck out the *Reynolds* privilege plea. The tone of the article was sensational. The status of the information on which it was based was rumour and speculation and it was not founded on any sort of formal inquiry. There was no urgency about the publication (as opposed to topicality and commercial expediency in promoting the book). The newspaper and the author of the article had taken no steps at all to verify the material or to seek the claimant's version. The author of the book (who seems to have been sued in respect of the article on the basis that he had caused its publication—[99]) had made some inquiries of the claimant in connection with the preparation of the book but, leaving aside the problems which arose from the different roles of the defendants in the publication of the *article*, these did not give a fair account of what was proposed to be alleged against him. As with *Jameel*, the background (drug taking in professional cycling) was undoubtedly a matter of public concern, but it did not follow from this that the defendants were under a duty to publish the allegations about the claimant. However, the Court of Appeal restored the defence. On the facts, the nature of the source material relied on by the article, the status of much of the information and the roles of and steps taken towards verification by the defendants required further elucidation by witness statements or at trial. Where the claimant makes a Pt 24 application in very general terms (see [31]–[34]) "a judge must be very careful to ensure that he does in fact accept as true everything asserted by the defendants (unless there is no reasonable prospect that some or all of it would be accepted as true)" (at [74]).

14.91   **Cases where privilege has been rejected.** There are a number of decisions in which the scope of the *Reynolds* privilege has been explored and defences based on it rejected.

In *Jameel (Mohammed) v Wall Street Journal Europe Sprl* [2005] EWCA Civ 74; [2005] 2 W.L.R. 1577 (appeal to House of Lords pending) the defendants published an article in which it was stated that the claimant's group of companies was on the list of those the accounts of which were being monitored by US authorities in connection with inquiries into terrorism. In holding that the publication was not the subject of qualified privilege (the defendants declined to seek to establish justification), Eady J. ([2004] EWCA Civ 37; [2004] E.M.L.R. 11) emphasised that *Reynolds* was based upon traditional principles of duty and interest and had not supplanted them with something else (see this Supplement, para.14.87). It was uncontroversial to say that combating terrorism was a matter of public interest but the issue was whether the public interest required at the time of publication that the defendants should identify the claimants as being on the list. There was no evidence of urgency in the publication and "the need for the public to be kept up to date is not to be confused with the quite understandable need of editors and journalists to obtain a scoop or to publish ahead of their rival newspapers" (at [44]); nor was there sufficient urgency to offset the fact that the claimant had been given no adequate opportunity to comment prior to publication (at [53]); according to the defendants' own story the United States had undertaken to keep the list confidential and if monitoring was taking place its object was likely to be undermined if the exercise was made public (at [55]); while journalists are not subject to government diktat in judging the public interest, cogent grounds were required to show why the public interest called for the confidentiality to be breached (at [58]). In upholding this decision the Court of Appeal said that the judge had been correct to reject "responsible journalism" as the sole test of *Reynolds* privilege (see this Supplement, para.14.87) and commented:

> "Assume, contrary to the judge's finding, that the publication of the article, names and all, would have been in the public interest if appropriate checks had been made. Quite apart from the jury's rejection of Mr. Dorsey's evidence in relation to his four sources, their rejection of his evidence of having sought the Jameels' comments on the morning before publication, coupled with the jury's finding that Mr. Dorsey was requested to give Mr. Jameel the time to comment were, so it seems to us, fatal to the appellants' case that they had satisfied the test of responsible journalism" (at [88]).

In *Miller v Associated Newspapers Ltd* [2004] EWHC 2799, QBD; [2004] E.M.L.R. 33 the defendants published an article critical of the handling by the claimant, a police officer, of an investigation into an accusation of sexual offences against two public figures. Eady J. struck out the plea of qualified privilege. The defendants claimed that the article was based on revelations by a police source from an "interim progress report" of an internal police inquiry. This was "a confidential and partially completed inquiry enjoying the status only of 'work in progress' " rather than a final and authoritative determination and was not of sufficient "status" under the fifth *Reynolds* factor to justify its disclosure to the public (at [21]). Nor was there any urgency about the disclosure. Furthermore, little had been done to verify the information, no attempt had been made to seek comment (even though the claimant would have been barred from responding to an inquiry, the police press office could have been approached) and the tone of the article was sensational. The imputations in the article were subsequently found to be substantially true (*Miller v Associated Newspapers Ltd* [2005] EWHC 557, QBD).

In *Galloway v Telegraph Group Ltd* [2004] EWHC 2786, QBD; [2005] E.M.L.R. 7 the defendants published articles conveying that the claimant, a member of Parliament, had been in the pay of Saddam Hussein, that he had diverted "oil-for-food" money for his own enrichment and that his conduct was tantamount to treason. The articles were founded on documents discovered in Baghdad after the occupation of the city and these were published in full by the newspaper, though no complaint was made in respect of them. The articles, however, in attributing motives of personal gain, went beyond the reporting of the contents of the documents and a call for an inquiry. Although the "Reynolds exercise" involves the weighing of all the factors to determine whether there is a duty to publish, the most significant element leading to the decision to reject the plea of privilege seems to have been the fact that the issue of personal enrichment was never put to the claimant in his interview with the newspaper prior to publication. Nor was he given sight of the Baghdad documents. It is also emphasised that while news can quickly become stale, this was not the sort of story interest in which would fade with time and attention was drawn to the warning by Lord Nicholls in *Reynolds* about the dangers of equating urgency with a newspaper's desire to safeguard a scoop:

"... in the absence of any additional safeguard for reputation, a newspaper, anxious
to be first with a 'scoop', would in practice be free to publish seriously defamatory
misstatements of fact based on the slenderest of materials. Unless the paper chose later
to withdraw the allegations, the politician thus defamed would have no means of
clearing his name, and the public could have no means of knowing where the truth lay.
Some further protection for reputation is needed if this can be achieved without a
disproportionate incursion into freedom of expression" ([2001] 2 A.C. 127 at 201).

The defendants relied on the decision of the European Court of Human Rights in *Selistö v Finland* [2005] E.M.L.R. 8, a striking decision (Eady J. in *Galloway* at [136]) in which the majority of the Court held that the criminal conviction of a journalist in respect of stories (which, in the general context of patient safety imputed by way of example that an unnamed but identifiable surgeon, who had been given no prior opportunity to comment, had been drunk on duty) violated Art.10 of the Convention. Perhaps it is best to say overall, as Eady J. did (at [148]), that the Court was concerned with the particular facts. However, it is also the case that the imputations were based upon a public police investigation document, albeit one which had not led to any proceedings; and, in the particular context of *Galloway*, the imputations about the surgeon were incidental and illustrative, whereas Mr Galloway was the centre-piece of the defendants' articles. Permission to appeal on qualified privilege and in particular on neutral reportage ([2005] EWCA Civ 435).

14.95   **The wider context.** *Ireland.* In *Hunter v Gerald Duckworth & Co. Ltd* [2003] IEHC 81 the plaintiffs were two of the "Birmingham Six", whose convictions in respect of a bombing had been quashed, and sued in respect of the publication of passages in a book the meaning of which, they alleged, was that they were not entitled to be treated as presumed to be innocent of the crime. On preliminary issues O'Caoimh J. rejected the contention of the second defendant, the author, that the claim should be struck out as an unwarranted interference with his right of freedom of expression under the Irish Constitution but concluded that:

> "the flexible approach represented by the decision of the House of Lords in *Reynolds v Times Newspapers Ltd.* is the most appropriate way of approaching the problems in the instant case, in the absence of a clear legislative framework. It is clear that in the context of Ireland being a democratic state, clear recognition has to be given to the right to freedom of expression. I believe that this right should not be undermined by the provisions of the Constitution relating to the protection of one's reputation. It is clear that the rights have to be construed on a harmonious basis. Nevertheless, it is clear that in certain cases, in the context of the democratic nature of the state, primacy may have to be given to freedom of expression. The approach adopted by the House of Lords has the merit of enabling the law to be developed on a case by case basis having regard to the requirements of the Constitution and the Convention which may inform the court in its approach to the interpretation of the Constitution. One must proceed on the assumption that the courts in addressing individual cases will have regard to the circumstances of each case and the nature of the rights pleaded by the parties and will be able to assess whether the right to freedom of expression contended for in any case is such that the Defendant may rely upon a plea of privilege or fair comment having regard to the evidence in any given case . . .
>
> In so far as judges are familiar with construing the law in light of the Constitution, and insofar as the decision whether to allow defences, including that of fair comment or privilege to go to a jury in any given case is one that is vested in the judge conducting the trial, I am confident that a judge can adequately deal with the requirements of the Constitution in reaching any such decision and, as circumstances ordain, in charging a jury in any particular case."

14.96   *Australia.* See Kenyon, "*Lange* and *Reynolds* Qualified Privilege: Australian and English Defamation Law and Practice" [2004] *Melbourne University Law Review* 13, which concludes that *Lange* has not had a major effect in improving the position of the media. For New South Wales see, however, the 2002 amendment of the Defamation Act referred to in note 2 of this paragraph, Main Work. A comparison with protections in Australian and US constitutional law is made in Weaver, R., Kenyon, A.T., Partlett, D.F., Walker, C., *The Right to Speak Ill* (Carolina Academic Press, Durham, 2005).

In the Australian Capital Territory s.66 of the Civil Law (Wrongs) Act 2002 now provides a general defence (other than in regard to matter imputing criminal behaviour) that the defendant has established that the matter was not published negligently (that is to say, that he took reasonable steps to ensure its accuracy *and* gave the plaintiff a reasonable opportunity for comment before publication).

Section (5) in the summary of Lange. In *Herald & Weekly Times v Popovic* [2003] VSCA 161 the Victoria CA stated that, subject to the jury finding primary facts which bear upon it, the issue of "reasonableness of conduct" of the publisher is a matter for the trial judge, not the jury, though, there having been no appeal on this issue, the appeal was dismissed on the basis that the trial judge had been correct to rule that there was no basis on which the jury could come to the conclusion on the facts that the publication was reasonable.

Honesty of purpose and not "reasonableness" remains the basis of protection by qualified privilege in cases of publication to a limited audience (*Szuty v Smyth* [2004] ACTSC 77 (complaint to professional body about plaintiff's conduct)).

Text to notes 91 et seq. In *Cornwall v Rowan* [2004] SASC 384; 90 S.A.S.R. 269 the Full Court summarised the then state of play on what is a governmental or political matter as follows at [623]:

"Relevantly for the purposes of this case, a communication about the elected representatives of Commonwealth and State governments and a communication about the conduct of those governments (including statutory authorities and public utilities who are obliged to report to the legislature or to a Minister who is responsible to the legislature) is a communication about a government or political matter. In our opinion, there is sufficient in *Lange* to conclude that, until the High Court says otherwise, the concept of a government or political matter includes a communication about the conduct of the elected representatives of State governments and the conduct of those governments even though the particular discussion does not have a bearing on matters of government at the Commonwealth level. In discussing such matters, private individuals or organizations may be defamed. Furthermore, a particular communication may contain no criticism of the elected representative or government if, for example, the author of the publication argues that the decision of the elected representative or government is right. However, if as a matter of characterisation, the publication is no more than an attack on a private individual or organization the communication is not a communication on or about a government or political matter. The fact that the communication is on or about a matter of public interest and is the subject of public debate is relevant but not of itself sufficient."

Hence, although the activities of a women's shelter were not matters of government or politics, a programme prompted by a decision to withdraw public funding of it was. *Cf. Conservation Council of SA Inc. v Chapman* [2003] SASC 398; 87 SASR 62.

In *Shave v West Australian Newspapers Ltd* [2003] WASC 83 it was held that an allegation that a Minister had misled an inquiry arguably concerned his role in that office even though it did not relate to the manner in which the plaintiff may or may not have carried out his ministerial duties. Hasluck J. said at [40] that:

"the question of whether a person is fit to hold public office is a matter that lies within the ambit of political discussion with the result that a plea of privilege pursuant to the *Lange* rule is available. To my mind, a persuasive distinction cannot be drawn in the circumstances of this case between the standing of the plaintiff as a person who gave evidence to the Inquiry and his status as a person who is holding office as a parliamentarian and Minister at the time the evidence was provided. The article cannot be regarded as confined to the narrow question of the plaintiff's personal integrity. It is in the nature of political discussion that there may be a degree of speculation as to whether a practising politician acted in a certain way under the influence of political considerations such as policies or partisan loyalty or pursuant to private concerns."

In *Herald & Weekly Times v Popovic* [2003] VSCA 161 (see note 91 for the case below) the Court was divided on whether the *Lange* privilege applied to criticism of the handling of a case by a magistrate. Winneke A.C.J. and Warren A.J.A. thought it was not a "government or political matter" except (*per* Winneke A.C.J. at [10]) "where the discussion impacts directly or indirectly on the executive government itself; whether in the exercise of its powers to appoint the officer, or in exercising or failing to exercise its powers to initiate the officer's removal". Gillard A.J.A. considered that it was a "government matter". See also *John Fairfax Publications Pty Ltd v O'Shane* [2005] NSWCA 164. *Cf. Peek v Channel Seven Adelaide Pty Ltd* [2004] SASC 425, 90 S.A.S.R. 522 (allegations about behaviour of counsel in a criminal trial arguably attracted the defence).

"It is arguable that the broadcast item goes to the heart of the public's confidence in the proper administration of justice. Its contents question the ability of the judiciary to attend to the fundamental obligation to exercise judicial power free from abuse of process. It is arguable that the broadcast item further touches upon the obligation of candour placed upon lawyers as officers of the court which is paramount to ensuring public confidence in the judicial system. It is arguable that the broadcast item constitutes discussion of government and political matters" (at [70]).

14.97   *Canada.* On the law under the Civil Code of Québec, see *Gilles E.Nérron Communication Marketing Inc. v Chambre des notaires du Québec* 2004 SCC 53; 241 D.L.R. (4th) 577; this Supplement, para.1.11.

14.98   *New Zealand. Notes 19 and 20.* See also *W v Westminster City Council* [2004] EWHC 2866, QBD at [91]. Although of the view that *Horrocks v Lowe* rather than *Lange* provided the basis of malice in English law, Tugendhat J. did refer (at [92]–[93]) to a passage in *Lange* (at [49]) which said that a greater degree of responsibility would be required for a statement to the world than for a statement to a limited group on a "no attribution" basis and, with reference to the facts of the case before him, went on:

"What is included in a Report for a Child Protection Conference is for publication in confidence to a small group of people with specific roles in the life of a child. While the publication can still cause grave harm, the extent of that harm can be mitigated by the subsequent actions of the defendants, and by the denials of the Claimant himself. It may not be a context in which the same very high degree of responsibility would be required as in, say, publication to all the world."

14.99   *South Africa.* In *Mthembi-Mahanyele v Mail & Guardian Ltd* [2004] ZASCA 67; 2004 (11) B.C.L.R 1182 the Supreme Court of Appeal of South Africa held that a cabinet minister did not lose his right to sue for defamation without proof of malice by virtue of his office. The Court also considered *National Media v Bogoshi* at some length, but was divided in its conclusions. In the majority in favour of the defendants, the thrust of the judgment of Lewis J.A. seems to be towards putting "political" speech in a separate category; whereas the decision of Ponnan A.J.A. turns on the view that in its context the publication could not be given a defamatory meaning. Mthiyane J.A. dissented: political speech was not in a special category, though in practice greater latitude might be allowed to it, and it was important not to downgrade the media's duty to seek comment or corroboration before publishing allegations.

SECTION 5. PRIVILEGED REPORTS AT COMMON LAW

(a) *Reports of judicial proceedings*

Reports of judicial proceedings. *Note 54.* The decision in *Bashford v Infor-* **14.102**
mation Australia (Newsletters) Pty Ltd was upheld by the High Court of Australia ([2004] HCA 5; 204 A.L.R. 193). The facts are, however, far removed from the illustration by Hodgson J.A. in note 54, since the publication in question *was* a report of proceedings in the ordinary sense but it was inaccurate because it attributed to the plaintiff a liability which had not in fact been found (he was not even a party to the proceedings). In effect there is an irrebuttable presumption that publication of a fair and accurate report is in the interest of society, whereas the hurdles which have to be surmounted to establish a privileged occasion on the basis of duty and interest impose severe demands on the publisher. This reasoning is entirely convincing in the context of the situation in Hodgson J.A.'s example of the reference, less so perhaps where, as in *Bashford*, the statement for which privilege is claimed is a volunteered one made to a large number of people as mere "background" to the general matter in which there is a reciprocity of interest. The communication in that case was about the law of copyright in safety data sheets, which was plainly a matter of legitimate interest to persons subscribing to a health and safety newsletter; the inaccurate statement sued on was that the plaintiff had been held liable for misleading or deceptive conduct in proceedings which had involved that copyright issue, whereas in fact he had not even been sued.

(b) *Reports of proceedings in Parliament*

Fairness and accuracy. *Nationwide News Pty Ltd v Moodie* [2003] WASCA **14.104**
273 concerned the qualified privilege under the common law of Western Australia for fair and accurate reports of proceedings of a parliamentary inquiry and the parallel privilege under s.354 of the Criminal Code (WA) for fair reports of statutory inquiries. Articles concerning the plaintiff's standing down as chief executive of hospitals in Perth referred to an allegation in a parliamentary inquiry in New South Wales, where the plaintiff had previously worked, that the plaintiff's control of a local health service there was like "the Mafia stranglehold over southern Italy". This was only a very small part of the proceedings of the inquiry and could not be described as an abridged or condensed report of them. However, it might be protected by privilege if it could be said that it was a report of part of the proceedings and not unfair or inaccurate in that context and it should not therefore be struck out. The question whether what was said in respect of the contents of the inquiry in New South Wales amounted to a fair and accurate report was one which should be held over for trial in the light of an examination of the whole of what took place in the inquiry.

Cornwall v Rowan [2004] SASC 384; 90 S.A.S.R. 269 considers what is a "report" of parliamentary proceedings under the overlapping privileges arising at common law and under s.7 of the Wrongs Act 1936 (SA). One television programme which made no reference to the proceedings was not a report even though it contained much material which had been presented to the Legislative Council: it was in the nature of debate between opposing parties rather than an attempt to recount what had passed in the Legislative Council. Nor was another programme taken as a whole a report, even though it began with a brief reference to material being tabled in the Legislative Council.

CHAPTER 15

QUALIFIED PRIVILEGE: STATUTE

SECTION 1. INTRODUCTION

In general. *Overlap of these statutory privileges with others, note 2.* See **15.1** *Jameel v Times Newspapers Ltd* [2005] EWHC 1219, QBD; this Supplement, para.13.35.

SECTION 2. PRIVILEGE CONFERRED BY SCHEDULE 1 TO THE DEFAMATION ACT 1996

(a) *Statements privileged under Schedule 1 without explanation or contradiction*

Public inquiries. For the absolute privilege in respect of ministerial inquiries **15.9** in the UK under the Inquiries Act 2005 see this Supplement, para.13.17.

Registers, etc. See *Jameel v Times Newspapers Ltd* [2005] EWHC 1219, **15.11** QBD; this Supplement, para.13.35 and the same paragraph on the possible effect on privilege of CPR, r.5.4.

(b) *Statements privileged under Schedule 1 subject to explanation or contradiction*

Local authority meetings, inquiries, etc. *Ad hoc local authority inquiries:* **15.17** *law reform.* See this Supplement, para.15.23.

SECTION 3. MISCELLANEOUS STATUTES CONFERRING QUALIFIED PRIVILEGE

Statutory qualified provisions. The following additional instances of statu- **15.23** tory qualified privilege have been found:

[89]

Education Act 2005, ss.11, 29.
Pensions Act 2004, ss.89, 205.
Protection of Children (Scotland) Act 2003 (asp), s.9.
Mental Health (Care and Treatment) (Scotland) Act 2003 (asp), s.20.
Education Act 2002, s.162A, inserted by Education Act 2005, Sch. 8.
Freedom of Information (Scotland) Act 2002 (asp), s.67.
Scottish Parliamentary Standards Commissioner Act 2002 (asp), s.17.

Ad hoc local authority inquiries: law reform. The Law Commission has examined and reported on the problems arising from ad hoc local authority inquiries (*In the Public Interest: Publication of Local Authority Inquiry Reports,* Law Com. No.289 (2004)). The draft Bill attached to the Law Commission's Report would create a new form of statutory privilege for the publication by the authority of the inquiry report. In summary, the privilege would apply where (a) before publication the authority took all reasonable steps to satisfy themselves that the inquiry was conducted fairly, or (b) even though they did not, the inquiry was conducted fairly (cl.12(1)). An inquiry is not to be treated as conducted fairly unless the person holding it bases his conclusions upon findings of fact, gives every person criticised in the report the opportunity to respond and fairly represents that response in the report (cl.12(4)). There are comparable provisions for publication of part of the report or a summary. Furthermore, a publication is not privileged if proved to be made with malice (cl.12(7)). The Bill would not limit or restrict a privilege which exists apart from it (e.g. at common law—see *Lillie v Newcastle City Council* [2002] EWHC 1600, QBD) but if the report is published to the public and the conditions in cl.12(1) are not satisfied, the authority would also lose the protection of the statutory qualified privilege under s.100H(5) of the Local Government Act 1972 or regulations made under s.22 of the Local Government Act 2000 (Main Work, para.15.23).

CHAPTER 16

MALICE AND QUALIFIED PRIVILEGE

SECTION 1. GENERAL

Malice and qualified privilege. In *Dorset Flint & Stone Blocks Ltd v Moir* **16.1**
[2004] EWHC 2173, QBD Eady J. at [49] warned that:

"allegations of malice, like allegations of fraud, need to be scrutinised with particular care to ensure that there is a sufficient evidential basis for alleging dishonesty or inviting such an inference. Such allegations should not be made formulaically by way of bare assertion or used as a tactical weapon to try to bludgeon people into submission or compromise. It is no good merely to say 'I have put a plea of malice on the record and it is up to the jury to decide'. There must be facts alleged which, if true, are more consistent with the presence of malice than with its absence."

The context is fair comment but the proposition must be equally applicable to qualified privilege.

Malice as "improper" or "indirect" motive. In *Rackham v Sandy* [2005] **16.4**
EWHC 482, QBD Gray J. said:

"[18] . . . [Counsel for the defendants] submits that malice arises if and only if it can be shown that the defendant was actuated by some improper motive. Knowledge of falsity is not a separate head of malice, still less is recklessness, it is simply a way of establishing an improper motive.
[19] I am of course bound by the decision in *Horrocks v Lowe*. But I respectfully agree with Gleeson CJ [in *Roberts v Bass*] that there is nothing in Lord Diplock's speech in that case which supports treating the defendant's knowledge of falsity or lack of belief in truth as being probative, of itself and without more, of malice. It may be said that the point is of limited practical significance since knowledge of falsity will almost always establish the existence of an improper motive. Nevertheless I accept that the question which I have ultimately to decide in this case is whether or not each of the Defendants was actuated by the improper motive of improperly removing [the claimant] from the Board of WRG or saving his own job with the company or preventing Candover from taking over WRG."

In *Conservation Council of South Australia Inc. v Chapman* [2003] SASC 398;
87 S.A.S.R. 62 at [301] Besanko J. summarised the effect of *Roberts v Bass* as follows:

"It seems to me a majority of the court rejected any suggestion that the absence of an honest belief was of itself always sufficient to constitute malice. The criterion for malice is whether there is an improper motive or purpose. The absence of an honest belief is, with other factors, relevant to whether an improper motive or purpose is made out. There is no reason to think that these principles do not apply generally, that is to say, whether the communication is a communication on a government or political matter or not."

Clover Bond Pty Ltd v Carroll [2004] WASC 216 is an example of improper motive (defendant's purpose to get plaintiff's service and maintenance business rather than to protect public) though the court treated the matter primarily as something outside the scope of the privilege.

See also *Cornwall v Rowan* [2004] SASC 384; 90 S.A.S.R. 269 (Full Court).

16.5   Matter believed to be true but purpose to injure. See also *Meade v Pugh* [2004] EWHC 408, QBD.

Note 45. See also *Friend v Civil Aviation Authority* [2005] EWHC 201, QBD at [237].

On the similarity (though not exact congruence) of malice in defamation and the absence of the "good faith" which is required where an employee makes a "protected disclosure" under the Employment Act 1996 (as amended) see *Street v Derbyshire Unemployed Workers' Centre* [2004] EWCA Civ 964; [2004] 4 All E.R. 839.

16.17   Unreasonable belief or carelessness in arriving at belief not malice. See also *Oliver v Chief Constable of Northumbria* [2004] EWHC 790, QBD.

Add to note 21. See also *Klason v Australian Capital Territory* [2003] ACTSC 104; 177 F.L.R. 216 (briefing note to Minister, defensive attitude towards plaintiff's complaints; fact that the briefing note "seems to have been drafted with scant concern to ensure that the Minister was given a fair and accurate account of the plaintiff's grievances, the extent to which they were well founded, or the distress which the Department's insensitive and unfair treatment may have caused him" not malice).

16.19   Matter not believed to be true: exceptional cases. In *W v Westminster City Council* [2004] EWHC 2866, QBD Tugendhat J. said that the true test in these cases was that posed by Lindley L.J. in *Stuart v Bell* at [1891] 2 Q.B. 351: "What, therefore, has to be ascertained is whether the defendant acted bona fide in the discharge of [the] moral duty which he owed . . . or whether he acted from some other unjustifiable motive—from some motive other than a sense of duty."

16.20   Malice and variant meanings. *Add to note 44.* See also *Klason v Australian Capital Territory* [2003] ACTSC 104; 177 F.L.R. 216.

SECTION 2. *REYNOLDS* PRIVILEGE

"If a particular publication passes the privilege test now [i.e. under *Reynolds*], it **16.21** is very difficult to envisage circumstances where there would be room for it to be overridden by malice": *Miller v Associated Newspapers Ltd* [2004] EWHC 2799, QBD; [2004] E.M.L.R. 33 at [10] *per* Eady J. See also *Jameel (Mohammed) v Wall Street Journal Europe Sprl* [2005] EWCA Civ 74; [2005] 2 W.L.R. 1577; this Supplement, para.14.86.

SECTION 3. CONCURRENT TORTFEASORS

Independent privilege. *Note 63.* On appeal in *Cornwall v Rowan* [2004] **16.24** SASC 384; 90 S.A.S.R. 269 the Full Court accepted that the law was as stated by Lord Denning M.R. in *Egger v Chelmsford*. It also held that the same principle must apply to the "extended *Lange* privilege" (see Main Work, para.14.96).

Derivative privilege. *Privilege of agents.* See *Richardson v Scwharzenegger* **16.25** [2004] EWHC 2422, QBD; this Supplement, para.14.55 which accords with the view of Lord Denning M.R. in *Egger v Chelmsford*.

OTHER DEFENCES

SECTION 1. THE OFFER OF AMENDS PROCEDURE

18.2   The Defamation Act 1996. *Note 9.* An offer of amends procedure is also found in the Australian Capital Territory in Pt 5.2 of the Civil Law (Wrongs) Act 2002.

18.6   The amount of compensation. See also this Supplement, paras 29.29, 33.52.

In *Nail v News Group Newspapers Ltd* [2004] EWCA Civ 1708; [2005] E.M.L.R. 12 the Court of Appeal upheld awards by Eady J. ([2004] EWHC 647, QBD; [2004] E.M.L.R. 20) under the offer of amends procedure. The matter complained of was a newspaper article and a book which made allegations about the claimant actor's sexual conduct, his personal life and his professional behaviour (see this Supplement, paras 2.19 and 2.20). The judge awarded £7,500 in respect of the book (most of the copies published were outside the limitation period) and £22,500 in respect of the newspaper article, applying a substantial discount of 50 per cent on account of the unqualified offer of amends. "If an early unqualified offer to make amends is made and accepted and . . . an agreed apology is published, there is bound to be substantial mitigation" (EWCA Civ at [41]).

In *Campbell-James v Guardian Media Group plc* [2005] EWHC 893, QBD the defendants published an untrue story that the claimant had been involved in command at the Abu Ghraib prison in Iraq, where abuse of detainees had taken place. Apart from causing considerable distress to the claimant, this largely nullified any hopes of his employment in the Middle East after retirement from the British Army. The defendants took a causal and off-hand approach to publishing an apology. Eady J. took the view that the starting point for damages would be £90,000, that the discount the defendants should receive for their offer of amends should be reduced because of their attitude and awarded £58,500 (a discount of 35 per cent).

Aspects of the defendants' behaviour also led to a reduction of the discount (40 per cent) in *Turner v News Group Newspapers Ltd* [2005] EWHC 892, QBD. In this case it was accepted that the *Burstein* principle (see note 80) was applicable to the setting of compensation under the offer of amends procedure. Provided the claimant had been given notice of the nature of the material the defendant proposed to introduce before accepting the offer and it was a genuine attempt to provide the court with material on which to assess the "value" of the claimant's reputation, it was not inconsistent with the procedure or an attempt to "justify by the back door". Eady J. said that:

> "given that the *Burstein* principle applies in s.3(5) assessment cases, it is almost inevitable that sometimes the steps which a defendant takes, albeit quite legitimately for the purposes of achieving a fair overall assessment, will add hurt to a claimant's feelings. That does not mean that the level of compensation goes up automatically. That would be to discourage defendants from seeking to deploy arguments based on *Burstein* or the more traditional mitigating factors. It would hamper settlements and undermine the utility of the 'offer of amends' procedure. The primary question . . . in any given case, [is] whether a claimant has behaved reasonably in raising any particular matters, rather than seeking to introduce irrelevant or scandalous matter to take impermissible advantage of the court's process. In the latter case, which in practice one imagines will be very rare, it would of course be right to reflect such aggravating conduct in quantifying the compensation. The test needs to be an objective one and cannot be solely determined by reference to the individual claimant's reaction" (at [55]).

See also this Supplement, para.27.25.

Knew or had reason to believe. The Court of Appeal dismissed an appeal **18.8** from the decision of Eady J. in *Milne v Express Newspapers* [2004] EWCA Civ 664; [2004] E.M.L.R. 24. The view taken in the Main Work is too cautious: the expression "had reason to believe" in s.4(3) is equivalent to the recklessness or conscious indifference which amounts to malice for the purposes of qualified privilege. Although the wording of the Act is not identical with that proposed by the Neill Committee, in the Court's view there was no indication that the intention of Parliament was to do anything other than implement the proposals of the Committee (at [48]).

> "There is, in our judgment, a powerful reason why the words in question should be construed as importing recklessness in Lord Diplock's sense [in *Horrocks v Lowe*]. If a claimant establishes malice on the part of a person who publishes a defamatory statement, he has the basis for a claim of aggravated, and possibly exemplary, damages. Mr Parkes accepted that, malice apart, compensation can be fully assessed and awarded under section 3(5). There would be little point therefore in relying on section 4(3), unless the requirement there was to establish malice. Recognising that some claimants might prefer a jury trial cannot alone have been the parliamentary purpose" (at [49]).

SECTION 3. CONSENT

Consent. While "consent" and "leave and licence" in this context appear to **18.15** mean the same thing, as far as *volenti non fit injuria* is concerned:

> "literally translated [it] means 'there can be no injury to the willing', it is usually loosely translated as 'voluntary assumption of the risk'. The introduction of the word

'risk' into the principle creates an ambiguity which could lead to error if used in that sense with respect to the intentional tort of libel. When a plaintiff consents to being defamed in the way in which it is alleged this plaintiff consented, he consents to the commission of an actual tort, the boundaries of which can be drawn by reference to the terms of his consent. He does not consent to the 'risk' of being libelled. He consents to the libel itself. He may, perhaps, consent to the risk of *injury* as, although injury is presumed to be the consequence of the publication of a libel, it is not inevitable that such publication will always lead to actual injury. Thus there could be a sense in which a person who consents to a libel does take a 'risk'. But that would be an unusual case."

Accordingly, "it is probably better if the term *volenti non fit injuria* was confined to the concept of the voluntary assumption of the risk of injury by a non-intentional tort" (*Frew v John Fairfax Publications Pty Ltd* [2004] VSC 311 at [16]–[17], *per* Bongiorno J.).

Note 84. See also *Crossland v Wilkinson Hardware Stores Ltd* [2005] EWHC 481, QBD at [70] (consent to publication of document in grievance procedure but not to its prior publication before claimant knew contents).

18.16   **Limits of doctrine.** In *Frew v John Fairfax Publications Pty Ltd* [2004] VSC 311 the plaintiff sent S a copy of his autobiography in circumstances where it was contended that there was an implied invitation to review it. Bongiorno J. held that:

"to avoid liability they must confine their publication of defamatory material about the plaintiff to what can be derived from the book itself, for they do not seek to plead anything the plaintiff has said or done which could possibly be construed as extending his consent to publication beyond that boundary. Whilst what may be published without liability by the defendants need not be confined to the actual words used in the autobiography, it must be substantially the same, for that is what it can be argued, the plaintiff consented to. It is certainly not arguable, on the pleading proposed by the defendants, that he consented to more. In particular, it could not be argued that he consented to exaggeration so as to permit the author of the article to write in more defamatory terms about the plaintiff than the plaintiff did about himself" (at [10]).

18.17   **Traps and challenges.** *Claimant procuring republication.* But see now *Jameel (Yousef) v Dow Jones & Co. Inc.* [2005] EWCA Civ 75; [2005] 2 W.L.R. 1614; this Supplement, para.6.1, where it is said that a limited publication like that in *Brunswick v Harmer* (note 95) might nowadays lead to the claim being struck out as an abuse of process. There were extensive submissions involving nearly 40 authorities in *Howe & Co. v Burden* [2004] EWHC 196, QBD (a case of a telephone conversation allegedly "set up" so that it could be recorded) which seems to have been directed to showing that "trap" publications *should* fall under the defence of consent but Eady J. declined to deal with the issue summarily.

SECTION 4. LIMITATION

18.18   **Basic principle and history.** *Current policy that defamation claims should be pursued with vigour. Mullan v Edwards* [2004] NIQB 83.

Subsequent publications. *Duke of Brunswick v Harmer*. But as to another   **18.19**
aspect of this case see this Supplement, para.6.1.

While for the purpose of assessing damages for a live cause of action (for
example where it alleged that the defendant was actuated by malice) it may be
permissible to consider the whole history of matters between the parties, the
court should not award damages in respect of the effect of a prior libel or slander
which is statute barred (*Murphy v Alexander* (2004) 236 D.L.R. (4th) 302, Ont.
CA).

Exercise of the discretion. *Amendment where existing claim*. Where there is   **18.26**
an existing claim, s.35 of the Limitation Act 1980 provides that:

> "except as provided by section 33 of this Act or by Rules of Court, neither the High
> Court nor any county court shall allow a new claim . . . to be made in the course of any
> action after the expiry of any time limit under this Act which would affect a new action
> to enforce that claim".

Since s.32A performs a similar function to s.33, the omission of any reference to
it in s.35 may be an oversight (*Wood v C.C. West Midlands* [2004] EWCA Civ
1638; [2004] E.M.L.R. 17 at [76]). However, CPR, r.17.4(2) provides that "the
court may allow an amendment whose effect will be to add or substitute a new
claim, but only if the claim arises out of the same facts or substantially the same
facts as a claim in respect of which the party applying for permission has already
claimed a remedy in the proceedings." In *Wood* this was held to cover an
amendment adding a claim for slander in a telephone conversation, the substance
of which was the same as a letter in respect of which the original libel proceedings (themselves time-barred but allowed to proceed by the s.32A discretion) had
been commenced. May L.J. expressed the opinion that the judge had been able
to allow the amendment by virtue of s.32A itself, r.17.4(2) and the general
discretion as to amendments in r.17.1. "In my judgment, the factors bearing on
the exercise of the discretion from each of these sources in the present case were
in substance the same. They were substantially encompassed in the terms of
section 32A" (at [84]).

On the exercise of the discretion see *Sarayiah v Suren* [2004] EWHC 1981,
QBD and *Maccaba v Lichtenstein* [2003] EWHC 1325, QBD.

In *Sarayiah* an attempt to add defendants after the expiry of the limitation
period under CPR, Pt 19 failed because the test of "necessity" under Pt 19 was
not satisfied. In refusing to exercise the discretion in the claimant's favour under
s.32A, Tugendhat J. took into account that: the claimant had a properly constituted claim against the first defendant and judgment against others would not add
to any vindication; there was no evidence that the claimant needed additional
defendants to provide any damages likely to be awarded; all defendants had a
reasonable prospect of establishing justification and the claim against one of
them was also very weak on other grounds; and the claimant was likely to be
made insolvent as a result of civil claims and faced having to make large
payments in respect of the criminal proceedings.

In *Maccaba* there were claims for slander, harassment and breach of confidence (misuse of private information). Two of the slander claims were time-
barred. Gray J. exercised his discretion under s.32A to allow these claims to
proceed.

(1) Since the defendant faced another seven timeous slander claims, the sting of which was comparable, the prejudice to him of having to face these two was limited. Although it might be argued that the claimant would lose little in view of the other seven claims, these two were more specific in that they identified the woman to whom he was alleged to have made improper advances.

(2) The defendant anyway faced the harassment claims, based on the same facts, which were not statute-barred. The jury would therefore hear a great deal about the two slanders in the context of the harassment claim and it would be artificial and confusing to excise them from the defamation claim. Although there was no adequate explanation of the delay in respect of the two slanders, it would be wrong to elevate the reason for the delay to the point where it became determinative of the application in favour of the defendant. The case may be said to illustrate the dangers of specifying special periods of limitation for particular causes of action, given the frequency of overlapping claims.

THOMSON

SWEET & MAXWELL

™

Thank you for purchasing **Gatley on Libel and Slander, 1st supplement to the 10th edition.**

Supplements to your main work

Gatley is supplemented regularly in order to keep your main work up-to-date with ongoing developments.

In order to receive your updating supplements to **Gatley** automatically on publication *you need to register*. Supplements will be invoiced on publication. You can cancel your request at any time.

How to register

Either complete and return this FREEPOST card, or, if you have purchased your copy of **Gatley** from a bookshop or other supplier, please ask your supplier to ensure that you are registered to receive your supplements.

Yes, please send me updating supplements to **Gatley on Libel and Slander, 10th edition** on publication, unless countermanded.

Name: _____

Organisation: _____

_____

Address: _____

_____

_____

Postcode: _____

Telephone: _____

Email: _____

S&M account number: (if known) _____

Signed: _____ Date: _____

LBU0975C

STANDING ORDERS

SWEET & MAXWELL

FREEPOST

PO Box 2000

ANDOVER

SP10 9AH

UNITED KINGDOM

CHAPTER 20

MALICIOUS FALSEHOOD

SECTION 1. INTRODUCTION

Generally. *Note 3.* In *Barratt International Resorts Ltd v Barratt Owners'* **20.1**
Group [2002] ScotCS 318 Lord Wheatley said:

"[24] . . . An action of damages for verbal injury is plainly now a well settled remedy
in Scots law. The term is recognised in a side title to section 14(b) of the Defamation
Act 1952 which applies to Scotland. It has been suggested (*Walker on Delict*, 2nd ed.
p. 902) that a more appropriate title for the present sort of action might be injurious or
malicious falsehood, although such descriptions may only reflect attempts to define
particular aspects of the nature of the various types of action for verbal injury. In
particular, such a suggestion might indicate that in all cases the words injurious and
malicious were interchangeable. In fact, an action of this kind may on one view require
the averment and proof of both malice and injury. These various terms originate from
English law from which much of the Scottish jurisprudence has developed. However,
from the authorities there now appears to be a settled Scottish position.
[25] . . . An action for verbal injury arises out of harm said to be done to a person
in his business relations by written or verbal falsehoods. That being so, it follows that
an action for interdict and *interim* interdict is competent against an apprehended delict
of this kind. The term 'verbal injury' is therefore distinct from defamation, which is the
remedy available to someone whose personal reputation has been injured by the
expression of written or verbal falsehoods. It is also distinct from *convicium* which is
concerned with the hurt to an individual's feelings and public reputation, by being
brought into public hatred, contempt and ridicule. Further, there are various types of
slanders, recognised principally in the English authorities, but which are of no concern
in the present case. Different considerations clearly apply to these various kinds of
action.
[26] . . . In respect of an action for verbal injury the delict consists in 'maliciously
communicating written or oral falsehoods calculated in the ordinary course to produce,
and in fact producing, actual damage' (*Walker* p. 902). The ingredients of such an action
are that false statements, either written or verbal, must be maliciously communicated to
third parties, which are calculated or likely to produce, and which in fact do produce,
actual damage to the pursuers' business interests. It is not necessary for the pursuers to
aver and prove that the defenders knew that the statements were false."

[99]

SECTION 2. MALICIOUS FALSEHOOD

20.7   **Malice.** "The question [in malicious falsehood] is whether the person communicating the information about the claimant was acting in good faith in doing so" (*Friend v Civil Aviation Authority* [2005] EWHC 201, QBD at [235] *per* Eady J.).

20.11   **Damage must be pecuniary.** *Damages for distress etc where pecuniary loss proved or presumed.* In *Murtough v Betham* [2004] NSWSC 753 Buddin J., having considered *Joyce v Sengupta* and *Khodaparast v Shad*, considered it unclear how far, if at all, the law now allowed recovery for non-pecuniary loss in cases of malicious falsehood.

20.13   **Damage: cases falling within section 3 of the Defamation Act 1952.** *Add*: In applying s.3 it is necessary to bear in mind the basic principle of company law that a wrong to a company is actionable by the company and not its individual members. So if a malicious falsehood is calculated to cause damage to a company that does not mean it is calculated to cause damage to the directors (*Dorset Flint & Stone Blocks Ltd v Moir* [2004] EWHC 2173, QBD, where Eady J. thought it conceivable that something might be done to cure the pleaded case but the action was dismissed in view of other deficiencies in it).

CHAPTER 21

OTHER CAUSES OF ACTION ARISING FROM STATEMENTS

SECTION 1. NEGLIGENCE

Limits on liability for negligence. For a situation in which there might be **21.5** liability for defamation (subject to the protection of qualified privilege) but no duty of care in negligence see *W v Westminster City Council* [2004] EWHC 2866, QBD; this Supplement, para.13.1.

Note 46. It has been suggested that *Wade v State of Victoria* may be inconsistent with the thrust of the High Court's decision in *Sullivan v Moody* (2001) 183 A.L.R. 404; *Cornwall v Rowan* [2004] SASC 384; 90 S.A.S.R. 269 at [694].

SECTION 2. PRIVACY, CONFIDENCE, DATA PROTECTION AND HARASSMENT

(a) *Introductory*

No protected right of privacy? It is now clear that there is no wrong of **21.9** invasion of privacy *as such* under English common law: see this Supplement, para.21.14.

(b) *Human Rights Act 1998*

The European Convention on Human Rights. The point has been made **21.12** elsewhere (this Supplement, para.1.2) that English lawyers have been accustomed to think of Art.8 of the Convention in terms of "privacy". Many situations which engage Art.8 cannot involve liability for defamation: there may be no statement of any sort, merely intrusion into private life; if there is a statement it may be embarrassing or offensive but not defamatory; even if it is defamatory it may be probably true or protected by absolute or qualified privilege. In any of these situations a claim for defamation will fail and in some it will fail *in limine*. However, Art.8 embraces the protection of reputation as well as privacy (see this Supplement, para.1.2) and the potential consequences are indicated by *W v Westminster City Council* [2004] EWHC 2866, QBD; [2005] 1 F.L.R. 816 (the first judgment) and [2005] EWHC 102, QBD (the second judgment). The judgments are to be read together ([2005] EWHC 102, QBD at [1]) (at the time of writing the available texts of the judgments are not numbered sequentially as is intended: *ibid.*).

The claimant was the father of a child by M. M had another child, S, who was on the defendants' Child Protection Register. A report prepared for a Case Conference referred to the relationship between the claimant and S, to the fact that the claimant had taken her for dinner to expensive restaurants and bought her gifts, and stated that during the "Core Assessment that was done last year professionals raised the concern that the [claimant] might be grooming [S] for prostitution". The claimant sued for libel. In the first judgment Tugendhat J. held that the statement was not protected by absolute privilege (see this Supplement, para.13.1). In the second judgment he held that the publication to the others at the Case Conference was on an occasion of qualified privilege and there was no malice. Although the defendants had contravened statutory guidelines about the investigation and reporting of such matters the defendants had acted in good faith in performing their statutory functions and the public interest required some latitude for mistakes. Hence the claim for libel failed. However, in the first judgment at [103] Tugendhat J. had suggested (though the point was not in fact argued) that in a case against a public authority:

> "it is possible, in an appropriate case, that a court might, in a claim under s.7 of the [Human Rights Act 1998, which enables proceedings to be brought against a public authority which has acted in a way incompatible with the claimant's Convention rights] be willing to investigate the truth or falsity of words complained of, and to grant some declaration, even if the claim is clearly one to which a defence of privilege would be available, if brought in libel. Comparison may be made with the Data Protection Act 1998, which was implemented to give effect to Art 8 rights in relation to personal information, and which made those rights available against anyone (if the statutory conditions are fulfilled) and not just against public authorities. Remedies of rectification and erasure are available under s.14, subject, of course, to the provisions of the Act. The focus of the Court's inquiry would not be confined, as it is in a libel action, mainly to the state of mind of the defendant, and to the proceedings only in so far as they could be relied on in aggravation of damages. The court would be asked to look at the proceedings as a whole"

After the first judgment, a new claim was added under the Human Rights Act, ss.7 and 8, alleging that the defendants knew or ought to have known that the claimant's rights would be infringed if the words complained of were published in the Report to the Case Conference, that such infringement would injure the claimant's reputation, would cause him distress and embarrassment and "would foreseeably cause serious damage to his family life", but they failed to take reasonable steps that would have avoided that infringement (at [2005] EWHC 102, QBD [168]).

The defendants' contention that the law of qualified privilege in libel was a complete code of public policy in this area and that it should therefore be equally applicable to a claim under the Human Rights Act, was rejected (*cf. Spring v Guardian Assurance*, Main Work, para.21.3, where a similar argument was rejected in the context of the relationship between defamation and the tort of negligence). In revealing the suspicions at the Case Conference in the presence of the mother and the claimant without considering the balance between the rights of the claimant and S and without investigation or consulting the claimant on the subject, the defendants, despite their good faith, had committed a breach of the claimant's Art.8 rights. However, the breach was not one "at the higher end of possible gravity" (at [241]), the claimant had received a reasonably prompt apology and retraction and the case was not one for the award of damages as opposed to a declaration. In the context of remedies under the Act, it may be noted that the House of Lords a few days later emphasised that the Strasbourg practice and not English scales of tort damages was the proper guide (*R. (Greenfield) v Secretary of State for the Home Department* [2005] UKHL 14; [2005] 2 All E.R. 240). The case concerns a violation of Art.6 but what is said on this point is plainly of wider application. Nevertheless, even if damages may be neither so frequent nor so large as in libel, a defendant may still find himself exposed on this basis to liability and substantial costs in circumstances where a claim for libel would fail. For example, had *W v Westminster* arisen through gross and prolonged carelessness and the material been more widely disseminated with more serious damage to the claimant, the outcome of the libel claim might have been the same but it does not follow that the same would have been true of the human rights claim. Furthermore, the fact that the balancing exercise between Art.8 rights and the public interest requires to be worked out on a case-by-case basis rather than by the application of fairly standardised categories means that it may be more difficult to have some cases dismissed at an early stage. However, it does not seem likely that any of the standard categories of absolute privilege (in particular, proceedings in Parliament—*cf. A v UK* (2003) 36 E.H.R.R. 51— judicial proceedings and contemporaneous reports of judicial proceedings) or the statutory "report" privileges under Sch.1 to the Defamation Act 1996 could be outflanked via a human rights attack.

Impact of the Act where there is no direct interference with a Convention   **21.14**
right by a public authority. There are three major appellate decisions considering the relationship of the Convention and the common law in the context of privacy.

In *Wainwright v Home Office* [2003] UKHL 53; [2004] 2 A.C. 406 the claimants were subjected to a strip-search conducted in an unauthorised manner while visiting a prison. This involved a battery on one of them but the dismissal of their claims in other respects was upheld. The House of Lords rejected the invitation to declare that at common law there was a tort of invasion of privacy. While in relation to the publication of personal information the law of confidence had certainly been expanded well beyond the traditional cases in which information had been imparted by one person to another, it had not expanded to the extent necessary to cover the case before the court; and while privacy was a value which underlay the existence of a rule of law (such as the law of confidence) and which might point the direction in which the law should develop, it was not a principle of law in itself capable without more of giving a cause of action for its infringement. The facts occurred before the coming into force of the Human Rights Act 1998 and, the defendants being a public authority, it was suggested in the Court of Appeal that the claimants would have had a strong case for damages under the Act on the basis of infringement of Art.8 of the Convention. Lord Hoffmann was more doubtful. On the facts the judge made no finding that the prison officers intended to cause distress or realised that they were acting without justification and said that they had acted in good faith and that the "deviations from the procedure laid down for strip-searches were, in my judgment, not intended to increase the humiliation necessarily involved but merely sloppiness". In Lord Hoffmann's view:

> "Although article 8 guarantees a right of privacy, I do not think that it treats that right as having been invaded and requiring a remedy in damages, irrespective of whether the defendant acted intentionally, negligently or accidentally. It is one thing to wander carelessly into the wrong hotel bedroom and another to hide in the wardrobe to take photographs. Article 8 may justify a monetary remedy for an intentional invasion of privacy by a public authority, even if no damage is suffered other than distress for which damages are not ordinarily recoverable. It does not follow that a merely negligent act should, contrary to general principle, give rise to a claim for damages for distress because it affects privacy rather than some other interest like bodily safety."

Cf., however, Baroness Hale in *Campbell v MGN Ltd* [2004] UKHL 22; [2004] 2 A.C. 457 at [133].

Campbell v MGN Ltd is a case about publication of personal information. The claimant, a model, had asserted that she did not take drugs. The defendants published a story to the effect that she was attending meetings of a group, Narcotics Anonymous, to receive therapy for drug addiction, gave details of the nature of the therapy and showed pictures of her in the street leaving meetings of the group. It was held that (as was in fact conceded) the publication of the fact that she was receiving therapy could be published without breach of confidence because while such information might normally be regarded as private, the defendants were entitled to publish it to rebut her denials of drug-taking. However, a majority of the House of Lords held that the defendants were not entitled to publish either the details of the therapy or the photographs. The details were akin to medical records and the revelation of the location of the therapy by the photographs might deter her from seeking further assistance from the group. For the minority, on the other hand, the additional information did not add significantly to the hurt which she suffered from the (justified) publication of the fact of her addiction. The court was divided, not on the general principles of law applicable but on their precise application to the facts (see *Douglas v Hello! Ltd (No.2)* [2005] EWCA Civ 595; [2005] 4 All E.R. 128 at [76]). The claim was based squarely and solely upon the common law of confidence. In fact the information came to the defendants either from a member of the claimant's entourage or another member of the therapy group so that the case would have fallen within the traditional idea that where information is imparted to A in confidence an obligation of confidence will also be imposed on B, to whom it has been imparted by A. However, the speeches rest on the assumption that the result would have been the same even if the information had been acquired by chance observation by the defendants themselves. Therefore the case decisively affirms the proposition that where the defendant publishes private information it is not now necessary that the claimant should have revealed this to him or to anyone else. In other words, the law now recognises "the artificiality of distinguishing between confidential information obtained through the violation of a confidential relationship and similar information obtained in some other way" (Lord Hoffmann at [46]).

> "This cause of action has now firmly shaken off the limiting constraint of the need for an initial confidential relationship. In doing so it has changed its nature . . . Now the law imposes a 'duty of confidence' whenever a person receives information he knows or ought to know is fairly and reasonably to be regarded as confidential. Even this formulation is awkward. The continuing use of the phrase 'duty of confidence' and the description of the information as 'confidential' is not altogether comfortable. Information about an individual's private life would not, in ordinary usage, be called 'confidential'. The more natural description today is that such information is private. The essence of the tort is better encapsulated now as misuse of private information" (Lord Nicholls at [14]).

These are judgments dissenting as to the result but not as to this principle.

In Convention terms there is of course a tension of competing rights between Arts 8 and 10, which requires a balancing exercise. The approach in *Campbell* has been summarised as follows in *Re S (A Child) (Identification: Restrictions on Publication)* [2004] UKHL 47; [2005] 1 A.C. 593 at [17]:

> "What does . . . emerge clearly from the opinions are four propositions. First, neither article *as such* has precedence over the other. Secondly, where the values under the two articles are in conflict, an intense focus on the comparative importance of the rights being claimed in the individual case is necessary. Thirdly, the justifications for interfering with or restricting each right must be taken into account. Finally, the proportionality test must be applied to each."

Douglas v Hello! Ltd (No.2) [2005] EWCA Civ 595; [2005] 4 All E.R. 128 is the substantive appeal (from [2003] EWHC 786 (Ch); [2003] E.M.L.R. 31 (liability) and [2003] EWHC 2629 (Ch); [2004] E.M.L.R. 2 (damages)) of the claims involved in the interlocutory proceedings referred to in this paragraph of the Main Work. The claimants D and J sold exclusive rights to publication of photographs of their wedding to the claimants *OK!*. Despite security precautions at the wedding, a paparazzo managed to infiltrate it and take photographs, which he sold to the defendants *Hello!*, a rival of *OK!*. *Hello!* published these photographs knowing, at least in broad terms, of the exclusive deal between *OK!* and D and J. The award of damages to D and J on the basis of breach of confidence was upheld (see this Supplement, para.21.15) but an appeal against a judgment in favour of *Hello!* was allowed (see this Supplement, para.21.16).

As to the claims of D and J, the Court of Appeal said that the effect of the cases culminating in *Campbell* was that "knowledge, actual or imputed, that information is private will normally impose on anyone publishing that information the duty to justify what, in the absence of justification, will be a wrongful invasion of privacy" (at [82]). The vehicle the English courts must use to give effect to the obligation under the Convention to protect one individual from an unjustified invasion of private life by another individual was the action "formerly described as breach of confidence" (see Lord Nicholls in *Campbell*, above) and now focused on misuse of private information. The facts that the occurrence of the wedding was common knowledge and that D and J had already sold exclusive rights in photographs of their wedding to *OK!* did not prevent the event being "private" for this purpose. The greater part of the damages awarded to D and J had in fact been for cost and inconvenience of having to deal at short notice with the selection of the authorised photographs to enable them to be published in *OK!* to meet the unauthorised publication in *Hello!*. This was much closer to the traditional confidence claim for disclosure of trade secrets because it arose from interference with their commercial exploitation of the wedding. The Court concluded that where "an individual has at his disposal information which he has created or which is private or personal and to which he can properly deny access to third parties, and he reasonably intends to profit commercially by using or publishing that information, then a third party who is, or ought to be, aware of these matters and who has knowingly obtained the information without authority, will be in breach of duty if he uses or publishes the information to the detriment of the [individual] (at [118]). However, the agreement between D and J and *OK!* was not such as to entitle *OK!* to sue for breach of confidence (this Supplement, para.21.15). Nor could *OK!* sue on the basis of unlawful interference with its business or unlawful interference with its contractual rights: while the interference with the rights of D and J would be unlawful means in tort for the purposes of a claim by *OK!* the conduct of *Hello!* was not aimed or directed at *OK!* in the sense required for these intentional wrongs.

Note 36. The scope of *Wilkinson v Downton* is discussed in *Wainwright v Home Office* (above). In *Wilkinson* the plaintiff suffered what would now be called psychiatric injury and since the demise of the rule that such harm was not compensable at all in negligence it is unnecessary to embark on the artificial extension of the concept of intention which was adopted in that case: the intentional infliction of such harm and the negligent infliction of it are both actionable, however exactly one classifies the cases. The negligent infliction of distress short of psychiatric injury is not actionable; whether such "harm" should be actionable in any circumstances if intentionally inflicted (at the moment it is not unless there is some form of trespass to the person) is left open by Lord Hoffmann (with whom the other members of the House agreed) but if this step were to be taken it would be necessary to limit the meaning of intention; and even on this basis, the requirement of a course of conduct in the Protection from Harassment Act 1997 "shows that Parliament was conscious that it might not be in the public interest to allow the law to be set in motion for one boorish incident [and] it may be that any development of the common law should show similar caution" (at [46]).

(c) *Confidence*

21.15   **Nature of law of confidence.** *Terminology.* The "adaptation" of the law of confidence to cover disclosures of private information even though it has not been voluntarily imparted by the subject of the information has led to a certain degree of judicial discomfort with "breach of confidence" (see *Campbell v MGN Ltd* and *Douglas v Hello! Ltd*, this Supplement, para.21.14). In *Douglas v Hello! Ltd (No.2)* the Court of Appeal referred to the action "formerly described as breach of confidence" ([2005] EWCA Civ 595 at [53]). However, later in the judgment the traditional expression is used several times (e.g. in the heading before [92], in [96], [99], [102], [103] and [107]) seemingly with reference to the present state of the law. However, what we have is a variant or off-shoot of an old cause of action, not a new tort. A supplement does not seem the right occasion to abandon the traditional terminology but the reader should bear in mind that the focus of the cases discussed here is "misuse of private information".

Classification. In *Campbell v MGN Ltd* [2004] UKHL 22; [2004] 2 A.C. 457 Lord Nicholls at [14]–[15] described the "expanded" wrong of breach of confidence involving publication of private information as a tort. However, in *Douglas v Hello! Ltd (No.2)* (this Supplement, para.21.14) the Court of Appeal, referring to the *Kitechnology* case (note 50) concluded "not without hesitation" that it was not a tort. They found persuasive the suggestion that it fell to be "categorised as a restitutionary claim for unjust enrichment" (at [97]). As in *Kitechnology* the issue was one of the conflict of laws (or at least related to that area), because the wedding took place in New York. However, the publication took place in England, so the matter was clearly covered by English law and the Court rejected the defendant's argument that because a publication by the photographer in New York would not (as was conceded) have been actionable there, *Hello!* could not be any worse off in respect of a publication of the photographs in England. The question whether the information was "private" was to be considered by reference to English law. The position in New York was relevant to the question of whether the claimants had a reasonable expectation of privacy in England, so that if, for example, the law of New York had provided a general public right to attend and take and publish photographs at anyone's wedding, D and J could not have contended that they had a reasonable expectation that such photographs would not be published here; but the law of New York provided no such thing and the absence of any legal remedy for publication there did not render the wedding a public occasion. Indeed, the judge's finding that under the law of New York the photographer was a trespasser was not challenged.

The classification of an award of damages for breach of confidence as a restitutionary remedy gives rise to some difficulty. A restitutionary claim is generally regarded as falling under one of two headings: "autonomous" restitution, as where recovery is sought of money paid under mistake or duress and "restitution for wrongs", such as torts or breaches of contract and including equitable wrongs. In either event, however, the claim is based on the fact that the defendant has been unjustly enriched at the claimant's expense. In *Douglas* the Court had no hesitation in saying that if *Hello!* had made a profit on the wrongful publication, D and J would have been entitled to an account of that profit. That would have been well in line with the approach in traditional trade secret cases, where an account of profits is a very apt remedy. In fact, however, *Hello!* made a loss on the exercise and what D and J were awarded damages for was (a) the distress suffered from the publication, and (b) the cost and inconvenience of making arrangements for the emergency publication by *OK!*. The first of these bears more than a passing resemblance to the categories where a tort is actionable per se (such as libel); it is difficult to see how either of them can be based on any enrichment of the defendant. It is submitted that the better view is that either this form of breach of confidence is a tort or, if it is not, it is an equitable wrong where the remedy follows the tort "pattern".

The legal nature of confidential (private) information. In *Douglas v Hello! Ltd (No.2)* (this Supplement, para.21.14) the claim of *OK!* for damages for breach of confidence failed in the Court of Appeal (as to the claim for damages under the economic torts, which also failed, see this Supplement, para.21.14). D and J had sold *OK!* the exclusive right to publish authorised photographs of the wedding approved by D and J, in other words, they granted them a licence to do what would otherwise have been wrongful in relation to those photographs. But what *OK!* was complaining of was the publication of other, unauthorised photographs. These had the effect of devaluing *OK!*'s licence rights (hence the claim under the economic torts) but in no sense had the defendants published private information about *OK!*. What the defendants had published was information about D and J in respect of which *OK!* had no rights (other than a contractual right against D and J that *they* should not publish any photographs so as to reduce the value of *OK!*'s rights). The "residual confidentiality" in the wedding remained in D and J and the claim being advanced by *OK!* was in fact at odds with that (at [136]).

It is, however, more difficult to accept the assertion, which seems unnecessary for the decision, that a right in private information is not a right of property and hence incapable of transfer (at [119]). D and J's:

"interest in the private information about events at the wedding did not amount to a right of intellectual property. Their right to protection of that interest does not arise because they have some form of proprietary interest in it. If that were the nature of the right, it would be one that could be exercised against a third party regardless of whether he ought to have been aware that the information was private or confidential. In fact the right depends upon the effect on the third party's conscience of the third party's knowledge of the nature of the information and the circumstances in which it was obtained" (at [126]).

However, no one could contest that an equitable interest in land or goods was "property" but it is a proprietary right which is defeated by the acquisition of the subject matter by a bona fide purchaser without notice (putting aside those cases where the principles of equity have been modified by a system of registration) and is not therefore binding on a third party "regardless etc." Furthermore, at least one case cited by the Court does seem squarely to support the proposition that rights in confidential information can be transferred so as to allow the transferee the right to enforce the confidence: *O. Mustad & Son v Dosen* [1964] 1 W.L.R. 109n.

21.16   **Remedies: injunction.** The decision of the Court of Appeal in *Cream Holdings Ltd v Banerjee* was reversed by the House of Lords ([2004] UKHL 44; [2005] 1 A.C. 253). "Likely" in s.12(3) creates no single standard.

"On its proper construction the effect of section 12(3) is that the court is not to make an interim restraint order unless satisfied the applicant's prospects of success at the trial are sufficiently favourable to justify such an order being made in the particular circumstances of the case. As to what degree of likelihood makes the prospects of success 'sufficiently favourable', the general approach should be that courts will be exceedingly slow to make interim restraint orders where the applicant has not satisfied the court he will probably ('more likely than not') succeed at the trial. In general, that should be the threshold an applicant must cross before the court embarks on exercising its discretion, duly taking into account the relevant jurisprudence on article 10 and any countervailing Convention rights. But there will be cases where it is necessary for a court to depart from this general approach and a lesser degree of likelihood will suffice as a prerequisite. Circumstances where this may be so include those . . . where the potential adverse consequences of disclosure are particularly grave, or where a short-lived injunction is needed to enable the court to hear and give proper consideration to an application for interim relief pending the trial or any relevant appeal" (at [22]).

In *Douglas v Hello! Ltd (No.2)* [2005] EWCA Civ 595; [2005] 4 All E.R. 128 (see this Supplement, para.21.14) the Court of Appeal had in earlier proceedings ([2001] Q.B. 967) discharged an interim injunction on the ground that damages would be an adequate remedy for the claimants D and J and *OK!*. D and J were ultimately awarded modest damages for breach of confidence and the claim of *OK!* was dismissed on appeal. The Court of Appeal has now said that in the light of subsequent decisions it was wrong to have discharged the injunction. D and J had an almost unanswerable claim for the protection of their privacy, perhaps enough to have justified summary judgment in their favour. The Court of Appeal in the earlier proceedings appeared to have assumed that the damages awarded would be much higher than they in fact were and, while the final award was unassailable in principle, they did not amount to an adequate remedy.

"The sum is also small in the sense that it could not represent any real deterrent to a newspaper or magazine, with a large circulation, contemplating the publication of photographs which infringed an individual's privacy. Accordingly, particularly in the light of the state of competition in the newspaper and magazine industry, the refusal of an interlocutory injunction in a case such as this represents a strong potential disincentive to respect for aspects of private life, which the Convention intends should be respected" (at [257]).

No prior relationship. *Douglas v Hello! Ltd (No.2)* [2005] EWCA Civ 595;   **21.19** [2005] 4 All E.R. 128 (see this Supplement, para.21.14) is a clear example of an obligation of confidence (though see this Supplement, para.21.15 as to terminology) arising without any prior relationship or "confiding". The information in *Campbell v MGN Ltd* [2004] UKHL 22; [2004] 2 A.C. 457 (see this Supplement, para.21.14) had originated with a person in a prior relationship with the claimant but the reasoning does not depend on this.

Note 88. See *Re S (A Child) (Identification: Restrictions on Publication)* [2004] UKHL 47; [2005] 1 A.C. 593; this Supplement, para.13.35.

Note 90. Photographs in public places. The photograph in *Campbell v MGN Ltd*, above, was taken in the street and was in itself innocuous but the majority of the House of Lords held that it was none the less "private" information in part because its close association with the venue of the therapy made it peculiarly intrusive and in part because of what it revealed about the location of that venue. It seems that the use of another photograph of the claimant taken on another occasion to illustrate the article would have been unobjectionable in law. However, there was some disagreement among the minority on a more general plane about the extent to which the law will restrain the use of photographs of people taken in public places even where the photograph reveals no other information. Lord Hope at [122] seems to suggest that the result in *Aubry v Editions Vice-Versa* (note 90) would be the same even in the common law, where there is no statutory right to control the use of one's image: one cannot complain if a photograph of a street scene is published in which one is merely an incidental presence, but one can complain of the publication of an unauthorised photograph taken in a public place where one is the main subject of it. *Cf.* Baroness Hale at [154]:

"Unlike France and Quebec, in this country we do not recognise a right to one's own image: cf. *Aubry v Editions Vice-Versa Inc* [1998] 1 SCR 591. We have not so far held that the mere fact of covert photography is sufficient to make the information contained in the photograph confidential. The activity photographed must be private. If this had been, and had been presented as, a picture of Naomi Campbell going about her business in a public street, there could have been no complaint. She makes a substantial part of her living out of being photographed looking stunning in designer clothing. Readers will obviously be interested to see how she looks if and when she pops out to the shops for a bottle of milk. There is nothing essentially private about that information nor can it be expected to damage her private life. It may not be a high order of freedom of speech but there is nothing to justify interfering with it."

A similar approach is taken by the New Zealand Court of Appeal in *Hosking v Runting* [2004] NZCA 34; [2005] 1 N.Z.L.R. 1. This case arose from the publication of innocuous photographs, taken in the street, of the infant children of the plaintiffs, a celebrity couple. The majority of the court was prepared to accept that the New Zealand common law had arrived at the position where it should recognise a wrong of misuse of private information (the New Zealand Bill of Rights Act deliberately omits any guarantee of privacy and the New Zealand Privacy Act 1993 does not create a remedy by civil action) but declined to find liability on the facts. There was no evidence that the publication of the photographs could produce any harm to the children, the photographs did no more than record information which was available to any passer-by in the street, no reasonable person could take offence a them and a person in a public place had no reasonable expectation of privacy in respect of innocuous photographs.

Cf. Stanton v Metro Corp. 357 F. Supp. 2d 369 (D. Mass. 2005). A photograph of the plaintiff taken at a high school "prom" was used as the header to an article which discussed teenage sexual behaviour. Although otherwise capable of being defamatory, the court with some reluctance held that a "disclaimer" in the article prevented this. A privacy claim failed because as a general rule publication of a photograph taken in a public place was not wrongful and Massachusetts did not recognise the "false light" version of privacy.

Lord Hope in *Campbell* relies on *Peck v United Kingdom* [2003] 36 EHRR 719 but that was a case of the applicant attempting to commit suicide and could therefore perhaps be brought within the concept of a "private act". However, the subsequent European Court of Human Rights case of *von Hannover v Germany* (2005) 40 E.H.R.R. 1 lends indirect support to Lord Hope's view.

The proceedings arose from the attempts in the German courts of the applicant, Princess Caroline of Hannover (née Grimaldi of Monaco) to restrain the publication in magazines of a number of series of photographs of her. The *Bundesgerichtshof* (Federal Court of Justice) restrained publication of photographs showing her in a restaurant courtyard with a man since in that respect they had retired to a secluded place away from the public eye. The *Bundesversfassungsgericht* (Federal Constitutional Court) further held that the issue of the publication of photographs of the applicant with her children required further consideration under the *Grundgesetz* (Basic Law) and remitted that aspect of the case. In fact the magazine subsequently undertook not to republish this group of photographs. However, the refusal of the *Bundesgerichtshof* to restrain the publication of the other photographs taken in open places frequented by the public was upheld. Although the applicant was the daughter of the Prince of Monaco she had no constitutional role in that territory and, while she fulfilled certain "representative" roles at formal events, the photographs did not relate to such occasions. Nevertheless, in the words of the *Bundesversfassungsgericht*:

> "General personality rights do not require publications that are not subject to prior consent to be limited to pictures of figures of contemporary society in the exercise of their function in society. Very often the public interest aroused by such figures does not relate exclusively to the exercise of their function in the strict sense. It can, on the contrary, by virtue of the particular function and its impact, extend to information about the way in which these figures behave generally—that is, also outside their function—in public. The public has a legitimate interest in being allowed to judge whether the personal behaviour of the individuals in question, who are often regarded as idols or role models, convincingly tallies with their behaviour on their official engagements.
>
> If, on the other hand, the right to publish pictures of people considered to be figures of contemporary society were to be limited to their official functions, insufficient account would be taken of the public interest properly aroused by such figures and this would, moreover, favour a selective presentation that would deprive the public of certain necessary judgmental possibilities in respect of figures of socio-political life, having regard to the function of role model of such figures and the influence they exert."

In two other sets of proceedings between 1997 and 2000 injunctions were refused against the publication of other series of photographs (including one of the applicant tripping over an obstacle at the Monte Carlo Beach Club) and the *Bundesversfassungsgericht* declined to entertain appeals.

The European Court of Human Rights unanimously held that the decisions of the German courts had, by setting too narrow a limit to the protection of privacy, led to a violation of Art.8 of the Convention. The majority opinion is, while startling to the tabloid media, at least simple. Even where the applicant is, as the German courts put it, an *absolute "Person der Zeitgeschichte"* (public figure par excellence/all purpose public figure) publication of even anodyne, inoffensive photographs taken where he is fully exposed to the public view can only be justified if that person is performing a public function or the publication contributes to some political or public debate.

> "[The] Court . . . considers that the decisive factor in balancing the protection of private life against freedom of expression should lie in the contribution that the published photos and articles make to a debate of general interest. It is clear in the instant case that they made no such contribution since the applicant exercises no official function and the photos and articles related exclusively to details of her private life.
>
> Furthermore, the Court considers that the public does not have a legitimate interest in knowing where the applicant is and how she behaves generally in her private life

even if she appears in places that cannot always be described as secluded and despite the fact that she is well known to the public.

Even if such a public interest exists, as does a commercial interest of the magazines in publishing these photos and these articles, in the instant case those interests must, in the Court's view, yield to the applicant's right to the effective protection of her private life" (at [76]–[77]).

The separate opinions of Judges Cabral Barreto and Zupancic are more cautious but also difficult to frame in terms of predictable rules to guide the behaviour of the press. For the former, it is clear that the public had a right to be informed about Princess Caroline's life, for "fame and public interest inevitably give rise to a difference in treatment of the private life of an ordinary person and a public figure" and he appears even to regard such information as capable of "contributing to a public debate"; furthermore, he is willing to accept that where the applicant is a role model the public has a legitimate interest in being able to judge whether their "private" behaviour tallies with the image they project, for example on official occasions. However, his conclusions on the individual photographs are surprising (at least to someone who has not seen them and has to rely on the descriptions in the report). The photograph of the applicant shopping in the market were not protected by any privacy right, nor were those of her fall at the Monte Carlo Beach Club, which were the only ones which might be regarded as embarrassing to her and which, moreover, were taken by long lens photography. Paradoxically, however, he regarded the photographs of the applicant horse riding and playing tennis as protected by Art.8. Judge Zupancic, while sharing his colleague's "hesitations" and accepting that "he who steps on to the public stage cannot claim to be a person entitled to anonymity", prefers a broad test of whether the matter being photographed is one which involves a "reasonable expectation of privacy", though he makes no attempt to apply this to the individual photographs. Neither separate opinion fits at all easily with the majority view that people "need to know exactly when and where they are in a protected sphere or, on the contrary, in a sphere in which they must expect interference from others, especially the tabloid press" (at [73]).

It is difficult to say how far the assumptions on which *Campbell* is built are consistent with the European Court of Human Rights' approach. Leaving aside the views of Lord Hope, it seems plain that if the particular story about Naomi Campbell had been illustrated with a photograph taken on another occasion the publication of it would not have been wrongful. *A fortiori*, therefore, the publication of a feature on Naomi Campbell's career, unconnected with drug taking and illustrated with innocuous photographs would not have been wrongful. Would it be wrongful under the *Hannover* dispensation? The very idea seems absurd because it would mean that the tabloid press would be confined to the publication of agreed, paid-for features of the *Hello!/OK!* type (with the rather obvious incidental effect of rendering "celebrity" a good deal more valuable a commodity). There is of course a clear difference between Naomi Campbell and the Princess of Hannover: it may fairly be said that the former built her career upon seeking publicity and the latter seems not to have sought it at all, the public interest in her being the product of her membership of the Grimaldi family and we cannot therefore be sure what the European Court of Human Rights would have said about the hypothetical case just posed. However, the general thrust of the majority judgment does seem in the direction of a rather "high-minded" view of the proper role of the media. Thus:

"The Court considers that a fundamental distinction needs to be made between report-ing facts—even controversial ones—capable of contributing to a debate in a democratic society relating to politicians in the exercise of their functions, for example, and reporting details of the private life of an individual who, moreover, as in this case, does not exercise official functions. While in the former case the press exercises its vital role of 'watchdog' in a democracy by contributing to 'impart[ing] information and ideas on matters of public interest' it does not do so in the latter case.

Similarly, although the public has a right to be informed, which is an essential right in a democratic society that, in certain special circumstances, can even extend to aspects of the private life of public figures, particularly where politicians are concerned, this is not the case here. The situation here does not come within the sphere of any political or public debate because the published photos and accompanying commentaries relate exclusively to details of the applicant's private life.

As in other similar cases it has examined, the Court considers that the publication of the photos and articles in question, of which the sole purpose was to satisfy the curiosity of a particular readership regarding the details of the applicant's private life, cannot be deemed to contribute to any debate of general interest to society despite the applicant being known to the public" (at [63]–[65]).

One may contrast what the *Bundesverfassungsgericht* said in the German proceedings:

"Nor can mere entertainment be denied any role in the formation of opinions. That would amount to unilaterally presuming that entertainment merely satisfies a desire for amusement, relaxation, escapism or diversion. Entertainment can also convey images of reality and propose subjects for debate that spark a process of discussion and assimila-tion relating to philosophies of life, values and behaviour models. In that respect it fulfils important social functions. . . . When measured against the aim of protecting press freedom, entertainment in the press is neither negligible nor entirely worthless and therefore falls within the scope of application of fundamental rights. . . .

The same is true of information about people. Personalization is an important journalistic means of attracting attention. Very often it is this which first arouses interest in a problem and stimulates a desire for factual information. Similarly, interest in a particular event or situation is usually stimulated by personalised accounts. Addition-ally, celebrities embody certain moral values and lifestyles. Many people base their choice of lifestyle on their example. They become points of crystallisation for adoption or rejection and act as examples or counter-examples. This is what explains the public interest in the various ups and downs occurring in their lives."

All one can say at this stage is that *von Hannover* has the potential to produce a very radical change in what the law regards as acceptable behaviour by the media, to an extent which would have been most unlikely to have got through Parliament.

The majority opinion in the European Court of Human Rights makes some play with the fact that for persons in the public eye the attentions of paparazzi may create a climate of continual harassment. It is true that in *some* cases in England that might fall within the statutory wrong of harassment (see para.21.31) but that would not serve in the generality of such cases: the legislation is built around the assumption that A is harassed by B, and not by a random succession of unconnected persons seeking to sell pictures or stories to the press.

Note 91. Various forms of voyeurism are now criminal offences under s.67 of the Sexual Offences Act 2003. The legislation incorporates the concepts of "reasonable expectation of privacy" and "private act", though the latter is a good deal narrower than in the civil law of confidence/privacy.

Venables case. See also *Green Corns Ltd v Claverley Group Ltd* [2005] EWHC 958, QBD.

21.20   **Information covered by the obligation.** In *Campbell v MGN Ltd*, this Supplement, para.21.14, the defendants were entitled to publish the fact of the claimant's treatment to rebut her assertions that she had not taken drugs. In *A v B*, 13 July 2005, QBD (no neutral citation currently available) Eady J. said at [17]:

> "i) In the context of personal information, which is treated differently in this respect from confidential information of a commercial nature, the fact that something has been published does not necessarily mean that further revelation cannot itself infringe the claimant's right to protect his privacy. That is especially the case perhaps where it is the defendant who has himself put the information into the public domain in the first place and would otherwise be enabling himself to profit from his own wrong (see *e.g. Att.-Gen. v Guardian Newspapers (No. 2)* [1990] 1 AC 109).
>
> ii) Where it is the claimant who has chosen to put personal information into the public domain, even though it may be such as to attract *prima facie* the protection of the law, it does not necessarily follow that it is open season for the media to publish any other information pertaining to the same subject matter (see *e.g. Douglas v Hello!* [2005] EWCA Civ 595). Individuals are permitted some degree of control over how much they choose to reveal."

And at [31]:

> "One has to recognise in this context that it is inherent in any communication of personal information to the public through the media that it may invite discussion. It would thus be unrealistic to confine future coverage to the precise details in the original revelations. People might wish to debate, for example, whether the revelations were accurate or whether they were so selective as to be misleading. It would be difficult to envisage circumstances in which this could be prevented on grounds of privacy."

Note 7. Thorpe v C.C. North Wales is considered in *Wood v C.C. West Midlands* [2004] EWCA Civ 1638; [2004] E.M.L.R. 17, a libel case arising out of police disclosure. See also *Green Corns Ltd v Claverley Group Ltd* [2005] EWHC 958, QBD.

On the lawfulness of "naming and shaming" schemes see *R. (Ellis) v C.C. Essex* [2003] EWHC 1321 and *R. (Stanley) v M.P.C.* [2004] EWHC 2229 (Admin).

21.21   **The public interest.** *"No confidence in iniquity"*. In *Campbell v MGN Ltd* [2004] UKHL 22; [2004] 2 A.C. 457 (this Supplement, para.21.14) it seems very likely that the claimant must have committed criminal offences in relation to her drug addiction and the defendants' editor had deposed that he considered her possible use of Class A drugs a valid reason for exposing her addiction. However, the only point at which criminality is mentioned in the House of Lords (at [151]) is in relation to the fact that her denials of drug taking entitled the defendants to "put the matter straight". In *Maccaba v Lichtenstein* [2004] EWHC 1579, QBD; [2005] E.M.L.R. 6 the claimant wrote unsolicited letters and poems to a young woman married to another man declaring his love for her and making a semi-serious proposal to pay her husband for her release. The woman consulted her rabbi, who disclosed the contents of the documents to the President of the claimant's synagogue. Gray J. dismissed the claim in respect of this disclosure. While in the normal way correspondence between A and B showing their feelings for each other woud be a prime candidate for the protection of the law, the claimant on these facts had no reasonable expectation of privacy in view of the impropriety of his conduct. In the alternative there was just cause for the limited disclosure which had taken place.

"There was a time when the defence of justification or just cause was expressed in the formula that the law of confidence cannot be invoked to prevent the disclosure of 'iniquity'. Iniquity is nowadays regarded as no more than one aspect of a broader defence of public interest or just cause. It seems to me that the letters and poems disclose facts which are 'iniquitous' " (at [7]).

In *A v B* , 13 July 2005, QBD (no neutral citation currently available) Eady J. said at [33]:

"for public policy reasons there would be powerful arguments against concealing, with the assistance of the court, information about one's criminal activities. This could not be an inflexible rule, as there *might* be circumstances in which the court would think it right for spent convictions or past acquittals not to be revealed to the general public. One example might be where the defendant was blackmailing the claimant. Never-theless, it would be hard to justify the concealment of information about (say) domestic violence or tax evasion simply because it has taken place behind closed doors. It could hardly be categorised as information in respect of which there would be a reasonable expectation of confidentiality. Nor would the law generally imply a duty of confidence. As it used to be said, 'there is no confidence in iniquity': see e.g. *Gartside v Outram* (1857) 26 L.J. Ch. 113. The courts might well baulk at assisting in the concealment of Class A drug consumption, especially if it has taken place in public. On the other hand, as Mr Spearman pointed out, the law is prepared to acknowledge in some circum-stances, as the *Campbell* case illustrates, that problems of addiction may be kept private—notwithstanding that it will often be implicit in such information that illegal supply must have occurred or other offences under the misuse of drugs legislation."

(d) *Data protection*

Data to which the Act applies. *Durant v Financial Services Authority* [2003] **21.24** EWCA Civ 1746; [2004] F.S.R. 28 arose from a claim to access to personal data under the Act and considers various matters on the scope of the 1998 Act.

What is "personal data"?

"Not all information retrieved from a computer search against an individual's name or unique identifier is personal data within the Act. Mere mention of the data subject in a document held by a data controller does not necessarily amount to his personal data. Whether it does so in any particular instance depends on where it falls in a continuum of relevance or proximity to the data subject as distinct, say, from transactions or matters in which he may have been involved to a greater or lesser degree. It seems to me that there are two notions that may be of assistance. The first is whether the information is biographical in a significant sense, that is, going beyond the recording of the putative data subject's involvement in a matter or an event that has no personal connotations, a life event in respect of which his privacy could not be said to be compromised. The second is one of focus. The information should have the putative data subject as its focus rather than some other person with whom he may have been involved or some transaction or event in which he may have figured or have had an interest, for example, as in this case, an investigation into some other person's or body's conduct that he may have instigated. In short, it is information that affects his privacy, whether in his personal or family life, business or professional capacity" (at [28] *per* Auld L.J.).

See also *Criminal Proceedings against Lindquist* (2003) Case C-101/01, ECJ, [2004] Q.B. 1014.

What is a "relevant filing system"? This is:

"limited to a system:

1) in which the files forming part of it are structured or referenced in such a way . . . as clearly to indicate at the outset of the search whether specific information capable of amounting to personal data of an individual requesting it under s 7 is held within the system and, if so, in which file or files it is held; and
2) which has, as part of its own structure or referencing mechanism, a sufficiently sophisticated and detailed means of readily indicating whether and where in an individual file or files specific criteria or information about the applicant can be readily located" (at [50] *per* Auld L.J.).

"Parliament intended to apply the Act to manual records only if they are of sufficient sophistication to provide the same or similar ready accessibility as a computerised filing system. That requires a filing system so referenced or indexed that it enables the data controller's employee responsible to identify at the outset of his search with reasonable certainty and speed the file or files in which the specific data relating to the person requesting the information is located and to locate the relevant information about him within the file or files, without having to make a manual search of them. To leave it to the searcher to leaf through files, possibly at great length and cost, and fruitlessly, to see whether it or they contain information relating to the person requesting information and whether that information is data within the Act bears, as Mr Sales said, no resemblance to a computerised search. It cannot have been intended by Parliament—and a filing system necessitating it cannot be 'a relevant filing system' within the Act. The statutory scheme for the provision of information by a data controller can only operate with proportionality and as a matter of common-sense where those who are required to respond to requests for information have a filing system that enables them to identify in advance of searching individual files whether or not it is 'a relevant filing system' for the purpose" (at [48]).

The question of the form in which the data is held is to be answered at the time of the request so that data which was once automatically processed but is now held in unstructured manual files is not covered. Nor is such data in manual files within the scope of the Act because it could easily be scanned into automatic equipment (*Smith v Lloyds TSB Bank plc* [2005] EWHC 246 (Ch)).

Durant also considers (1) the data controller's position where the request would include information about a third party (2) the court's discretion on requiring a data controller to comply with a request.

As from January 1, 2005 (SI 2004/3122, implementing the Freedom of Information Act 2000, s.68(1), (2)(a) and adding para.(e) to s.1(1) of the 1998 Act) any recorded information held by a public authority and not falling with paras (a)–(d) of s.1 of the 1998 Act is "data". However, such manual data are very largely exempt from the Data Protection Principles: see s.33A of the 1998 Act, as inserted from January 1, 2005 by s.70(1) of the Freedom of Information Act 2000.

Freedom of Information Act 2000. Since *Durant* arose from access rights to personal data, it should be noted that the Freedom of Information Act 2000 is now fully in force from January 1, 2005 (SI 2004/3122). Under this a person may request access to personal information about a third party held by a public authority. However, such information is exempt if it is personal data and either:

(a) its disclosure other than under the Freedom of Information Act would:

    (i) contravene any of the Data Protection Principles; or

    (ii) contravene the right to prevent processing of data likely to cause damage or distress (s.10 of the Data Protection Act 1998); or

    (iii) in the case of manual data, would contravene any of the Data Protection Principles if the exemptions relating to manual data held by public authorities (see above) were ignored; or

(b) the information is exempt from the data subject's right of access under the Data Protection Act 1998.

These exemptions are by no means necessarily absolute: thus a public authority faced with a request from A for information relating to B may have to make an assessment of whether, for example, it would be a breach of confidence to disclose the information.

Compensation. In *Sofola v Lloyds TSB Bank plc* [2005] EWHC 1335, QBD **21.27** Tugendhat J. held that it was arguable that (a) refusal of banking facilities, and (b) detention falling short of false imprisonment were "damage" for the purposes of s.13.

(e) *Harassment*

The Protection from Harassment Act 1997. *Overlap with defamation.* See **21.31** this Supplement, para.25.15.

Note 39. On the current status of *Wilkinson v Downton* see this Supplement, para.21.14.

Note 49. Daiichi UK Ltd v Stop Huntington Animal Cruelty [2003] EWHC 2337, QBD; [2004] 1 W.L.R. 1503 confirms that a corporate body is incapable of being harassed within the meaning of the Act.

Conflict of laws. In *Potter v Price* [2004] EWHC 781, QBD, where threatening emails were sent from England to the claimant in Thailand and where there were concurrent claims under the 1997 Act and s.40 of the Administration of Justice Act 1970 (harassment of debtors), it was held that for the purposes of s.11 of the Private International Law (Miscellaneous Provisions) Act 1995 "significant elements" of the tort occurred in England, because the claimant frequently returned here and distress was an ongoing thing.

Employment and Vicarious liability. Although the 1997 Act says nothing on this matter, in accordance with general principle an employer is vicariously liable for conduct by an employee which contravenes the Act, including conduct directed at fellow employees, provided there is a sufficiently close connection between the conduct and the employment (*Majrowski v Guy's and St Thomas's NHS Trusts* [2005] EWCA Civ 251; [2005] I.R.L.R. 340).

In addition to the 1997 Act, there are now various statutory provisions making it unlawful for an employer to subject a person to harassment in relation to employment. Details are beyond the scope of this work, but typical is s.3B of the Disability Discrimination Act 1995, added by the Disability Discrimination Act 1995 (Amendment) Regulations 2003, SI 2003/1673: a person subjects another to harassment where, for a reason which relates to the disabled person's disability, he engages in unwanted conduct which has the purpose or effect of violating the disabled person's dignity, or creating an intimidating, hostile, degrading, humiliating or offensive environment for him.

Standard of proof. Although civil liability under the 1997 Act is founded on conduct which amounts to a crime, the standard of proof in civil proceedings is the ordinary civil one of a balance of probabilities (*Jones v Hipgrave* [2004] EWHC 2901, QBD). Although there is some degree of overlap and similarity between the 1997 Act and the grounds for making an anti-social behaviour order under the Crime and Disorder Act 1998 ("that the person has acted . . . in an anti-social manner, that is to say, in a manner that caused or was likely to cause harassment, alarm or distress to one or more persons not of the same household as himself") and under the 1998 Act, although the proceedings are civil the standard of proof is the criminal one, there are also significant differences between the purposes and scope of the two pieces of legislation.

CHAPTER 22

CRIMINAL LIBEL

SECTION 4. REFORM OF THE LAW

The contemporary usage of criminal libel. More cases may arise because of **22.14** the possibility of publishing via the internet which reduces the usual "quality controls" present with larger media outlets and also produces publishers who are entirely without means for the purposes of civil process. See Carter, E.L., "Outlaw speech on the internet" (2005) 21 *Santa Clara Computer & High Technology Journal* 289.

Responses to the Criminal Defamation Bill. (2) The post-Human Rights Act **22.16** attitude to criminal libel may be indicated by the Privy Council in *Worme v Commissioner of Police of Grenada* [2004] UKPC 8. It is not as dismissive as some might have foretold. The editor and publisher of a newspaper in Grenada were charged with a crime of intentional libel concerning allegations of mis-spending money during a recent election in order to "bribe" people to vote for him. The appellants argued unsuccessfully that a crime of libel was in general unnecessary and unjustified in a modern democracy and that the particular offence under scrutiny (s.252(2) of the Criminal Code) breached the Grenadian constitution because it did not require the prosecution to establish that the defamatory matter was untrue. The Privy Council held on the latter point that the statutory language had to be interpreted in accordance with the normal burden of proof in criminal trials and the constitutional presumption of innocence. If a defendant raised a defence such as justification and there was evidence to support it, then the prosecution must prove both that the defamatory matter was untrue and that it was not for the public benefit that it was published (at [25], [31]). On the general point, the Privy Council emphasised not only the freedom to publish material discussing political matters and the affairs of public figures, but also the public interest in protecting the reputations of public figures from being debased falsely (at [42]). The existence of a civil remedy for damages no more rendered unnecessary a crime of intentional libel than did the existence of the tort of conversion rendered the crime of theft unnecessary (at [43]). The Privy Council felt further assured in its support for the crime of libel since the offence was maintained by democratic societies such as England, Australia and Canada, so there was no reason Grenada should be left out in the cold (at [43]).

[119]

(3) As a postcript to the Canadian case of *R. v Lucas* (1998) 157 D.L.R. (4th) 423 (*cf. R. v Stevens* (1995) 96 C.C.C. 3d 238, Man. CA; *R. v Gill and Waugh* (1996) 35 C.C.R. 2d 369, Ont. Ct. GD) Lucas' attempt to overturn his conviction was dismissed in *Lucas v Dueck* (2002) 214 Sask. R. 213.

Recent cases on criminal libel in Commonwealth jurisdictions include the following. In Australia, there is the case of *Byrnes v Barry* [2003] ACTSC 0054 (citing para.22.10 of the Main Work), where the applicant for leave was portrayed as an ex-convict, ex-bankrupt and unethical businessman; leave was nevertheless refused on the grounds that criminal defamation should only be prosecuted in the most exceptional circumstances and where the publication can be shown to be vile or intemperate as well as inimical to the public welfare. Other relevant factors included whether there was a danger of disorderly reprisals, whether there was significant damage to personal or business reputation and whether the applicant had the means to bring civil process. A case from Singapore is *Sulochana D/O Tambiah Dirumala Sakkrawarthi v Rajalakshmi Ramoo* [2003] SGHC 299, where a conviction was sustained for calling her estranged husband's new partner a prostitute; factors affecting the sentence of one month included the nature of the defamatory remark, the conduct, position and standing of the defamed party, the mode and extent of the publication and the remorse of the defendant.

For a recent survey of the usage of criminal libel in the US, see Media Law Resource Center, *Criminalizing Speech about Reputation* (MLRC Bulletin 1, New York, 2003). Attempts to secure a declaration of unconstitutionality of the relevant offences in Kansas, one of the more zealous jurisdictions, failed in *Thomas v City of Baxter Springs, Kansas* 369 F. Supp. 2d 1291 (2005) and *How v City of Baxter Springs, Kansas* 369 F. Supp. 2d 1300 (2005), actions which also seem to illustrate that local authorities may suffer criminal defamation. Action to strike down the criminal libel statutes in Colorado and Puerto Rico were also dismissed (on procedural grounds) in *Mink and The Howling Pig v Salazar* 344 F. Supp. 2d 1231 (2004) and in *Soto v Rodriguez* 306 F. Supp. 2d 120 (2004).

The Report of the (Irish) Legal Advisory Group on Defamation (Ministry of Justice, Dublin, 2003) continues to pursue the notion of a more confined offence with the following elements:

(i) a person without lawful authority or reasonable cause;
(ii) intentionally and with malice publishes a false statement in relation to a natural person;
(iii) that statement was calculated to damage gravely and has damaged gravely the reputation of that person; and
(iv) was calculated to cause and has caused serious harm to the mind of the person who was the subject of the statements.

22.17 **Responses to "poison pen letters", "character assassination" and harassment: the Malicious Communications Act 1988 and the Protection from Harassment Act 1997.** (1) Note 32: The Telecommunications Act 1984, s.43 is to be replaced by the Communications Act 2003, s.127.

CHAPTER 23

THE EUROPEAN CONVENTION ON HUMAN RIGHTS AND LIBEL

SECTION 1. BACKGROUND

Relationships with United Kingdom law under the Human Rights Act **23.4**
1998. The impact of s.12 in relation to a claim to an interim injunction was
examined in *Cream Holdings Ltd v Banerjee* [2004] UKHL 44; [2005] 1 A.C.
253 (see further, this Supplement, para.21.16) and in *Greene v Associated
Newspapers Ltd* [2004] EWCA Civ 1462; [2005] 1 All E.R. 30 (see further, this
Supplement, para.25.6).

Convention applicants. The case of *Steel and Morris v United Kingdom* **23.5**
(No.2), Application No.68416/01, 15/02/05 (see further, this Supplement, par-
a.8.16) confirms, as stated previously, that it is open to trading companies to
bring applications under the Convention for the protection of their reputation.
However, the bounds of acceptable comment will be wider in the case of
powerful multinational companies such as McDonalds, since the public interest
in their affairs is heightened (at [94], [95]).

Convention procedures. There remains concern about the ability of the **23.7**
Convention system to cope with the ever-increasing workload, especially the
influx of cases from Eastern Europe. Therefore, a further Protocol to the Convention has been agreed in 2004: Protocol No.14 to the Convention for the Protection of Human Rights and Fundamental Freedoms, amending the control system
of the Convention, ETS 194 (ratified by the UK in January 2005 but not yet in
force). When it comes into force, it will allow a single judge to declare admissibility, will insert a new ground of inadmissibility (that the applicant suffered no
significant disadvantage), will avoid the repetition of litigated issues, and will
allow admissibility and merits to be ruled upon simultaneously.

SECTION 2. THE RIGHT TO REPUTATION AS A CONVENTION RIGHT

The basis for the right to reputation in the Convention. A number of cases, **23.10**
both domestic and international, have emphasised Art.8 as the basis for the right
to reputation (see also this Supplement, para.21.12). At the international level, in
Radio France v France, Application No.53984/00, 30/03/2004, para.31, the

European Court of Human Rights declared that "the right to reputation is included among the rights protected by Art.8 of the Convention in so far as it is an element of the right to respect for private life". The case was not argued on the basis of Art.8, but a later case, *Zollman v United Kingdom*, Application No.62902/00, 2003-XII at [16] mixed in the claim under Art.8 the right to "honour and reputation" with the right to private life arising from an allegedly untrue statement made by a government Minister. Though involving a defence of absolute privilege, the fact that the case was argued under Art.8 did not make a difference to the outcome not least because the exceptions under Arts 8(2) and 10(2) are identical. But this commonality of exceptions may not always produce a commonality of outcomes, as illustrated by *W v Westminster City Council (No.1)* [2004] EWHC 2866, QBD; *(No.2)* [2005] EWHC 102, QBD. See further, this Supplement, paras 9.16, 21.12, 23.16.

In domestic law, the Court of Appeal has expressed itself to be "content to assume" that "a person's right to protect his/her reputation is among the rights guaranteed by . . . Art.8" (*Greene v Associated Newspapers Ltd* [2004] EWCA Civ 1462; [2005] 1 All E.R. 30).

One potential problem with this path to protection of reputation concerns the effect of the decision under Art.8 concerning the photographing of a famous person in *Von Hannover v Germany*, Application No.59320/00, 24/06/2004 (see further, this Supplement, para.21.19). The strong statements in the judgment distinguishing "reporting facts—even controversial ones—capable of contributing to a debate in a democratic society relating to politicians in the exercise of their functions, for example, and reporting details of the private life of an individual" (at [63]) would presumably apply to the printed word just as it applies to photographs, as would the warning that it takes "certain special circumstances" to be legitimate to reveal the private details of public figures (at [64]). This approach appears less robust than statements under Art.10 about the need to encourage speech about public affairs and the special role of the press therein (see this Supplement, para.23.18).

23.13   **Problems of excessive enforcement of the right to reputation.** The size of damage awards was considered in *Independent News & Media and Independent Newspapers Ireland Ltd v Ireland*, Application No.55120/00, 16/06/05 (see further, this Supplement, para.9.3) when the newspapers published stark allegations of criminal activities and sympathies with violent Communist oppression and anti-Semitism against Proinsias de Rossa, a political leader engaged in negotiations to form a coalition government in 1992. The original jury award of 300,000 Irish pounds (IR£) was confirmed by the Supreme Court, which was determined to be more respectful of jury discretion than it believed was evident in contemporary English jurisprudence. The European Court took due account of the gravity of the libel, the effect on the libelled person, the extent of the publication and the conduct of the litigation which required the libelled person to endure three long and difficult trials; all in all, an award "going to the top of the bracket" was within the margin of appreciation [129].

The size of the award of damages was in breach of Art.10 in *Steel and Morris v United Kingdom (No.2)*, Application No.68416/01, 15/02/05 (see further, this Supplement, para.9.2). Though the sums awarded were modest in objective terms (£36,000 and £40,000), they became disproportionate when compared to the meagre incomes and resources of the two applicants. This reasoning is, of course, entirely inconsistent with the English law's compensatory approach to general damages which is based on loss and not means.

As well as limits on damage awards in civil cases, the European Court demands proportionality in the punishment at the end of a criminal process. As applied to criminal libel, this precept was taken to mean in *Sabou and Pircalab v Romania*, Application No.46572/99, 28/09/04, that the deprivation of parental rights as an automatic part of the punishment of imprisonment breached Art.8 as the offence was wholly unrelated to the care of children. Remarkably, the European Court did not condemn the sentence of 10 months' imprisonment, though the accusation of corruption by the president of the court of first authority of Baia Mare was indeed a serious allegation which might be viewed as akin to the (dormant) English common law offence scandalising the court. Later sentences of that kind of length have been struck down. In *Cumpǎnǎ and Mazǎre v Romania*, Application No.33348/96, 17/12/04, newspaper articles accused local officials of taking backhanders and bribes relating to awarding unlawfully a contract to a company for impounding illegally parked vehicles or trailers. The punishments for criminal libel, imprisonment for seven months and disqualification from journalism for one year (later removed by presidential pardon) were in breach of Art.10, especially because of the disqualification, though the convictions were viewed as proper owing to the lack of factual base for such grave allegations. In *Skala v Poland*, Application No.43425/98, 25/05/03, a sentence for criminal insult of eight months' imprisonment arising from a letter written by a prisoner to the president of a regional court to complain about one of the judges he had encountered; words such as "irresponsible", "clowns", "cretins" and "bully" were used. The sentence was viewed as disproportionate, but the offence of insult, which did not require publication beyond the victim, was not.

Problems of inadequate procedural support for the right to reputation. **23.15** (4) The unavailability of legal aid in libel litigation has given rise to complaints both by plaintiffs and defendants. As for complaints by defendants, the Commission concluded in *Steel and Morris v United Kingdom (No.1)* that its absence was not unfair (Application No.21325/93; (1993) 18 E.H.R.R. C.D. 172). That conclusion warranted further consideration in view of the facts that the applicants were ultimately unsuccessful in their defence, having endured the longest ever libel trial in English legal history (at 313 days, and culminating in a 762-page judgment, see *The Times*, June 20, 1997—the full High Court judgment is available at *www.mcspotlight.org/case/trial/verdict/index.html*). A further application, *Steel and Morris v United Kingdom (No.2)*, Application No.68416/01, 15/02/05 (see further Hudson, A., "Free speech and equality of arms—the decision in Steel & Morris v United Kingdom" [2005] EHRLR 301) was therefore mounted and proved successful in 2005, when the Court found that the extraordinary complexity of the case meant that the absence of paid legal assistance could not be reconciled with the concept of equality of arms. Three points should be noted. The first is that the same reasoning could presumably apply to plaintiffs facing corresponding complexity. The second is that the Court emphasised that the finding would not affect all cases. In particular, it contrasted, rather than condemned the earlier judgment in *McVicar v UK*, Application No.46311/99, 2002-III. The third point is that the *McLibel* domestic litigation took place when the blanket refusal of legal aid under Legal Aid Act 1988 was in force. Since that time, there have been introduced contingent fee arrangements. In addition, while the presumption remains that civil legal aid should not be granted in respect of claims in defamation (para.1(a)(f) of Schedule), there is a residual power for the exceptional funding of cases under s.6(8) of the Access to Justice Act 1999. The Lord Chancellor's guidance to the Commission requires that "there is a significant wider public interest . . . in the resolution of the case and funded representation will contribute to it", or that the case "is of overwhelming importance to the client", or that "there is convincing evidence that there are other exceptional circumstances such that without public funding for representation it would be practically impossible for the client to bring or defend the proceedings, or the lack of public funding would lead to obvious unfairness in the proceedings" (Legal Services Commission, Funding Code Guidance (2003), p.22). In all, the judgment may be seen as requiring no more than nuanced reforms, assuming that the *McLibel* case can be depicted as exceptional, which it certainly was by the Lord Chancellor in response to the judgment (House of Lords Debates, vol.669, col.1099, February 22, 2005, Lord Falconer).

23.16   **Equal treatment in the protection of reputations.** Robust protection for the absolute privilege afforded to Parliamentary debate has once again been indicated in *Zollman v United Kingdom*, Application No.62902/00, 2003-XII. The Zollman brothers, who ran an international diamond business based in Belgium and South Africa, were condemned by Mr Peter Hain, Minister of State at the Foreign and Commonwealth Office, in the House of Commons for breaching sanctions imposed by the UN Security Council on the export of Angolan diamonds by UNITA. The condemnation was duly published in Hansard (HC Debs. vol.217, col.273 WH, February 17, 2000) and thereafter published in various media outlets. The case was argued primarily on the basis of Art.6, but the Court found no breach, especially under Art.6(1) on the basis that "the special importance of safeguarding the freedom of expression of the elected representatives of the people, stating that in a democracy, Parliament or such comparable bodies are the essential *fora* for political debate and that very weighty reasons must be advanced to justify interfering with the freedom of expression exercised therein" at [14]. The Court was further persuaded by the fact the Parliamentary privilege is more limited than several Continental versions and is kept within well-defined bounds through the rules of contempt of Parliament and the discipline of the Speaker. Nor did the recourse to "naming and shaming" amount to any form of discrimination in comparison to British citizens who would be subject to normal regulatory or criminal proceedings.

Other forms of "state immunity" which are insufficiently proportionate to the operational needs of the branches of government will fall foul of Art.10. An example is *Colombani v France*, Application No.51279/99, 2002-V. In the context of the Moroccan application for EU membership, the European Commission commissioned the Observatoire Géopolitique des Drogues to compile a report on cannabis production and the measures being taken to eradicate it. The report reached the public domain in 1995, whereupon *Le Monde* published an article about it with the headlines "Morocco, world's leading exporter of cannabis" and "King Hassan II's entourage implicated by confidential report". This article not inconsiderably annoyed King Hassan II, who pressured the French authorities to take criminal proceedings. As a result, the editor-in-chief of *Le Monde* and the author of the article, were prosecuted and convicted on charges of insulting a foreign head of State contrary to s.36 of the Freedom of the Press Act of July 29, 1881 (s.26 of the same Act covers insulting the President of the French Republic). The European Court of Human Rights began with the proposition that those in political life lay themselves open to close scrutiny by journalists and the public at large and must display a great degree of tolerance (at [56]) . But what was crucial in this case was that the applicants were not able to rely on any defence of justification, despite the existence of a soberly expressed and well-researched report which might have supported their assertions. In short, s.36 "amounts to conferring on foreign heads of State a special privilege that cannot be reconciled with modern practice and political conceptions" (at [68]) and so is not necessary in a democratic society under Art.10(2).

Section 3. INFRINGEMENT OF CONVENTION RIGHTS BY THE PROTECTION OF REPUTATION

Restrictions on the right to free expression. (1) Concern for the protection of speech about political affairs and political leaders has again been confirmed. In *Scharsach v Austria*, Application No.39394/98, 2003-XI, a journalist and a news magazine publisher were convicted of criminal libel arising from an article which questioned whether the right-wing Austrian Freedom Party was a suitable coalition partner. Some of its members were referred to as "closet Nazis". The European Court considered that the national courts had failed to consider the political context and the categorisation of the statements as value judgments. It distinguished the case of *Wabl v Austria*, in which use of the epithet, "Nazi" had also been impugned, on the basis that *Wabl* involved civil not criminal sanctions (at [42]). In *Wirtschafts-Trend Zeitschriften-Verlags GMBH v Austria*, Application No.58547/00, 22/06/04, the ubiquitous weekly magazine *Profil* published an article concerning the author of a book who was criticised for pardoning Jörg Haider's belittlement of the Nazi concentration camps as "punishment camps". The Austrian Regional Court (*Landesgericht*) had ordered compensation and the forfeiture of the issue. The European Court has declared admissible the subsequent complaint.

But it remains possible to go too far in speech about politicians. The stark allegations of criminal activities and sympathies with violent Communist oppression and anti-Semitism against Proinsias de Rossa, a political leader engaged in negotiations to form a coalition government in 1992, in *Independent News & Media and Independent Newspapers Ireland Ltd v Ireland*, Application No.55120/00, 16/06/05, were not protected by Art.10.

(2) Discussion of public affairs of wider interest are protected under Art.10, but the level of protection seems to be less potent than with outright party political discussion. An illustration is the prosecution of Radio France arising from articles in its magazine, *Le Point*, to the effect that the former deputy Mayor of Paris, Michel Junot, had collaborated in the deportations of Jews during 1942–43 while he served as a sub-prefect (*Radio France v France*, Application

23.18

No.53984/00, 30/03/2004). The French courts found that there had been an offence of the offence of slandering a public servant. The European Court did not doubt the serious public interest in the attitudes and performance of a senior official (at [34]). But it would not disturb the verdict of the French court that the charges contained in the transmissions message lacked strict adherence to the objective facts, especially because of the indication that Junot actually admitted to having organised the departure of a convoy, albeit that it was later made clear that he refuted that allegation (at [38]). Likewise, in *Chauvy v France*, Application No.64915/01, 29/06/04, the applicant was the author of a book entitled, *Aubrac-Lyon 1943*, which was published in 1997. It contained material from the investigation of Klaus Barbie, the regional head of the Gestapo, which cast doubt on accounts of resistance members and alleged collaboration, including by Raymond Aubrac. The allegations were discussed, and it was accepted that there was no evidence in the archives to substantiate the accusations of Barbie against Aubrac but that they did reveal that the accounts of Aubrac were in part unreliable. Actions for criminal and civil libel were begun, which resulted in the imposition of fines, damages and the order to insert a legal notice in the book. The European Court found no reason to disagree with the domestic courts which were found to have engaged in "meticulous analysis of the book" (at [77]).

More encouragement for speech was shown in *Vides Aizsardzības Klubs v Latvia*, Application No.57829/00, 27/05/04. An environmental protection group had addressed a resolution to a local authority about coastline protection. It included allegations that a local council chair had authorised illegal work. An independent report had confirmed that there was illegal development in the area and that the chair had made erroneous decisions. The order to pay damages breached Art.10. It is not easy to reconcile this outcome with the *Radio France* case, decided just a couple of months previously. Aside from the peculiar facts of the cases, the existence of independent verification of the sting of the allegations and the fact that the Latvian applicant sought primarily to engage through democratic processes and not the media could be viewed as objective differences.

(4) The Court's attachment to the fact/value distinction remains strong and is illustrated by *Pedersen and Baadsgaard v Denmark*, Application No.49017/99, 17/12/03. Two TV programmes, "Convicted of Murder" and "The Blind Eye of the Police" questioned the soundness of X's conviction for the murder of his wife (he was acquitted after spending 10 years in prison) and focused disapproval upon named police officers for the suppression of evidence. The criticism, which prompted a conviction for criminal libel, was depicted as involving factual statements which were not viewed as properly researched and so did not fall within the protection of Art.10. On the facts, this result appears harsh (partly reflected in the 9–8 split in the Court), as there was considerable research into the case files and also the programme had implied a range of possibilities in the criticised investigation and left open possible explanations and responsibility for the alleged miscarriage.

Another example of the difficulties caused by the distinction is *Selistö v Finland*, Application No.56767/00, 16/11/04, where the Court treated as "fact" the details of interviews with the partner of a deceased patient of a surgeon accused of unprofessional conduct. The interviews were indeed "fact"—they had taken place and been accurately reported—but the allegations in the interviews were of course contentious. In some ways, this position on "fact" is reminiscent of the notion of "reportage" (see also this Supplement, paras 14.87, 14.91).

In *Ukraine Media Group v Ukraine*, Application No.72713/01, 29/03/05, critical newspaper articles about two presidential candidates in the 1999 elections were categorised as value judgments, which amounted to political rhetoric expressed in strong, polemical, sarcastic language. Ukrainian law failed to distinguish fact and value, and so there was a breach of Art.10.

(5) The manner of expression does not in principle reduce the protections of the Convention, and the Court has emphasised the right to offend, shock or disturb. Its resolve in these matters is being tested following a declaration of admissibility in *Vereinigung Bildender Künstler Wiener Secession v Austria*, Application No.68354/01, 30/06/2005. The paintings are reproduced in the report on the European Court website). An association of artists organised an exhibition, "The century of artistic freedom" (*"Das Jahrhundert künstlerischer Freiheit"*). The exhibits included the painting "Apocalypse" by the Austrian painter Otto Mühl, which showed a collage of numerous persons in public life, such as Mother Teresa, the Austrian cardinal Hermann Groer and the former head of the Austrian Freedom Party Mr Jörg Haider. Their heads and faces, taken from newspaper photographs, were superimposed on painted bodies engaging in a variety of sexual exploits. The Austrian courts issued an injunction against further exhibition of the painting and ordered payment of compensation on the basis of s.78 of the Copyright Act (Urheberrechtsgesetz 1936) which arises where injury would be caused to the legitimate interests of a person.

A less exotic case was *Alves Costa v Portugal*, Application No.65297/01, 25/03/04. A conviction for libel was sustained following the publication of an open letter in a newspaper to the director of a medical treatment. The author complained of the poor standard of care for his daughter, who had died, and said the director of the centre was a person only moved by her own personal interests and image and without regard for ethical or professional principles. These expressions overstepped the permissible bounds of Art.10. By comparison, in *Selistö v Finland*, Application No.56767/00, 16/11/04 (see further, this Supplement, paras 14.84, 14.91), a newspaper journalist's articles about the unprofessional conduct (including the consumption of alcohol) of an unnamed (but identifiable) surgeon which resulted in the death of a patient were based on interviews with the partner of the deceased and on statements from an aborted pre-trial criminal investigation. Differences from *Alves Costa* included that the articles were based in large part around factual statements which were drawn in part from public documents which the journalist could rely upon without further verification. The fact that the journalist had been selective in the use of sources—the articles did not clearly explain the findings of the National Medico-Legal Board which concluded that no charges should be brought (though that outcome was mentioned)—did not detract from the value of the expression. Furthermore, the articles sought to draw out general points of public interest about medical standards from the particular case.

(7) The maintenance of the authority of the judiciary and judicial process has been prominent as a countervailing interest to free speech. In *Lešník v Slovakia*, Application No.35640/97, 2003-IV, the applicant was seeking to have criminal proceedings instituted against another businessman for fraud. When no progress was made, he wrote to the district prosecutor, making unsubstantiated allegations

of, *inter alia*, incompetence, corruption and abuse of authority. The case, including the contents of the letter, were discussed by a newspaper. The criminal conviction of the applicant for insult was within Art.10, the public prosecutor being viewed as part of the judicial machinery in the broader sense of that term. The fact that it was the letters and not the newspaper report of them which were impugned is, however, disturbing, as pointed out in the dissenting judgments of two of the five European judges. In this respect, the defences of qualified privilege in English law may go further than Art.10, especially when dealing with Continental offences of insult of officials (see *Skala v Poland*, Application No.43425/98, 25/05/03). Another example of the protection now extended to public prosecutors is *Perna v Italy*, Application No.48898/99, 2003-V. A journalist was convicted of criminal libel arising form article written in *Il Giornale* about the Principal Public Prosecutor in Palermo which claimed he was loyal to the Italian Communists and had a mission to destroy former premier Giulio Andreotti and to take over prosecutions all over Italy. As there was no attempt at factual justification, the conviction did not breach Art.10. Nor could the language be said to be "symbolic" (the equivalent of mere abuse) (at [47]). See also *Skala v Poland*, Application No.43425/98, 25/05/03; *Ukraine Media Group v Ukraine*, Application No.72713/01, 29/03/05.

In any event, moderately expressed criticism must be protected, as in *Amihalachioaie v Moldova*, Application No.60115/00, 20/04/04, where the chairman of the Moldovan Bar Association was required to pay an administrative fine for disrespect when he criticised in a newspaper the decision of the Constitutional Court that the law requiring lawyers to be members of the Association to be unconstitutional, including the observation that "The Constitutional Court's decision will produce total anarchy in the legal profession . . . the question he asks himself is whether the Constitutional Court is constitutional . . . the judges of the Constitutional Court . . . do not regard the European Court of Human Rights as an authority." This could be described as "a certain lack of regard for the Constitutional Court [but not] as grave or as insulting" (at [36]).

In the application of this strand of reasoning, practising lawyers acting in the course of their duties may have more leeway than most, as is illustrated by *Steur v Netherlands*, Application No.39657/98, 2003-XI. The applicant, a practising lawyer, acted for a client of Surinamese origin who was suspected of having unlawfully received social security benefits and of forgery and who was subjected to criminal and civil proceedings. In the civil proceedings, the applicant declared that a social security investigating officer had obtained statements from his client by means of improper pressure. The officer responded by filing a disciplinary complaint; the lawyer was found guilty but no sanction was imposed. The European Court found a breach of Art.10 on the basis of the principle that "the limits of acceptable criticism may in some circumstances be wider with regard to civil servants exercising their powers than in relation to private individuals" (at [40]). It was further impressed that the criticism was limited to actions involving the applicant's client, was confined to the courtroom and did not amount to a personal insult. Above all it was "difficult to reconcile with his duty as an advocate to defend the interests of his clients and could have a 'chilling effect' on the practice of his profession" (at [44]).

A further qualification to judicial protection emerged in *Hrico v Slovakia*, Application No.49418/99, 20/07/04. Where a presiding judge of the Supreme

Court was an electoral candidate, then there was greater leeway for disrespectful criticism of his judgments—epithets such as "tragicomic farce", "shameful judgment", "strange reasoning" and "legal farce".

Speech which encourages violence is invariably unacceptable. In *Gunduz v Turkey*, Application No.59745/00, 2003-XI, the leader of Tarikat Aczmendi (an Islamic sect) criticised in a newspaper an Islamic intellectual known for his moderate views and called his supporters comic and deserving to have "one brave man among the Muslims to plant a dagger in their soft underbelly and run them through twice with a bayonet". Even as a metaphor, such language will not rouse any support from the European Court.

(8) Required standards of journalism are illustrated by *Harlanova v Latvia*, Application No.57313//00, 03/04/03. A journalist published two articles containing allegations against the President of the Central Council of the Old Orthodox Church. The gist was that the President has misappropriated funds for his own private business purposes. The facts were gathered from a church report and from a letter written by a Member of Parliament. But as the church was divided on the facts, the European Court stated that the journalist should have researched further. The established stream of cases about journalistic standards is in stark contrast to the statement in *Selistö v Finland*, Application No.56767/00, 16/11/04 at [59] (see further, this Supplement, para.14.84) to the effect that "it is not for the Court, any more than it is for the national courts, to substitute its own views for those of the press as to what techniques of reporting should be adopted by journalists". In the circumstances, the dictum should be understood as allowing the equivalent of a margin of appreciation for journalists' choice of words and phrases but not to be expressing disinterest in their professional methods or standards.

Applying European Human Rights standards to English legal restrictions   **23.19**
on speech. That English law is broadly compliant was confirmed in *Ashworth Hospital Authority v MGN Ltd* [2002] UKHL 29; [2002] 1 W.L.R. at [73]. In *Galloway v Telegraph Ltd* [2004] EWHC 2786, QBD; [2005] E.M.L.R. 7 at [132] (see further, this Supplement, para.14.84) it was asserted that the *Reynolds* doctrine is Convention compliant. A comparison with protections in Australian and US constitutional law is made in Weaver, R., Kenyon, A.T., Partlett, D.F., Walker, C., *The Right to Speak Ill* (Carolina Academic Press, Durham, 2005).

The contention that the rule that the claimant has no burden of proof in relation to loss or damage breaches Arts 6 and 10 of the Convention was considered and rejected in *Steel and Morris v United Kingdom (No.2)* Application, No.68416/01, 15/02/05. See further *Jameel v Wall Street Journal Europe Sprl (No.2)* [2005] EWCA Civ 74; [2005] 2 W.L.R. 1577 (and see this Supplement, para.8.16). The applicants claimed that the domestic proceedings and their outcome were disproportionate under Art.10 given, *inter alia*, that the applicants bore the burden of proving the truth of the matters set out in their factsheet about "What's wrong with McDonald's?". This complaint was not sustained (at [93]). The Court followed its decision in *McVicar v United Kingdom*, Application No.46311/99, 2002-III, and the general precept that matters of evidence, especially in civil cases, are for national authorities to settle (see *G v France*, Application No.11941/86; 57 DR 100 at [1]). The (Irish) Law Reform Commission Report on the Civil Law of Defamation proposed to put on the plaintiff the burden of proof that the matter contained in the publication was defamatory (which also means that its falsity must be established) and that the defamatory matter concerned the plaintiff (LRC 38, Dublin, 1991, para.3.13). The subsequent Report of the Legal Advisory Group on Defamation (Ministry of Justice, Dublin, 2003, paras 21–22) suggested that there should be no substantive change in the law concerning the presumption of falsity. However, all plaintiffs in defamation proceedings should, in future, have to file, within a specific period of time, an affidavit which would verify the particulars of their claim. Failure to file such an affidavit could, in certain circumstances, result in the claim being struck out.

23.21   **Procedural safeguards for persons exercising freedom of expression.** Decisions about the admissibility of evidence in libel litigation will be largely left to national authorities (*Perna v Italy*, Application No.48898/99, 2003-V).

CHAPTER 24

THE INITIAL STAGES

Section 1. INTRODUCTION

Risks. *Add after the first sentence a new note 3a*: For an unusual exception to **24.2** the no-skeleton rule, note the case of *Polanski v Conde Nast*, in which the Paris-based claimant was awarded £50,000 by a jury on July 22, 2005 despite not being able to give evidence in person because of the risk of extradition to the USA in respect of a conviction for under-age sex (a difficulty which led to an interlocutory appeal to the House of Lords: [2005] UKHL 10; [2005] 1 W.L.R. 637).

Defences. *Add at the end of the final paragraph of 24.4*: This passage was **24.3** criticised as "despondent" in *Jameel v Wall Street Journal (No.2)* [2004] EWHC 37, QBD [2004] E.M.L.R. 11 by Eady J., who was mindful of Lord Nicholls' words in *Reynolds v Times Newspapers Ltd* [2001] 2 A.C. 127 at [202E–F]: " . . . the extent of this uncertainty should not be exaggerated. With the enunciation of some guidelines by the court, any practical problems should be manageable".

Add to note 21: See now also *Armstrong v Times Newspapers Ltd* [2005] EWCA Civ 1007; *Jameel (Mohammed) v Wall Street Journal* [2005] EWCA Civ 74; [2005] 2 W.L.R. 1577; *Wood v Chief Constable of West Midlands Police* [2004] EWCA Civ 1638; [2005] E.M.L.R. 20; *Miller v Associated Newspapers* [2003] EWHC 2799.

Defendant's response. *Add after the second sentence a new note 23a*: On the **24.11** circumstances in which it may be reasonable from a costs assessment perspective to instruct specialist London solicitors as against a provincial firm, see *Gazley v News Group Newspapers* [2004] EWHC 2675, QBD.

Repeated statements. *Add*: The perils of starting multiple actions against **24.19** different defendants are illustrated by the decision in *Pedder v News Group Newspapers* [2004] E.M.L.R 19, in which a claim was struck out as an abuse after an almost identical claim against another newspaper had been litigated to trial and lost. That illustrates the need to identify the most serious libel and proceed against the defendant responsible. An alternative may be to start proceedings against all the intended targets and then apply under CPR, r.3.1(2)(f) for a stay of all actions but one until that action is resolved by trial or settlement.

SECTION 3. JURISDICTION

24.21   **Publisher not present in England and Wales.** The presumption of damage in libel cases, which is a factor of central importance in cases where a claimant wishes to have his action against a foreign publisher tried in England, has been challenged (so far unsuccessfully) in two related cases in the Court of Appeal. The arguments in each case were quite different. In *Jameel (Mohammed) v Wall Street Journal* [2005] EWCA Civ 74; [2005] 2 W.L.R. 1577, it was argued that English law, to be compatible with Art.10 of the ECHR, had to require proof of special damage as an essential element of a cause of action in libel by a corporation. That argument was rejected. In *Jameel (Yousef) v Dow Jones* [2005] EWCA Civ 75; [2005] 2 W.L.R. 1614, it was accepted by the defendant that damage could be presumed in a claim by a corporation where there has been significant publication of a defamatory article: the argument was that this was very different from presuming damage irrebuttably as a matter of law, and that if a defendant could show that no damage had been done, it ought to be able to do so. That argument also was rejected, but from the defendant's point of view it hardly mattered, since the action was stayed as an abuse. However, the defendants in *Jameel (Mohammed) v Wall Street Journal* have obtained leave to appeal from the House of Lords, and the appeal is expected to be heard in April 2006.

Add to note 50: See also *King v Lewis* [2004] EWCA Civ 1329; [2005] E.M.L.R. 45.

Add to note 52: See also *King v Lewis*, above; *Richardson v Schwarzenegger* [2004] EWHC 2422, QBD. In *King v Lewis*, the Court of Appeal observed that:

> "The global publisher should not be too fastidious as to the part of the globe where he is made a libel defendant. We by no means propose a free-for-all for claimants libelled on the Internet. The court must still ascertain the most appropriate forum; the parties' connections with this or that jurisdiction will still have to be considered; there will be cases (like the present) where only two jurisdictions are really in contention. We apprehend that . . . in an Internet case the court's discretion will tend to be more open-textured than otherwise; for that is the means by which the court may give effect to the publisher's choice of a global medium" ([2004] EWCA Civ 1329; [2005] E.M.L.R. 45 at [31]).

It is worth noting that the court rejected "out of hand" [34] a submission that the intention of the defendant as to the particular jurisdiction which he had targeted should be a factor in ascertaining the appropriate forum.

24.29   *Forum non conveniens. Add to note 73*: See *Jameel (Yousef) v Dow Jones* [2005] EWCA Civ 75; [2005] 2 W.L.R. 1614, a case where there was no substantial tort because of insignificant English publication (probably only five internet hits, two of which were by subscribers who did not know the claimant, and three of which were by members of the claimant's camp).

See also *King v Lewis* [2004] EWCA Civ 1329, where the Court of Appeal accepted that authority requires the court to decide objectively the most appropriate forum for the conduct of the litigation, and that this question should be decided before and without reference to consideration of any juridical advantage which the claimant might enjoy by suing in England, but found it difficult to grasp the idea of a principle which first enjoins ascertainment of the appropriate forum, but then permits a claimant to sue in an inappropriate forum for reasons of juridical advantage ([2004] EWCA Civ 1329; [2005] E.M.L.R. 45 at [38]).

Application of principle in defamation cases. Although the starting-point for **24.30** ascertainment of the appropriate forum is to identify the place where the tort has been committed, which will by definition be England in a case where leave to serve out has been given on the basis of publication here, "The more tenuous the claimant's connection with this jurisdiction (and the more substantial any publication abroad), the weaker this consideration becomes" (*King v Lewis* [2004] EWCA Civ 1329; [2005] E.M.L.R. 45 at [27]).

In *Jameel (Yousef) v Dow Jones* [2005] EWCA Civ 75; [2005] 2 W.L.R. 1614, the court found that no real and substantial tort had been committed within the jurisdiction. The claimant had English connections, but it appeared that there were probably only five English-based subscribers to the *Wall Street Journal On-Line*, which published the article complained of: two of those did not know the claimant, and the other three were in the claimant's camp. It was not legitimate for the claimant to justify the English proceedings by praying in aid the effect that they might have in vindicating his reputation outside England, so on any view the damage and vindication would be minimal.

"The cost of the exercise will have been out of all proportion to what has been achieved. The game will not merely not have been worth the candle, it will not have been worth the wick . . . It would be an abuse of process to continue to commit the resources of the English court, including substantial judge and possibly jury time, to an action where so little is now seen to be at stake" ([69]–[70]).

Claimants, resident, etc. in UK. A stay was also refused to an American **24.31** defendant sued for words attributed by the *Los Angeles Times* to a spokesman for Arnold Schwarzenegger during the 2003 Californian gubernatorial campaign (*Richardson v Schwarzenegger* [2004] EWHC 2422, QBD). The claimant sued on publication in hard copies distributed in England and on English internet publication. Factors relevant to the judge's decision included the facts that the claimant, a UK citizen who was resident in England, worked there and was widely known there, but had no comparable reputation elsewhere, including in the USA. Moreover, the underlying events (relevant if justification was pleaded) took place in London. Nonetheless, the judge had some sympathy for the submissions of counsel for the applicant, who identified the question for the court as follows:

"This case is about whether a spokesman for a foreign politician in a local election campaign who was asked by a foreign newspaper to respond on behalf of the foreign electoral candidate to allegations concerning the past conduct of that candidate, and who provided a response that is immune from suit under local law and is protected by qualified privilege under our system of law in circumstances in which malice is not and could not reasonably be alleged, should nevertheless be amenable to the exorbitant jurisdiction of the English court . . . ."

This summary was "seductively put as though it were a new scenario free from authority. But it would seem to ignore . . . clear and recently stated principles of English law" (*per* Eady J. at [28]).

In particular, it took no account of the Court of Appeal's decision in *King v Lewis* [2004] EWCA Civ 1329; [2005] E.M.L.R. 45. In that case, an American boxing promoter, resident in Florida, sued a New York lawyer for words spoken on two Californian websites about New York litigation. The Court of Appeal found no error of law in Eady J.'s conclusion that leave to serve out had been rightly given, the claimant having a substantial reputation and a financial and business connection in England, and the evidence having shown that the two websites were popular in England and frequently accessed by English residents.

24.32   **Examples (1).** It is worth noting that the House of Lords did not question the propriety of Roman Polanski's action against Condé Nast in respect of the English publication of 53,000 copies of *Vanity Fair*, even though the principal circulation was in the USA (1.13 million copies), and even though he was a French citizen, resident in France, who had not set foot in England since February 1978. Lord Nicholls observed that, given his international reputation, there was no question of his libel action being an abuse of the process of the court. Indeed, Condé Nast did not suggest otherwise (*Polanski v Condé Nast Publications Ltd* [2005] UKHL 10 at [12]).

24.34   **Problems over US enforcement of English judgments.** *Add to note 96*: In the result, the decision of the District Court in *Yahoo! Inc. v La Ligue Contre le Racisme et L'Antisemitisme (LICRA)* was overturned by a majority of the US Court of Appeals, 9th Circuit (379 F. 3d 1120), on the ground that the District Court had no personal jurisdiction over the French appellants until they asked the court to enforce their French judgment. However, it was ordered on February 10, 2005 that the case be reheard by the *en banc* court of the US Court of Appeals, 9th Circuit. The case was argued before the *en banc* court in March 2005 and the opinion of the court is awaited.

24.35   **Scotland and Northern Ireland.** The tension between the two conflicting decisions of Drake J. was resolved by the judgment of Tugendhat J. in *Lennon v Scottish Daily Record* [2004] EWHC 359, QBD; [2004] E.M.L.R. 18. The claimant was a Celtic footballer who sued the *Daily Record* over English sales of an article about his supposed misbehaviour in Newcastle, and the defendant newspaper applied to stay the action on the ground that Scotland was the more appropriate forum. The judge held that he did have jurisdiction to order a stay of proceedings brought in England on the grounds of *forum non conveniens*. The position was, and remains, that no legislation allocating jurisdiction within the UK will be inconsistent with the Brussels Convention, or the Lugano Convention, or the Judgments Regulation, because those instruments allocate jurisdiction between member states: Scotland on the one hand, and England and Wales on the other, are separate jurisdictions but not separate member states.

Add to note 99: In *Lennon v Scottish Daily Record* (above), Tugendhat J. considered that the reasoning in the passage in Dicey & Morris (*The Conflict of Laws*, 2nd supplement to 13th ed., para.12–014) referred to in note 99 was addressed to a different factual scenario from that where a claimant sued a Scots company in England on English publication of a Scots newspaper. In his view, the authors had in mind a situation where a defendant was domiciled (for instance) in the Republic of Ireland, and Art.1 of the Judgments Regulation would require it to be sued in Ireland, subject to the right under Art.5 to sue in the place where the harmful event occurred. If the action was brought against the Irish defendant for publication of a newspaper distributed by it in England, the English courts would be, by Art.5(3), the courts of the place where the harmful event occurred. If the question then arose whether the English court was entitled to stay the action on the ground that Scotland was a more appropriate forum, the answer might depend on whether "the place" within Art.5(3) was the UK, or a part of the UK, i.e. England. If the former, it would not be inconsistent with the Judgments Regulation to stay the English proceedings in favour of Scotland; but if the latter, then there plainly would be an inconsistency. The opinion of the authors of Dicey & Morris was that "place" in Art.5(3) refers to a part of the UK, for instance England or Scotland. Since the rightness of that opinion was not argued before him, Tugendhat J. did not express a view upon it.

SECTION 4. OTHER COMPLAINTS PROCEDURES

PCC Code of Practice. The PCC Code of Practice is frequently reviewed and **24.38** updated, and the latest version was ratified by the PCC on June 13, 2005. (The Code may be found on the PCC website at *www.pcc.org.uk/cop/intro.html.*)

Accuracy. The wording of clause 1 has been altered slightly, but there is no **24.40** substantive change. The press must take care not to publish inaccurate, misleading or distorted information, including pictures, and a significant inaccuracy, misleading statement or distortion must be corrected promptly and with due prominence, and, where appropriate, an apology must be published.

Privacy. Clause 3 of the updated Code makes clear that the entitlement to **24.41** respect for correspondence includes digital communications. More significantly, the old proscription of the use of long lens photography to take pictures of people on private places without their consent has been replaced by a rule that it is unacceptable to photograph individuals in private places without their consent. Photography plainly includes telephoto photography, so the effect of the change is to extend the scope of the Code's protection of privacy.

By contrast, it is curious to note that the protection of the children of celebrities appears to have been subtly undermined. Previously, where material about the private life of a child was published, there had to be justification for publication other than the fame, notoriety or position of the child's parents or guardian. The new cl.6(v) provides that editors must not use the fame, notoriety or position of a parent or guardian as "sole justification" for publishing details of a child's private life. In other words, fame, notoriety and position can now be a justification, albeit not the only one.

The related rules on subterfuge and the use of listening devices have been brought together in a new cl.10, which (subject to the public interest exception) forbids the press to seek to obtain or publish material acquired by using hidden cameras or clandestine listening devices, or by intercepting private or mobile telephone calls, messages or emails, or by the unauthorised removal of documents or photographs. It also provides that engaging in misrepresentation or subterfuge can generally be justified only by reference to the public interest, and then only where the material cannot be obtained by other means.

Add to note 8: The public interest exception has been slightly broadened. It is now stated to include, but not to be confined to (1) detecting or exposing crime or serious impropriety (apparently wider than the previous "serious misdemeanour"), (2) protecting public health and safety, and (3) preventing the public from being misled by an action or statement of an individual or organisation. Whenever the public interest is invoked, the PCC will require editors to demonstrate fully how the public interest was served.

Add to note 9: The relevant clause is now cl.10, combining the old cll.8 and 11.

Add to note 10: See now the new cl.10, which makes clear that misrepresentation can only be justified when it is in the public interest.

24.41   **Procedure for Complaint.** *Add to note 12*: The time for complaint is now within two months of the article or of the end of "effective" correspondence with the editor.

24.43   **Broadcasting Standards Commission, Fairness and Privacy Code, Privacy**
24.46   **under the Code, Procedure.** Delete these paragraphs. The Broadcasting Standards Commission ceased operations on December 28, 2003 and its functions were transferred to the Office of Communications (Ofcom) on the following day.

24.47   **Independent Television Commission and Radio Authority Programme Codes.** *Delete this paragraph*. The Independent Television Commission and the Radio Authority ceased to exist on December 18 and December 29, 2003 respectively, and their functions were transferred to the Office of Communications (Ofcom) with effect from December 29, 2003.

24.48   **Ofcom.** Ofcom came into existence on December 29, 2003 and from that date assumed the functions of the "legacy regulators", the Broadcasting Standards Commission, the Independent Television Commission, the Radio Authority, the Office of Telecommunications and the Radiocommunications Agency.

Ofcom's new Broadcasting Code applies to television and radio programmes broadcast on and after July 25, 2005: before that date, programmes continued to be regulated under the relevant "legacy" code. The Code, which may be found on the Ofcom website (*www.ofcom.org.uk/tv/ifi/codes/bcode/#content*), covers standards in programmes, sponsorship, fairness (s.7) and privacy (s.8). The fairness and privacy sections of the Code must be observed by all broadcasters, including the BBC and S4C.

The Privacy section of the Code (s.8) has the aim of ensuring that broadcasters avoid any unwarranted infringement of privacy both in programmes and in the process of obtaining material which is included in programmes. It provides (cl.8.1) that any infringement of privacy in programmes, or in connection with obtaining material included in programmes, must be warranted. That requirement imposes a duty on broadcasters to show why the infringement is warranted, and (if the justification is the public interest) to show that the public interest out-weighs the right to privacy. Examples of public interest include revealing or detecting crime, protecting public health or safety, exposing misleading claims made by individuals or organisations, or disclosing incompetence that affects the public.

Under the heading "Private lives, public places and legitimate expectation of privacy", the Privacy section sets out the practices which broadcasters are to follow. "Legitimate expectation of privacy" will vary:

> "according to the place and nature of the information, activity or condition in question, the extent to which it is in the public domain (if at all) and whether the individual concerned is already in the public eye. There may be circumstances where people can reasonably expect privacy even in a public place. Some activities and conditions may be of such a private nature that filming or recording, even in a public place, could involve an infringement of privacy. People under investigation or in the public eye, and their immediate family and friends, retain the right to a private life, although private behaviour can raise issues of legitimate public interest".

The Ofcom Code is drafted in more general terms than the PCC Code, and in consequence its principles are less specific (although the Guidance Notes sup-plied for each section give more concrete examples of the kind of behaviour which will and will not amount to breach). For example, in s.8 there is no equivalent of the PCC Code's rule against photographing individuals in private places without their consent. One exception is a rule that (unless "warranted": cl.8.2) information which discloses the location of a person's home or family should not be revealed without permission. However, the Code does require that any infringement of privacy in the making or broadcasting of a programme needs consent (unless the infringement is warranted: cll.8.5–8.6), and it proscribes surreptitious filming or recording (which includes the use of long lenses, and recording telephone conversations without the other party's knowledge: cl.8.13), again unless warranted. Normally, surreptitious filming or recording will only be warranted if there is prima facie evidence of a story in the public interest, there are reasonable grounds to suspect that further material evidence could be obtained, and it is necessary to the credibility and authenticity of the pro-gramme.

Broadcasters are obliged (cl.8.21) to pay particular attention to the privacy of children under the age of 16, who do not lose their rights to privacy because of the fame or notoriety of their parents or because of events in their schools. Consent must be obtained from a parent or guardian where a child under 16 is featured in a way that infringes privacy, unless the subject matter is trivial or uncontroversial and the participation minor, or it is warranted to proceed without consent.

The Fairness section of the Ofcom Broadcasting Code (s.7) aims to ensure that broadcasters avoid unjust or unfair treatment of individuals or organisations in programmes. That generally entails (cl.7.3) giving potential contributors full details of the nature and purpose of the programme, the kind of contribution which they are expected to make, and the areas of questioning which they will face, with the broad object of ensuring that an informed consent is given. However, there is provision for withholding some of that information when justifiable in the public interest. There is an obligation to take reasonable care in factual programmes (cl.7.9) to ensure that material facts have not been presented, disregarded or omitted in an unfair way, and that anyone whose omission could be unfair has been offered an opportunity to contribute, and programmes such as dramas and factually based dramas should not portray facts, events, individuals or organisations in an unfair way (cl.7.10). Clause 7.11 provides that if a programme alleges wrongdoing or incompetence or makes other "significant allegations", those concerned should normally be given an appropriate and timely opportunity to respond. Misrepresentation and deception (including surreptitious filming or recording) should not normally be used (cl.7.14), unless it is in the public interest to use material obtained in that way and it cannot reasonably be obtained by other means.

Ofcom will consider complaints about partiality, inaccuracy, offensiveness, harmfulness, unfairness and breach of privacy. In the case of the BBC and SC4, it will consider issues relating to fairness and privacy, and harm and offence. There does not appear to be any provision for oral hearings: complaints are resolved by written submissions. Ofcom has the power to uphold complaints, and also (but only in the most serious cases) to order that the programme should not be repeated, to order the broadcast of a correction or a summary of the decision, or to impose a fine. Indeed, it can even shorten or withdraw a licence (not in the case of the BBC, S4C or Channel 4), although this must be supposed to be a sanction of last resort.

24.49   **Advertising.** From November 1, 2004, the regulation of broadcast advertising content was contracted out by Ofcom to the Advertising Standards Authority (Broadcast) Ltd (ASAB) under the provisions of The Contracting Out (Functions Relating to Broadcast Advertising) and Specification of Relevant Functions Order 2004, SI 2004/1975, having previously been the responsibility of the ITC and the Radio Authority. In consequence there are now separate TV and Radio Advertising Codes, for which the Broadcast Code of Advertising Practice (BCAP) is responsible, in addition to the existing CAP Code for non-broadcast advertisements. Ofcom has also contracted out its enforcement powers, so that ASAB can require a licence holder to exclude an advertisement or certain descriptions of advertisements from its programme service (see Communications Act 2003, s.325(5)). Ofcom retains its powers under the Broadcasting Acts 1990 and 1996 and the Communications Act 2003 to order the broadcast of a correction or statement of findings, to impose a financial penalty or to shorten or revoke a licence.

Delete note 45.

24.50   **Complaint procedure.** *Add to note 49*: The 1988 Regulations have been further amended by SI 2003/3183.

INTERIM INJUNCTIONS

SECTION 1. GENERAL PRINCIPLES

Jurisdiction. *Add note 4a*: Almost invariably interim injunctions are granted **25.1** in prohibitory form, to restrain the threatened or repeated publication of defamatory statements about the claimant. Exceptionally a publisher might be ordered to withdraw, say, a book or pamphlet from distribution or circulation, or, if it was within his power, to cause copies he had distributed to be returned to him. However, in *Chin Bay Ching v Merchant Ventures Pte Ltd* [2005] S.G.A. 29; [2005] SLR 142 the Singapore Court of Appeal indicated, albeit making no express ruling, that in an appropriate case a mandatory interim injunction ordering a defendant to publish a correction might be granted. In support of this view the court cited *TV3 network Ltd v Eveready New Zealand Ltd* [1993] 3 NZLR 435 in which Gault J. had stated (in a defamation case) that there was "no jurisdictional bar to an injunction cast in mandatory form". Gault J. had observed that such an injunction had been granted in *Hermann Loog v Bean* (1884) 26 Ch D 306 though it would seem that the order in this case was made to effect the redelivery to the plaintiff of some letters which the defendant had wrongly directed the Post Office to deliver to him, rather than to obtain the publication of a correction of a defamatory statement. As the court's statutory powers under the offer to make amends procedure and the summary disposal procedure do not extend as far as ordering the defendant to publish a correction, it seems unlikely that any judge would consider that by virtue of his general powers to grant injunctions contained in s.37(1) of the Supreme Court Act 1981 he was enabled to make such an order.

Delicate nature of jurisdiction. *Add to note 7*: These four conditions were **25.2** applied by Tugendhat J. in *Coys Ltd v Autocherish Ltd* [2004] EWHC 1334, QBD; [2004] E.M.L.R. 25.

Defence of justification. Section 12(3) of the Human Rights Act 1998 and **25.6** Art.8 of the European Convention for the Protection of Human Rights and Fundamental Freedoms have been used as weapons to challenge the continued validity of the rule in *Bonnard v Perryman*. Both challenges have been repulsed. See *Coys Ltd v Autocherish Ltd*, above, and *Greene v Associated Newspapers Ltd*

[2004] EWCA Civ 1462; [2005] E.M.L.R. 10 discussed further, at paras 25.19 and 25.19a of this Supplement.

25.15   *Examples (2). Add to note 56*: In *Georgallides v Etzin*, unreported, July 12, 2005, G made an application under the Protection of Harassment Act 1997 for an order restraining E, who alleged he was owed money by G, from organising protests with placards and leaflets outside G's restaurant. Gray J. granted a limited injunction, commenting that though the words on the placards were defamatory of G he was satisfied that the application was not an attempt to circumvent the rule in *Bonnard v Perryman* but to prevent G from being harassed.

25.18   **Section 12(3).** The House of Lords have now ruled (*Cream Holdings Ltd v Bannerjee* [2004] UKHL 44; [2005] 1 A.C. 253) that the term "likely" was not to be given a rigid definition, but was to be applied pragmatically to the circumstances of each individual case. Lord Nicholls explained, at [22]:

> "Section 12(3) makes the likelihood of success at the trial an essential element in the court's consideration of whether to make an interim order. But in order to achieve the necessary flexibility the degree of likelihood needed to satisfy section 12(3) must depend on the circumstances. There can be no single, rigid standard governing all applications for interim restraint orders. Rather, on its proper construction the effect of section 12(3) is that the court is not to make an interim restraint order unless satisfied the applicant's prospects of success at the trial are sufficiently favourable to justify such an order being made in the particular circumstances of the case. As to what degree of likelihood makes the prospect of success 'sufficiently favourable' the general approach should be that the courts will be exceedingly slow to make interim restraint orders where the applicant has not satisfied the court he will probably ('more likely than not') succeed at trial. In general, that should be the threshold an applicant must cross before the court embarks on exercising its discretion, duly taking into account the relevant jurisprudence on Art. 10 and any countervailing Convention rights. But there will be cases where it is necessary for a court to depart from this general approach and a lesser degree of likelihood will suffice as a prerequisite."

Their lordships held that the single judge had been in error, not necessarily in his construction of s.12(3), but in his finding that that there was no public interest justification for the publishing of the material the subject of the injunction and thus had misdirected himself when exercising his discretion. Exercising this discretion afresh (which the Court of Appeal had not done) their lordships took the view that the claimant's prospects of success were not sufficiently likely to justify making an interim restraint order, and they discharged the injunction.

25.19   **The effect on the rule in *Bonnard v Perryman*.** In *Coys Ltd v Autocherish Ltd* (see para.25.2 of this Supplement) the claimant submitted that s.12(3) of the Human Rights Act 1998 applied to defamation actions and as construed, by the Court of Appeal in *Cream Holdings v Bannerjee* [2003] EWCA Civ 103; [2003] 3 W.L.R. 999 (the House of Lords had not as yet heard the appeal), had the effect of changing the law so that where a defendant was resisting an interim injunction on the grounds that he intended to plead and prove justification the court was bound to investigate the merits of that defence, and decide whether despite such defence the claimant had real prospects of succeeding at trial. If the claimant passed this threshold test the court could exercise its discretion to grant an injunction. Tugendhat J. rejected that submission citing with approval this paragraph of the Main Work as well as suggesting that he was probably bound by the decision of the Court of Appeal in *Holley v Smyth* [1998] Q.B. 726. In *Greene v Associated Newspapers Ltd* [2004] EWCA Civ 1462; [2005] E.M.L.R. 10 the Court of Appeal disposed of a similar argument robustly. Referring to the first principles of statutory interpretation which excluded "the dismantling of judge-made law by stealth", the Court concluded (at [66]):

> "We therefore have no hesitation in holding that there is nothing in s.12(3) of the Human Rights Act 1998 that can properly be interpreted as weakening in any way the force of the rule in *Bonnard v Perryman*."

Article 8 of ECHR and the rule in *Bonnard v Perryman*. Following the   **25.19A**
pronouncement by the ECtHR in *Radio France v France* (2005) 40 E.H.R.R. 29 that the rights protected under Art.8 included the right to reputation, it was contended by the claimant in *Greene v Associated Newspapers Ltd* [2004] EWCA Civ 1462; [2005] E.M.L.R. 10 that where there was an application for an interim injunction to restrain a threatened publication of defamatory allegations the court had to adopt a "rights-based approach" which would involve a careful investigation of the importance of the competing rights of reputation and freedom of expression in the particular circumstances of the case. This would inevitably exclude the routine application of the rule in *Bonnard v Perryman* as that would amount to granting the right of freedom of expression (Art.10) precedence over the rights protected under Art.8. The Court of Appeal was unimpressed. It accepted the submission of the defendant that in a defamation case where the defence of justification is raised the claimant's right to a fair reputation is put in issue. But, "one cannot speak sensibly of the violation of that right until it is established at trial" (at [76]). Furthermore, while some damage may be done to the claimant by permitting the publication of what may later turn out to be false, the damage "pales into insignificance compared with the damage which would be done to freedom of expression and the freedom of the press if the rule in *Bonnard v Perryman* was relaxed" (at [78]). Accordingly, there was nothing in the ECHR that required the rule to be done away with.

Section 12(4). *Add new note to section 12(4)(1), 69a*: In *Re X, Y (Children)*   **25.21**
[2004] EWHC 762 (Fam); [2004] E.M.L.R. 29 Munby J. stated that the extent to which material had become available to the public was a relevant factor to which the court was to have regard in considering the grant of injunctive relief, but was not determinative. Although the general practice was for injunctions to be qualified with a public domain proviso, there were circumstances where such a qualification was inappropriate. (This was an application for a *contra mundum* injunction to restrain publication of information relating to a father, a convicted paedophile, and his two children at the time of the criminal trial of the father's identical twin brother on charges of raping and indecently assaulting boys under 16.)

Section 2. Practice and Procedure

25.23   **Introduction.** It should be noted that it is now permissible to join a party to a claim by description rather than by name and to grant an injunction against such a person. This was sanctioned in *Bloomsbury Publishing Group v News Group Newspapers Ltd* [2003] EWHC 1205; [2003] 1 W.L.R. 1633, concerned with the theft, and attempted sale of extracts to newspapers, of an unpublished *Harry Potter* book. It would surely be an appropriate procedure to follow where, for example, there was evidence of the distribution of anonymous defamatory leaflets, or the display by persons whose identities are unknown of defamatory posters or placards.

Section 4. Injunctions to Restrain Statements Prejudicial to the Fair Trial of an Action

25.38   **Contempt and confidence.** *Note 29*: The correct name of the case is *Att-Gen v Punch & Others* [2003] 1 A.C. 1046.

CHAPTER 26

PARTICULARS OF CLAIM

SECTION 2. PREFATORY AVERMENTS

Prefatory averments. *Add at end of note 17*: See also *Jameel v The Wall*   **26.4**
Street Journal Europe Sprl [2003] EWHC 2945, QBD; [2004] 2 All E.R. 92 in
which Eady J. rejected the contention that a foreign corporation could not
maintain a claim in defamation unless it could prove it had been caused actual
financial loss by the publication at issue. The Court of Appeal "endorsed and
commended" Eady J.'s judgment (*Jameel (Mohammed) v Wall Street Journal
Europe Sprl* [2005] EWCA Civ 74; [2005] 2 W.L.R. 1577) at [116]–[118] and
also rejected a new submission by the defendant that any corporation, domestic
or foreign, needed to establish special damage as a condition for suing in
defamation: [113]. Nonetheless, in cases where the claimant is a foreign corporation and its trading reputation in this jurisdiction may be in issue, it would be
advisable to provide particulars of this trading reputation (see *Jameel (Mohammed) v Wall Street Journal Europe Sprl (CA, No.2)*, above, at [98] (recording that
one of the conditions for an award of damages by the jury to the corporate
claimant was a finding that "the Jameel Company had a trading reputation in
England") and the observations of the court at [113]–[118].

SECTION 3. PUBLICATION

Details of publication: libel. *Add at end of note 24*: With regard to internet   **26.5**
publication, see also *Loutchansky v Times Newspapers Ltd (No.2)* [2001] EWCA
Civ 1805; [2002] Q.B. 783; *Jameel (Yousef) v Dow Jones & Co. Inc.* [2005]

EWCA Civ 75; [2005] 2 W.L.R. 1614; *Steinberg v Pritchard Englefield (a firm)* [2005] EWCA Civ 288 and *Hewitt v Grunwald* [2004] EWHC 2959, QBD at [72]–[74].

SECTION 4. THE WORDS PUBLISHED

26.13   **Setting out words complained of.** *Add at end of note 55*: See also *Jennings v Buchanan* [2004] UKPC 36; [2005] 1 A.C. 115 at [5].

SECTION 5. FOREIGN PUBLICATION

26.18   **Publication in a foreign language.** *Add at end of note 76*: For the position in Malaysia, see *Dato' Seri Tiong King Sing v Datuk Justine Jinggut* [2003] 6 M.L.J. 433.

SECTION 6. THE MEANING OF THE WORDS

26.20   **Pleading meanings.** *Add at end of note 81*: In *Jameel v Times Newspapers Ltd* [2004] EWCA Civ 983; [2004] E.M.L.R. 31, Sedley L.J. observed at [12]: "No issue arises before us about the need for a claimant to situate at least his highest pleaded meaning at one of these three levels: see now the judgment of Brooke L.J. in *Chase v News Group Newspapers Ltd* [2003] E.M.L.R. 11 at [45]." So much is uncontroversial. However, Sedley L.J. went on to say: "For my part I would think it high time that claimants were required to plead their levels of meaning in the alternative, especially since the decision in *Bennett* [*v News Group Newspapers Ltd* [2002] E.M.L.R. 39]." Longmore L.J. expressly "echoed this view" at [43].

This view *is* controversial, and problematic. First, both the decisions invoked in support of it were concerned principally with *Lucas-Box* particulars, that is, particulars of meaning which it might be open to a defendant to plead in the context of a defence of justification, and not the manner in which a claimant might frame his case on meaning. Secondly, in practical terms, it is difficult to see what interest a claimant could have in pleading "levels of meaning in the alternative", rather than identifying the single highest or gravest defamatory meaning he contends a particular allegation bears. This has long been standard practice, and for good reason: it is unlikely to be in the claimant's interest to be equivocal about the "level of meaning" at trial.

In these circumstances, it is suggested that the new *Jameel* requirement of pleading alternative meanings in particulars of claim should be confined to cases where the claimant is uncertain about the level of meaning attributable to the allegation in question. In such cases, in compliance with CPR PD 53, para.2.3(1), the claimant ought to plead alternative levels of meaning expressly. In cases where the claimant has a clear-cut case on what has been alleged against him, it is contended that there is no reason to depart from the standard practice of pleading the single, highest meaning.

Pleading innuendoes. *Add to note 88*: See also *Winnel v Snow* [2003] ACTSC   **26.22**
94.

Miscellaneous considerations. *Add to note 94*: For the extent to which juries   **26.24**
in Victoria are constrained by the pleaded imputations, see *Waters v WA News-papers* [2004] VSC 124.

Section 9. Damages

Damages. *Add to note 9*: This principle applies just as much to corporations   **26.27**
as it does to individuals: *Jameel (Mohammed) v Wall Street Journal Europe Sprl*
[2005] EWCA Civ 74; [2005] 2 W.L.R. 1577. However, whether the claimant is
an individual or a corporation, where the defendant can demonstrate that the
publication at issue caused the claimant's reputation no or minimum actual
damage, an action based on such a publication will be stayed as an abuse of the
process: *Jameel (Yousef) v Dow Jones & Co. Inc.* [2005] EWCA Civ 75; [2005]
2 W.L.R. 1614.

Where damage must be pleaded. *Add at end of paragraph*: A corporate   **26.28**
claimant may not claim aggravated damages in respect of conduct by the
defendant subsequent to publication alleged to have aggravated or exacerbated
the defamation because such damages required injury to feelings, which a
corporation could not suffer (new note 22A).

New note 22A: *Collins Stewart Ltd v The Financial Times Ltd (No.2)* [2005]
EWHC 262, QBD at [31].

Special damage. *Add to note 24*: In *Collins Stewart Ltd v The Financial Times*   **26.29**
Ltd [2004] EWHC 2337, QBD; [2005] E.M.L.R. 5, a claim for special damages
was struck out on the grounds that a fall in the market capitalisation of the
claimant company was considered too uncertain a basis for an assessment by the
court of the quantum of damages occasioned by an alleged libel.

Section 12. Malicious Falsehood

Generally. *Add to note 54*: Now see Eady J.'s observations on and application   **26.39**
of these principles in *Hewitt v Grunwald* [2004] EWHC 2959, QBD at
[23]–[27].

Section 13. Amendment of Particulars of Claim

Permission necessary. *Add to note 68*: See also *Wood v Chief Constable of the*   **26.41**
West Midlands Police [2004] EWCA Civ 1638; [2005] E.M.L.R. 20, where May
L.J. at [66]–[86] gave detailed consideration to the question of whether the trial

judge (Tugendhat J.) had been right to permit the claimant to amend his case at trial to introduce a new claim for slander, a cause of action in respect of which the limitation period had long since expired. (The Court of Appeal concluded that the judge had and dismissed the defendant's appeal against that decision.)

CHAPTER 27

DEFENCE

[With a view to avoiding confusion, the following decisions in libel claims featuring Mohammed or Yousef Jameel as a claimant, set out here in chronological order, will be referred to in this Chapter of the Supplement:

Jameel v The Wall Street Journal Europe Sprl [2003] EWHC 2302, QBD, Eady J., October 7, 2003;

Jameel v Times Newspapers Ltd [2003] EWHC 2609, QBD, Gray J., November 7, 2003;

Jameel v The Wall Street Journal Europe Sprl [2003] EWCA Civ 1694, [2004] E.M.L.R. 6, CA, November 26, 2003.

Jameel v The Wall Street Journal Europe Sprl [2003] EWHC 37, QBD; reported as *Jameel v The Wall Street Journal Sprl (No.2)* [2004] E.M.L.R. 11 (Eady J., ruling on qualified privilege at trial, January 20, 2004);

Jameel v Times Newspapers Ltd [2004] EWCA Civ 983; [2004] E.M.L.R. 31, CA, July 21, 2004.

Jameel v The Wall Street Journal Europe Sprl [2005] EWCA Civ 74; reported as *Jameel (Mohammed) v Wall Street Journal Europe Sprl* [2005] 2 W.L.R. 1577, CA, February 9, 2005, appeal from Eady J.'s ruling on qualified privilege at trial.]

SECTION 2. PLEA OF JUSTIFICATION

When to plead this defence. *Add to note 23*: Now see Eady J.'s observations **27.5** on and application of these principles in *Hewitt v Grunwald* [2004] EWHC 2959, QBD at [23]–[27].

Justifying the words in their natural and ordinary meaning. *Add at end of* **27.7** *paragraph*: It is also not permissible to plead a *Lucas-Box* meaning in the form of a hearsay statement, *e.g.* to seek to justify a defamatory publication in the meaning that "A said that B murdered C" (where B is the claimant) (new note 41A, see below).

Add at the beginning of note 32: As Sedley L.J. neatly encapsulated the point in *Jameel v Times Newspapers Ltd* [2004] EWCA Civ 983; [2004] E.M.L.R. 31 at [26]: "the permissible mode of justification of a libel arises out of the question of meaning".

Add at the end of note 34: Now, for the position in New South Wales, see *John Fairfax Publications Pty Ltd v Jones* [2004] NSWCA 205.

Add at the end of note 35: With regard to *Templeton v Jones* [1984] 1 N.Z.L.R 448, now see *Haines v TV New Zealand* [2004] NZAR 513.

Add at the end of note 36: There have been significant developments—some not readily comprehensible or reconcilable with others—in the jurisprudence relating to the three "tiers" or levels of defamatory meaning in the context of pleading *Lucas-Box* particulars. Although the three-tier analysis has its roots in *Lewis v Daily Telegraph* [1964] A.C. 264, as Sedley L.J. observed in *Jameel v Times Newspapers Ltd* [2004] EWCA Civ 983; [2004] E.M.L.R. 31 at [10], "The elevation of this taxonomy of meanings into legal categories is recent". It seems that now a pleader will in general be required to "pitch" his *Lucas-Box* meaning at one of these three levels: *Chase v News Group Newspapers Ltd* [2002] EWCA Civ 1772; [2003] E.M.L.R. 11 at [45] (although see *Miller v Associated Newspapers Ltd* [2005] EWHC 21, QBD for a case in which Eady J. accepted that all three levels of meaning were "in play" ([8]–[9]).

With regard to the question of the meanings it is open to a defendant to attribute to a defamatory publication, Gray J. in *Jameel v Times Newspapers Ltd* [2003] EWHC 2609, QBD at [23]–[25] identified certain distinctions between level 2 ("reasonable grounds to suspect") and level 3 ("grounds to enquire or investigate") meanings. The Court of Appeal later that year in *Jameel v The Wall Street Journal Europe Sprl* [2003] EWCA Civ 1694; [2004] E.M.L.R. 6, cited Gray J.'s analysis, ostensibly with approval, at [19], albeit that Simon Brown L.J. at [20] observed that the difference between levels 2 and 3 was "not perhaps an entirely satisfactory distinction". Importantly, however, Simon Brown L.J. recognised at [21] that the reason it might be necessary to decide on whether a publication was capable of bearing a level 2 or a level 3 meaning was "in order to determine whether the plea of justification is permissible *given the differing character of justification evidence required for the respective levels*" (emphasis added). See also Simon Brown L.J. at [16] recognising that where a defence of justification that incorporates a level 3 meaning is raised, it may be important for the court to rule at the interlocutory stage on whether the words are capable of bearing that lower level meaning "so as to control the evidence properly adducible at trial". In other words, the significance of the answer to the question of whether a publication is capable of bearing a level 2 or 3 meaning, according to the Court of Appeal, is that it may affect how a defendant goes about—and is permitted by the court to go about—justifying what he has published. How so? For an answer to this question, see para.27.10 of this Supplement.

In the meantime, the Court of Appeal in *Musa King v Telegraph Group Ltd* [2004] EWCA Civ 613; [2004] E.M.L.R. 23 permitted the defendant to plead and justify a *Lucas-Box* meaning that "the police suspected the claimant of involvement in terror-related activities" on the grounds that it could be equated with a permissible level 3 meaning (see [29]–[33], *per* Brooke L.J.). *Quaere* whether a meaning that "the police suspected . . . " can really be "equated" with a level 3 "grounds to suspect or investigate" meaning. Moreover, the Court of Appeal's approval of this form of meaning in *Musa King* sits somewhat unhappily with the principle derived from Eady J.'s decision in *Hamilton v Clifford* [2004] EWHC 1542, QBD set out in para.27.10 of this Supplement, which itself purported to be an application of *Musa King*.

In *Armstrong v Times Newspapers Ltd* [2004] EWHC 2928, QBD, Eady J. ruled that the publication complained of was not capable of bearing a meaning lower than a level 2 meaning and struck out the *Lucas-Box* particulars in so far as they sought to advance a lower, level 3 meaning. In so doing, the judge subjected to yet further scrutiny "the precise nature of the third tier of gravity" and the question of why it was permissible as a defamatory meaning at all (at [5]–[10]). The ruling on meaning had a knock-on effect on the particulars of justification, substantial parts of which were struck out. For an account of this aspect of Eady J.'s judgment, see note 60 to para.27.10 of this Supplement.

Add new note 41A: To do so would be to infringe the "repetition rule", which is a rule governing not only what facts and matters a defendant is entitled to plead and prove in support of a defence of justification, but that also circumscribes the permissible range of *meanings* a defendant can seek to justify: *Hamilton v Clifford* [2004] EWHC 1542, QBD at [33], *per* Eady J. For an account of how the "repetition rule" constrains the pleading of particulars of justification, see para.27.10 and, specifically, note 60 to para.27.10 in this Supplement.

Pleading particulars. *Add at the end of note 56*: For a recent invocation of the   **27.10**
principles embodied in *Polly Peck plc v Trelford* [1986] Q.B. 1000 and *Rechem International Ltd v Express Newspapers plc, The Times*, June 19, 1992, CA, in "managing" a defence of justification, see *McKeith v News Group Newspapers Ltd* [2005] EWHC 1162, QBD; [2005] E.M.L.R. 32.

Add at the end of note 58:

> "If it had truly been intended . . . to accuse the claimant of dishonesty in respect of her theories and nutritional advice, it would surely have been spelt out as such a serious accusation requires . . . It is, of course, elementary that a person can mislead innocently or negligently or dishonestly. If such an allegation is to be made in a plea of justification, it behoves the pleader to identify whether a culpable state of mind is said to be applicable to the instant case. Moreover, if there is to be an allegation that misleading statements or representations had been made dishonestly, it would be necessary to set out the facts from which that state of mind is to be inferred" (*McKeith v News Group Newspapers Ltd* [2005] EWHC 1162, QBD; [2005] E.M.L.R. 32 at [26]–[27], *per* Eady J.).

Add at the end of note 59: For a discussion of the application (or non-application) of the "repetition rule" to justification of level 3 ("grounds to enquire or investigate") meanings, see note 60 to para.27.10 in this Supplement.

Add at the end of note 60: Eady J.'s distillation of the principles governing the pleading of level 2 "reasonable grounds to suspect" meanings in *Musa King v Telegraph Group Ltd* [2003] EWHC 1312, QBD was quoted by the Court of

Appeal in that case ([2004] EWCA Civ 613; [2004] E.M.L.R. 23 at [22] with apparent approval.

In answer to the question posed at the end of this footnote in the Main Work, the significance of whether a publication bears or is capable of bearing a level 2 or a level 3 meaning, according to the Court of Appeal in *Jameel v The Wall Street Journal Europe Sprl* [2003] EWCA Civ 1694; [2004] E.M.L.R. 6 at [21], is that it may affect the permissible scope of justification. To ascertain the effect the level of meaning may have on the ambit of particulars of justification, it is instructive to go back to Gray J.'s decision in *Jameel v Times Newspapers Ltd* [2003] EWHC 2609, QBD.

Gray J. ruled that the publication at issue was capable of bearing no defamatory meaning higher than a level 3 ("grounds to enquire or investigate") meaning. Having so ruled, he went on to hold that that the "conduct" rule (see *Shah v Standard Chartered Bank* [1999] Q.B. 241 and the explanation of that rule in para.27.10 of the Main Work) applied to justification of a level 3 meaning only if the publication made some allegation about the claimant's conduct. Otherwise, as in the case he was deciding, it did not apply and it was permissible for the defendant to seek to justify with reference to facts and matters which did *not* focus on the claimant's conduct ([22]–[28]). Moreover, Gray J. held that the "repetition rule" (see para.27.10 of the Main Work) did not apply to justification of a level 3 meaning. Having observed that where one was considering a level 3 meaning, the grounds for enquiry or investigation did not have to be shown to be "objectively reasonable", the judge held at [30] that it was "difficult to see how in principle hearsay material may not be relied on to support the contention that sufficient grounds exist for enquiry or investigation".

The Court of Appeal ([2004] EWCA Civ 983; [2004] E.M.L.R. 31) reversed Gray J.'s ruling on meaning, holding that the publication was capable of bearing both a level 2 and a level 3 meaning. Having done so, the claimant did not pursue his appeal against the judge's ruling on the applicability of the "repetition rule" to level 3 meanings (and there was no appeal against the "conduct" rule decision). Nonetheless, Sedley L.J. at [30] was at pains to record his view *obiter* that:

> "the consequences of so holding [that the 'repetition rule' has no application to level 3 meanings] are disquieting. It means that, so long as a slur on an individual's reputation is cast in level [3] terms, it can be justified by reliance on the bare fact of assertions made by others, without any need to make them good."

His conclusion was that there were "strong practical reasons" why the repetition rule should apply to level 3 meanings.

In *Musa King v Telegraph Group Ltd* [2004] EWCA Civ 613; [2004] E.M.L.R. 23 (decided after Gray J.'s ruling in *Jameel v Times Newspapers Ltd* [2003] EWHC 2609, QBD and the Court of Appeal's decision in *Jameel v The Wall Street Journal Europe Sprl* [2003] EWCA Civ 1694; [2004] E.M.L.R. 6 but before the Court of Appeal's decision in *Jameel v Times Newspapers Ltd* [2004] EWCA Civ 983, [2004] E.M.L.R. 31) the Court of Appeal permitted the defendant to justify a *Lucas-Box* meaning that "the police suspected the claimant of involvement in terror-related activities" on the grounds that it could be equated with a permissible level 3 meaning (see [29]–[33] *per* Brooke L.J.). Particulars of justification which pleaded the facts that the claimant had been placed on a list of police suspects and that the claimant's home had been raided by the police, struck out by the judge (see [2003] EWHC 1312, QBD, *per* Eady J.), were reinstated on the basis that they were capable of justifying the level 3 meaning. *Quaere* whether the Court of Appeal's decision on the facts of the case can be reconciled with Eady J.'s synthesis of the principles governing the pleading of "reasonable grounds to suspect" meanings to which the Court of Appeal apparently gave its imprimatur. If the logic of the Court of Appeal's reasoning as regards its decision on the facts were followed, what would stand in the way of a defendant—wishing to circumvent the disciplines that govern the justification of a level 2 meaning—pleading in the alternative a "lower" level 3 meaning and justifying that? (In a more recent case, *Armstrong v Times Newspapers Ltd* [2004] EWHC 2928, QBD, Eady J. put a stop to what he plainly perceived to be an attempt by a defendant to do just this (see [27]–[28]) of his judgment in particular.) A more satisfactory basis for the court in *Musa King* to have allowed the disputed particulars of justification to stand, it is submitted, is that in a case where (a) the article complained of made express reference to the fact the claimant was on a police list of suspects and that his flat had been raided by the police, and (b) the defendant was already properly justifying a "reasonable grounds to suspect" meaning (which only demands a *focus* on the claimant's conduct), it would have been wholly unjust and unreal to preclude the defendant from establishing before the jury key facts bearing on suspicions about the claimant which were expressly referred to in the article sued on. In *Miller v Associated Newspapers Ltd* [2005] EWHC 21, QBD, Eady J. adopted such a pragmatic approach (albeit he avowed reliance on the Court of Appeal's decision in *Musa King*!) in allowing the defendant to amend its case to justify that the claimant at the date of publication was in fact "suspected of ... neglect of duty".

For a detailed analysis and application of the principles governing level 2 justification, including the requirement that the grounds pleaded must be objectively reasonable, see *Hamilton v Clifford* [2004] EWHC 1542, QBD, at [36]–[52], *per* Eady J. Note in particular what the judge said at [38]–[39]:

> "It was apparently accepted in *Musa King*, as a general proposition, that the mere fact that someone has said that a claimant is guilty, or that someone believes it to be so, cannot in itself constitute reasonable grounds to suspect. Mr Moloney queried the authority for that proposition, but it would appear to follow from the need for the grounds pleaded to be tested by objective criteria. The point is closely related to the repetition rule. The fact that someone has asserted 'X is guilty of murder' does not in itself go to provide reasonable grounds for suspicion. Something more is required ... The essence of May L.J.'s remarks in *Shah* was that the setting out of subjective views and judgments is irrelevant to the establishment of grounds to suspect, which are to be judged objectively."

Eady J. held that the fact the person making the defamatory assertion "X is guilty of murder" was—on his own account—an eye-witness does not, of itself, affect the position ([40]).

In *Armstrong v Times Newspapers Ltd*, above, Eady J., having ruled that the publication at issue was not capable of bearing any meaning lower than a level 2 meaning, proceeded to excise from the lengthy particulars of justification (102 paragraphs' worth) all the material that failed to comply with the principles governing level 2 justification. These rulings were not challenged by the defendant on appeal ([2005] EWCA Civ 1007 at [36]).

SECTION 3. PLEA OF FAIR COMMENT

27.13 **Pleading fair comment.** *Add to note 69*: See also *Hamilton v Clifford* [2004] EWHC 1542, QBD at [53]–[62] for a useful gloss on the principles to be derived from the line of recent authority on the defence of fair comment starting with *Branson v Bower* [2001] EWCA Civ 791; [2001] E.M.L.R. 32. In terms of the interrelation between the defences of fair comment and justification, Eady J. stated at [60] that:

> "It should perhaps be emphasised that nothing in the *Branson* decisions was intended to conflict with or undermine the repetition rule. They were not supposed to provide a way round the disciplines which the law imposes in respect of factual allegations which are objectively verifiable . . . For reasons of policy . . . one is not permitted to seek shelter behind a defence of fair comment when the defamatory sting is one of verifiable fact. Depending on the meaning of the particular words complained of, a defendant has either to justify the primary factual allegation . . . or comply with the necessary disciplines to establish 'reasonable grounds to suspect'. Fair comment does not provide an escape route in such circumstances."

27.16 **Pleading matter of public interest.** *Add at the end of note 75*: See also *Anderson v Ah Kit* [2004] WASC 194.

SECTION 4. PLEA OF PRIVILEGE

27.18 **Defence must be specially pleaded.** *Add at the end of note 77*: In *Jameel (Mohammed) v Wall Street Journal Europe Sprl* [2005] EWCA Civ 74; [2005] 2 W.L.R. 1577 at [18], the Court of Appeal observed that the pleading requirement imposed by CPR PD 53, para.2.7 "can be a weighty one where a defendant relies on *Reynolds* privilege, for there may be many different circumstances relied upon in support of the defence". For the matters which a defendant is required to plead in support of this species of qualified privilege, see new para.27.19A in this Supplement.

Delete from note 79: the references to *Reynolds* qualified privilege and see new para.27.19A in this Supplement.

27.19 **Basis of privilege to be stated.** *Note 81*: Now see new para.27.19A in this Supplement.

27.19A **Pleading *Reynolds* privilege.** Where a defendant newspaper or other publisher claims that its dissemination of defamatory material to the public took place on an occasion covered by the species of qualified privilege elaborated by the House of Lords in *Reynolds v Times Newspapers Ltd* (new note 84A), it must demonstrate why the nature of the subject matter of the publication was such that it was in the public interest for it to be published (new note 84B). The defendant must also set out the circumstances of the publication said to support publication in public interest (new note 84C), existing at the date of publication (new note 84D), such as the seriousness of the allegation, the extent to which it was a matter of public concern, the source (new note 84E) and the status of the information, the steps taken to verify it, the urgency of the matter and the steps taken to obtain and print the claimant's side of the story. Responsible journalism, in all the circumstances, must be demonstrated (new note 84F). In an appropriate case, it may be necessary or at least admissible for a defendant to plead and prove a subjective belief in the truth of its publication in order to establish a defence of *Reynolds* privilege (new note 84G). In such a case, the defendant should expressly identify the meaning it contends the individuals responsible for the publication understood it to bear (new note 84H).

New note 84A: *Reynolds v Times Newspapers Ltd* [2001] 2 A.C. 127. In *Jameel (Mohammed) v Wall Street Journal Europe Sprl* [2005] EWCA Civ 74; [2005] 2 W.L.R. 1577, the Court of Appeal at [18] *et seq.* directly addressed the question: "What must a defendant plead and prove to establish *Reynolds* privilege?" The specific pleading requirements identified by the Court of Appeal in this judgment are extracted in new notes 84B to 84H below. At the outset of its analysis, however, the Court of Appeal made the following preliminary observations (at [18]): " . . . it is common ground that the test involves consideration of whether the publication was in the public interest and whether, in the particular circumstances, it was a product of responsible journalism. It is also common ground that the non-exhaustive list of material circumstances drawn up by Lord Nicholls . . . in *Reynolds* at p.205 has to be considered."

New note 84B: *Jameel (Mohammed) v Wall Street Journal Europe Sprl* [2005] EWCA Civ 74; [2005] 2 W.L.R. 1577 at [87].

The correct legal test for *Reynolds* privilege has been the subject of considerable debate. The principal "fault-line" of this debate has been whether a defendant asserting *Reynolds* privilege has to plead and prove either (a) that it was under a duty to publish, or (b) merely that it had satisfied the requirements of "responsible journalism" described by the Court of Appeal in *Loutchansky v Times Newspapers Ltd (No.2)* [2001] EWCA Civ 1805; [2002] Q.B. 783. This debate came to a head in the case of *Jameel v The Wall Street Journal Europe Sprl*.

At the trial of the action, Eady J. ruled that the defendant's publication did not attract a defence of *Reynolds* privilege. As recorded in the Court of Appeal's judgment on the appeal from that decision (*Jameel (Mohammed) v Wall Street Journal Europe Sprl*) at [44], Eady J.

"considered the publishers' suggestion that *Reynolds* had reduced the test of qualified privilege to the question of whether the publication of the article in question constituted 'responsible journalism'. He concluded that it had not. The fundamental test laid down by *Reynolds* was whether it was in the public interest for the article to be published and, the obverse of this, whether the publisher had a social or moral duty."

On appeal, the defendant renewed its complaint that Eady J. had applied too stringent a test and had failed to apply the "correct test" of "responsible journalism" it contended had been laid down by the Court of Appeal in *Loutch-ansky v Times Newspapers Ltd (No.2)* [2001] EWCA Civ 1805; [2002] Q.B. 783, at [36]. The Court of Appeal in *Jameel* resolved this dispute as to the correct test as follows (at [87]):

> "We agree with the judge that the phrase *responsible journalism* is insufficiently precise to constitute the sole test for *Reynolds* privilege. It seems to us that it denotes the degree of care that a journalist should exercise before publishing a defamatory statement. The requirements of responsible journalism will vary according to the particular circumstances and, in particular, the gravity of the defamation. Responsible journalism must be demonstrated before *Reynolds* privilege can be established. But there is a further element that must be demonstrated. The subject matter of the publication must be of such a nature that it is in the public interest that it should be published. This is a more stringent test than that the public should be interested in receiving the information; see *A v B plc* [2002] EWCA Civ 337; [2003] Q.B. 195, 208D."

So much is clear. However, the Court of Appeal, having expressly recorded Eady J.'s observation that the obverse of publication being in the public interest was that the publisher had a social or moral duty to publish (see [44] and [86]), chose not to comment on it. The Court of Appeal certainly did not *dissent* from Eady J.'s view, but nor did it expressly approve it. *Quaere* where this leaves authorities such as *Miller v Associated Newspapers Ltd* [2003] EWHC 2799, QBD; [2004] E.M.L.R. 33 in which Eady J. emphasised that the focus and touchstone of a properly pleaded defence of *Reynolds* privilege should be whether, objectively, at the time of publication, the defendant was under a duty to publish the words complained of to the general public, irrespective of their truth or falsity (see, in particular, at [8] and [19]–[20]). See also *Galloway v Telegraph Group Ltd* [2004] EWHC 2786, QBD; [2005] E.M.L.R. 7 at [31]. Certainly Eady J. himself has not interpreted *Jameel (Mohammed) v Wall Street Journal Europe Sprl*, above, as effecting a change in the law in this regard and continues to apply the "duty" test as key determinant of whether or not a publication attracts *Reynolds* privilege (see *McKeith v News Group Newspapers Ltd* [2005] EWHC 1162, QBD at [54]–[56]). In *Armstrong v Times Newspapers Ltd* [2005] EWCA Civ 1007 (decided almost three months after *Jameel (Mohammed) v Wall Street Journal Europe Sprl*), the Court of Appeal did not criticise him for doing so (see at [68]).

On May 6, 2005 the defendant in *Jameel v The Wall Street Journal Europe Sprl* obtained permission to petition the House of Lords in relation to the correct test for *Reynolds* qualified privilege. Perhaps their Lordships will grasp the nettle the Court of Appeal chose to leave alone and inject some much needed certainty into this area of law.

New note 84C: See CPR PD 53, para.2.7 and the observations on its application to *Reynolds* privilege defences in note 77 of this Supplement. The plea of the circumstances of publication should focus on, or at least address, Lord Nicholls's non-exhaustive list of relevant circumstances in *Reynolds* at [205].

In *Miller v Associated Newspapers Ltd* [2003] EWHC 2799, QBD; [2004] E.M.L.R. 33, Eady J. at [7] sounded a salutary warning with regard to pleading *Reynolds* qualified privilege:

"Since the decision of their Lordships in *Reynolds* . . . there has been something of a tendency to plead qualified privilege in rather waffly generalities and these require close scrutiny. There is an undesirable trend to plead in rather vague terms and then to try to avoid the sanctions of Pt 24 by resorting to the dicta of Sir Thomas Bingham M.R. in *E (A Minor) v Dorset County Council* [1995] 2 A.C. 233 to the effect that in an area of developing jurisprudence an order striking out should not be made. That is an important principle, but it is not to be regarded as a mantra that will guarantee a way round the disciplines of pleading."

In *Armstrong v Times Newspapers Ltd*, above, the Court of Appeal observed at [74] that Eady J. was "right to direct himself that such defences required close scrutiny".

The "repetition rule" (see para.27.10 of the Main Work and paras 27.7 and 27.10 in this Supplement, especially the discussion in note 60 to para.27.10 of this Supplement) does not apply to the defence of *Reynolds* qualified privilege (*Galloway v Telegraph Group Ltd*, above at [36], citing *Mark v Associated Newspapers Ltd* [2002] EWCA Civ 772; E.M.L.R. 38 at [33]–[35] and *Al-Fagih v HH Saudi Research Marketing (UK) Ltd* [2001] EWCA Civ 1634; [2002] E.M.L.R. 13 at [36]). For the interrelationship between the "repetition rule" and defence of *Reynolds* qualified privilege for "neutral reportage", see *Galloway v Telegraph Group Ltd*, above at [122]–[145].

In *Armstrong v Times Newspapers Ltd*, above, Eady J. at [94] emphasised the importance of considering and pleading particulars of *Reynolds* qualified privilege separately from particulars of justification and not confusing the two. In cases where both defences were relied on by a defendant, the two ought not to be treated as "interchangeable". As the judge observed:

"[The claimant's counsel] took particular issue with the first paragraph of the particulars, which merely purports to include all the preceding particulars which have gone to support the particulars of justification . . . If I may say so, it is a somewhat sloppy approach to use this cross-over technique as though particulars of justification were simply interchangeable with a case on *Reynolds* privilege."

The Court of Appeal endorsed the judge's criticism of this pleading technique on the (successful) appeal from the decision to strike out the defence of qualified privilege ([2005] EWCA Civ 1007 at [25]). For another plea of qualified privilege that was found to be unsatisfactory for similar reasons, see *McKeith v News Group Newspapers* [2005] EWHC 1162, QBD; [2005] E.M.L.R. 32 at [44], [53].

New note 84D: See *Loutchansky v Times Newspapers Ltd* [2001] EWCA Civ 536; [2002] Q.B. 321, where it was held that a media defendant who claims to have been entitled to publish in the public interest may not rely on matters in support of that plea which arose after publication or about which it did not know at the time of publication. See also *McKeith v News Group Newspapers Ltd* [2005] EWHC 1162, QBD; [2005] E.M.L.R. 32 at [36] and [43]–[47].

New note 84E: See *Gaddafi v Telegraph Group Ltd* [2000] E.M.L.R. 431, where it was held that in the new climate created by *Reynolds* it was very important that the claimant should have adequate particulars in order to evaluate the prospects of the defence succeeding. However, the defendant will not be required to elaborate on the status or identity of his sources where to do so would infringe the important principles which protect a defendant from revealing his source. In *Gaddafi* itself, Hirst L.J. expressed disquiet at allowing a *Reynolds* defence to go forward in which the defendant had not identified the sources of the article complained of. The Court of Appeal nevertheless considered that to refuse to do so would offend against the fundamental rule that journalists should not, without good reason, be compelled to reveal their sources. For further information and observations on how the court should approach cases where a defendant, in support of a plea of *Reynolds* privilege, seeks to rely on sources he declines to identify, see CPR, r.53.3, Gray J. in *Loutchansky v Times Newspapers Ltd (No.4)* [2001] E.M.L.R. 38 at [50] and Eady J. in *Jameel v The Wall Street Journal Europe Sprl* [2003] EWHC 2302, QBD, at [18]–[20], quoted and substantially approved by the Court of Appeal in the appeal from that decision (*Jameel v The Wall Street Journal Europe Sprl (CA, No.1)* [2003] EWCA Civ 1694; [2004] E.M.L.R. 6); see at [4] and [32].

New note 81F: Jameel (Mohammed) v Wall Street Journal Europe Sprl [2005] EWCA Civ 74; [2005] 2 W.L.R. 1577 at [87] (quoted in full in new note 84B above).

New note 81G: Jameel (Mohammed) v Wall Street Journal Europe Sprl [2005] EWCA Civ 74; [2005] 2 W.L.R. 1577 at [27]–[29]:

> "It seems to us that, in seeking to demonstrate that a publication accords with the requirements of responsible journalism, a publisher will almost certainly wish to adduce evidence of the subjective belief of those responsible for the publication . . . Issues of subjective belief which hitherto have only been relevant where malice is in issue now become relevant to the inquiry of whether responsible journalism has been exercised . . . [this] suggest[s] that it may be necessary or at least admissible for a defendant to allege and prove subjective belief in order to establish a defence of *Reynolds* privilege."

For this reason, so the Court of Appeal proceeded to state, at [31]:

> "It is important that the pleadings should make clear where a defendant is relying on reasonable belief in the truth of matters published, or their implications, and where he is not. It is also important that the claimant should make clear whether or not he denies that the belief was held, or whether he merely contends that the belief was not reasonable."

In *McKeith v News Group Newspapers Ltd* [2005] EWHC 1162, QBD; [2005] E.M.L.R. 32, Eady J. observed at [38] that: "More targeted pleadings in these respects would, apart from anything else, assist the parties in identifying individual issues of fact requiring an answer from the jury." In striking out the pleaded defence of qualified privilege in the *McKeith* case, Eady J. also stated at [39]:

> " . . . there seems to be force in the submission that a defendant's advisers need to comply with these disciplines [as identified in *Jameel (Mohammed) v Wall Street Journal Europe Sprl* at [29]–[31]] in order to set up a defence of *Reynolds* privilege, the pleading of which can so often descend into woolly generalities."

In this context, see also *McKeith* at [50].

A situation in which it would probably not be appropriate for a defendant to plead a subjective belief in the truth of its publication is where it was asserting that its publication constituted "neutral reportage" (see *Jameel (Mohammed) v Wall Street Journal Europe Sprl*, above at [19]–[20], citing *Al-Fagih v HH Saudi Research Marketing (UK) Ltd*, above), assuming, that is, a defence of "neutral reportage" "exists under English law" (see *Jameel (Mohammed) v Wall Street Journal Europe Sprl*, above, at [22]). This view also seems to be supported by the observations of Eady J. in *McKeith v News Group Newspapers Ltd*, above at [37].

New note 84H: The notion that it might be sensible for a defendant relying on *Reynolds* privilege, in appropriate circumstances, to identify the meaning he attributed to the publication at issue seemed implicit in the decision of the Privy Council in *Bonnick v Morris* [2002] UKPC 31; [2003] 1 A.C. 300; see, in particular, at [22]–[25]. Now, since a defendant seeking to rely on a defence of *Reynolds* privilege is required in all but "neutral reportage" cases to plead the subjective belief the persons responsible for the publication at issue had in the truth of its contents and explain why that belief was reasonable (see new note 84G above), pleading the meaning the defendant understood the article to bear would appear to be integral to fulfilling this requirement. Explicit support for this proposition can be derived from *McKeith v News Group Newspapers* [2005] EWHC 1162, QBD; [2005] E.M.L.R. 32 at [40]–[41].

SECTION 6. MITIGATION OF DAMAGES

Mitigation of damages. *Add at end of paragraph*: Where a defendant makes 27.25 an unqualified offer to make amends under s.2 of the Defamation Act 1996, should he wish, if the offer is accepted, to rely at any subsequent hearing to assess the compensation due to the claimant under s.3(5) of the Defamation Act 1996 on "background contextual material" he claims bears on the claimant's reputation, it would be advisable for him to serve on the claimant a statement of case setting out the facts and matters on which he intends to rely (new note 4A).

Add to note 98: See *Voon Lee Shan v Sarawak Press Sdn Bhd* [2003] 690 MLJU 1 for a case in which the Malaysian equivalent of the defence under s.2 of the English Libel Act (Lord Campbell's Act) 1843 was considered.

Add to note 3: See now Eady J.'s analysis in *Turner v News Group Newspapers Ltd* [2005] EWHC 892, QBD; [2005] E.M.L.R. 25 at [19] *et seq*. Note in particular the judge's observation at [25]:

"I am not persuaded that a defendant need always establish a direct causal link between the 'background context' and the fact of publication: that would be likely to lead to over-elaborate analysis in some cases, and detract from the flexibility which the Court of Appeal in the *Burstein* case clearly intended."

New note 4A: This practice was adopted conveniently and approved in *Turner v News Group Newspapers Ltd* [2005] EWHC 892, QBD; [2005] E.M.L.R. 25; see, in particular, at [18].

SECTION 10. AMENDMENT OF DEFENCE AND COUNTERCLAIM

27.34   **Granting of permission in discretion of court.** *Add to note 28*: See also *W v Westminster City Council* [2004] EWHC 2812, QBD at [32]–[43]. Despite the fact the defendants delayed for four months after the proposed amendments had first been discussed until the eve of the date fixed for the trial of the action before making their application for permission to revise their defences of qualified and absolute privilege, Tugendhat J. considered at [41] he "really [had] . . . no choice" but to permit the amendment. A key factor telling in favour of this conclusion (at [42]) was that the second defendant's entitlement to a fair trial could "only be met" by permitting her to respond to the claimant's case of malice against her in the manner envisaged in her amended case.

SECTION 12. APPLICATION FOR FURTHER INFORMATION

27.39   **Demand must not be disproportionate.** *Add to note 60*: See also the observations of the Court of Appeal in *Musa King v Telegraph Group Ltd (Practice Note)* [2004] EWCA Civ 613; [2005] 1 W.L.R. 2282 (reported as *King v Telegraph Group Ltd (Practice Note)* at [63].

CHAPTER 28

REPLY AND DEFENCE TO COUNTERCLAIM

SECTION 3. PLEADING AN AFFIRMATIVE CASE IN REPLY GENERALLY

Pleading an affirmative case. *Add after penultimate sentence in paragraph*: **28.3**
When responding in a Reply to a defence of qualified privilege, the pleader
should take care to distinguish matters only relevant to the question of whether
the publication at issue attracts a privilege from matters only germane to malice,
and not to confuse the two (insert new note 5A).

New note 5A: For a discussion of this distinction, see *Oliver v Chief Constable
of Northumbria* [2003] EWHC 2417, QBD; [2004] E.M.L.R. 32 at [34]–[42].

Other illustrations. *Add at end of note 8*: Now see *Milne v Express News-* **28.4**
papers [2004] EWCA Civ 664; [2005] 1 W.L.R. 772 in which the Court of
Appeal, dismissing the claimant's appeal from the decision of Eady J. ([2002]
EWHC 2564; [2003] 1 W.L.R. 927), held that a claimant who wished to rebut the
defence under s.4 of the Defamation Act 1996 by establishing that the defendant
had had reason to believe the statement complained of was false within the
meaning of s.4(3) of the Act needed to plead and prove that the defendant was
recklessly indifferent to the truth or falsity of the relevant statement.

SECTION 4. MALICE

Malice. *Add after first sentence of second paragraph*: The court will be **28.5**
sceptical about pleas of malice in which the claimant pitches the meaning high
and then asserts that the defendant did not or could believe that high meaning to
be true, and so is malicious (new note 11A).

New note 11A: See *Crossland v Wilkinson Hardware Stores Ltd* [2005] EWHC
481, QBD, *per* Tugendhat J., citing *H v Chief Constable of H* [2003] EWCA Civ
102 at [56] and [63], where the Court of Appeal said that the court should be
ready to find that the words complained of mean what they say and no more.

Add at end of note 12: "Carelessness of expression or carelessness in making a defamatory statement never provides a ground for inferring malice" (*Roberts v Bass* (2002) 194 A.L.R. 161 at [103], cited with approval by Gray J. in *Oliver v Chief Constable of Northumbria* [2003] EWHC 2417, QBD; [2004] E.M.L.R. 32 at [135].

APOLOGY, OFFER OF AMENDS AND COMPROMISE

Section 1. Apology

Nature of an apology. *Add to note 9*: The sufficiency of an apology will be **29.2** considered by the judge when assessing compensation under the offer to make amends procedure. See para.33.52 of this Supplement.

Publicising the apology. In *Nail v Newsgroup Newspapers* [2004] EWHC **29.3** 647, QBD; [2004] E.M.L.R. 20 Eady J. stated:

" . . . there is no point in endlessly haggling or niggling about the size or location of an apology. The important thing is to achieve vindication as quickly and effectively as possible . . . I believe the important elements of the apology are that it was published relatively quickly after the proceedings were issued, at the top of the page, and that it was relatively eye-catching" [69].

Section 2. Settlement

Statements in open court. Where a defendant makes a payment into court **29.5** under CPR Pt 36, which is accepted, it will generally be the case that the costs of any formal application by the claimant to make a unilateral statement, and those of making the statement, will be paid by the defendant as an integral part of the costs of the action (*Phillips v Associated Newspapers Ltd* [2004] EWHC 190, QBD; [2004] 1 W.L.R. 2106).

CPR and settlement. *Note 17.* How this sub-rule should be applied was **29.6** considered by the Court of Appeal in *Trustees of Stokes Pension Fund v Western Power Distribution* [2005] EWCA Civ 854; [2005] 3 All E.R. 775 in which the defendant had offered by letter a certain sum in settlement of a trespass claim, which was refused, and the judge awarded less, but ruled that the offer did not afford the claimant any protection in relation to costs because it had not been followed by a payment in under Pt 36. The Court of Appeal held that an offer to settle a money claim should usually be treated as having the same effect as a payment into court if the offer was expressed in clear terms, was open to acceptance for at least 21 days and otherwise accorded with the substance of a Calderbank offer, was a genuine offer, and if the defendant was good for the money when the offer was made. Each of the conditions were satisfied in the instant case, so the court ordered the claimant to pay the defendant's costs from 21 days after the date of the offer.

SECTION 3. PART 36 PAYMENTS AND OFFERS

29.17   **When an offer or payment may be made.** In the light of the decision in *Trustees of Stoke Pension Fund v Westerns Power Distribution* (see note 17 to para.29.6 of this Supplement), some modification is required to the statement in the Main Work that "a defendant's offer to settle the damages element of a defamation claim *must* be made by way of a Pt 36 payment" (emphasis added). Rule 36.3(1) does state that "an offer by a defendant to settle a money claim will not have the consequences set out in this Part unless it is made by way of a Part 36 payment". But in the case mentioned above the Court of Appeal ruled that if the necessary conditions it specified were fulfilled, a court in exercising its discretion under r.44(3) and having regard to r.44.3(4)(c), should give an offer to settle a money claim otherwise than by a Pt 36 payment the same effect as a Pt 36 payment.

29.18   **Acceptance of offer or payment.** *Add to note 75.* In *Pell v Express Newspapers* [2004] EWCA Civ 46 the defamation action was settled by the claimant's acceptance of a Pt 36 offer. Almost a year later the claimant sought to challenge an interlocutory costs order made against him before settlement when he had been refused permission to amend. The Court of Appeal refused permission to appeal, declaring that, assuming the settlement was not a formal bar to challenging the judge's order for costs, what the claimant was attempting to do was wholly disproportionate and contrary to the interests of justice. If interlocutory orders could be challenged by way of appeal on the ground of alleged deceit, without the result of the trial or settlement being disturbed then the finality of judgments would be gravely undermined and the appeal process subverted.

29.24   **Verdict and costs.** *Note 93. Add:* but not in every case (see *Rackham v Sandy* [2005] EWHC and note 78 of para.35.17 of this Supplement). In *Read v Edmed* [2004] EWHC 3274, QBD the judge awarded indemnity costs to the claimant in a personal injury action where his Pt 36 offer to settle an issue of liability at a given proportion of his claim had been refused and the court gave judgement for precisely that proportion of the claim.

SECTION 4. OFFER OF AMENDS

29.27   **Definition.** *Add to note 13*: *Cleese v Clark* is now reported at [2004] E.M.L.R. 3.

29.29   **Compensation.** The question of how far the making of an offer of amends should go to mitigate the amount of compensation awarded to the claimant was considered by the Court of Appeal in *Nail v News Group Newspapers Ltd* [2004] EWCA Civ 1708; [2005] 1 All E.R. 1040.

At first instance, Eady J. had assessed the proper level of compensation for libels in the *News of the World* and in a book published by HarperCollins. The libels were summed up by the claimant's counsel as mapping out a life in which the claimant had progressed "from being a dog meat eating yob, who engaged in grubby and obscene sexual behaviour, to heartless prima donna". The judge took the view that the offer of amends regime was a process of conciliation, so that the very adoption of the procedure had a major deflationary effect on the appropriate level of compensation. Media defendants who act promptly when confronted with a claim are entitled to expect that the level of compensation will be "healthily discounted". His starting point was to consider what he would have awarded for the libels following a notional trial at which there had been no significant aggravation (such as a plea of justification) and no significant mitigation (such as an apology); to assess how much the particular libel is worth on the scale of gravity, having regard to what he called the current conventional ceiling of £200,000; and then to make a significant reduction to take account not only of any actual apology but also of the defendant's very willingness to use the offer of amends route. In the event, he settled on £45,000 as the notional trial award for the newspaper libel, and reduced that figure by half to £22,500.

This approach was endorsed by the Court of Appeal. The court accepted that if an early unqualified offer to make amends is offered and accepted, and an agreed apology published, there is bound to be substantial mitigation (which May L.J. regarded as a less colourful synonym of Eady J.'s "healthy discount"), for the defendant has capitulated at an early stage, the claimant knows that his reputation has been repaired as far as it can be, and he is relieved of the anxiety and the costs risk of contested proceedings. There was a hint from May L.J. that the award might have been higher ("The possibility that another judge might have reached a somewhat higher amount does not mean that Eady J.'s conclusion was wrong"), but there was no error of principle, and no basis for the court to interfere.

If the defendant treats a serious complaint casually, and publishes an apology which is late or off-hand, the discount for making an offer of amends will be less: in *Campbell-James v Guardian Newspapers Ltd* [2005] EWHC 893 Civ, Eady J. considered that the starting-point for a very grave libel on a distinguished British soldier, of whom it was falsely suggested that he had been in some way linked to the abuses at Abu Ghraib prison in Baghdad, was £90,000, which (in view of the newspaper's dismissive attitude) he reduced by 35 per cent for offer of amends purposes to a figure of £58,500.

In *Turner v News Group Newspapers Ltd* [2005] EWHC 892, QBD, a case about a *News of the World* article which alleged, broadly speaking, that the claimant was a "swinger" and wife-swapper, the court applied the principle in *Burstein v Times Newspapers Ltd* [2001] 1 W.L.R. 57, CA for the first time in an offer of amends context, and admitted evidence of directly relevant background context. However, that went not to the discount applicable to the offer of amends procedure but to the award which Eady J. fixed as his starting point at a notional trial, which was £15,000. Presumably the judge's model of a notional trial without significant aggravation or mitigation (see *Nail*, above) has been adapted to accommodate the potentially substantial mitigatory effect of *Burstein* evidence. Eady J. did not think it right to penalise the defendant for introducing the *Burstein* material, but taking into account the fact that Mr Turner was first treated dismissively and then told that the newspaper had no reason to believe that its allegations were false, he fixed the discount at 40 per cent and the award at £9,000. (Note that the single Lord Justice, Sedley L.J., has given the claimant permission to appeal.)

In *Nail v News Group Newspapers Ltd* an important point of practice was raised about the scope of argument as to meaning at the offer of amends hearing. Eady J. held that where there is an unqualified offer, the parties "generally need to work on the basis that the words complained of bore the pleaded meanings". He disagreed with counsel for the defendant, who submitted that it remained the task of the court to form its own view on the precise meanings. He agreed that any exaggerated or distorted meaning should be ignored, but he expected that if such circumstances arose, the defendant would have made the challenge clear by making a qualified offer. "It would seem unfair on a claimant who accepts an unqualified offer to find that the court dismisses his meanings as untenable when it comes to assessing the damages" ([2004] EWHC 647, QBD at [26]). May L.J. approved this approach, and what he described as the judge's refusal to admit much of the evidence which the parties (in fact it was primarily, if not entirely, the defendant) had sought to adduce in aggravation and mitigation. "Claimants should . . . plead the full substance for which they seek redress: defendants who wish to make amends for significantly less than that full substance should make appropriate qualifications to their offer" (*per* May L.J., [2004] EWCA Civ 1708 [2005]; 1 All E.R. 1040 [15]).

Add to note 23: *Cleese v Clark* is now reported at [2004] E.M.L.R. 3.

Add to note 28: *Cleese v Clark* is now reported at [2004] E.M.L.R. 3. For the limited role of disclosure in the offer of amends process, see *Rigg v Associated Newspapers Ltd* [2003] EWHC 710, QBD; [2004] E.M.L.R. 4.

29.31   **Rejection of offer of amends.** *Add to note 32*: The claimant's appeal from Eady J.'s judgment was dismissed by the Court of Appeal (*Milne v Express Newspapers Ltd* [2004] EWCA Civ 664; [2005] 1 W.L.R. 772), which considered that his construction of s.4(3) was entirely correct, for the reasons which he gave.

CHAPTER 30

PRE-TRIAL APPLICATIONS

SECTION 2. RULINGS ON MEANING

Principles to be applied. Forensic consideration of the meaning of words has **30.5** acquired a new shorthand since the impact of the decisions of the Court of Appeal in *Bennett v News Group Newspapers Ltd* [2002] E.M.L.R. 39 (decided four years before it was reported) and *Chase v News Group Newspapers Ltd* [2002] EWCA Civ 1772; [2003] E.M.L.R. 11, which have introduced the language of level (or "tier") 1, 2 and 3 meanings into legal debate. In very broad terms, they may be understood as meanings which impute (1) guilt, (2) reasonable grounds to suspect the claimant of guilt, and (3) grounds to investigate the claimant. As Sedley L.J. pointed out in *Jameel v Times Newspapers Ltd* [2004] EWCA Civ 983; [2004] E.M.L.R. 31 at [10]:

"The elevation of this taxonomy of meanings into legal categories is recent. It is correct to say that as long ago as 1963, in *Lewis v Daily Telegraph Ltd* [1964] A.C. 234, a libel action arising out of an article headlined 'Fraud squad probe firm', it was recognised, at least by Lord Devlin, that such an allegation might operate on any of three levels, each distinctly capable of justification: the fact of an inquiry, the existence of reasonable grounds for suspicion, and guilt. But, although the practice (criticised by Lord Devlin, *loc. cit.*, 287) has persisted of letting a claimant plead only his highest meaning and then argue for any lesser one, it was not until the decision of this court in *Bennett v News Group Newspapers* that recognition was accorded to these three classes as being legally distinct."

Jargon apart, the underlying principles have not changed, and indeed the *Skuse* and *Gillick* formulations have been repeatedly followed and endorsed (see note 14 below).

However, the Court of Appeal has given a strong indication that first instance judges should be slower to rule out pleaded meanings, particularly at the level 2/level 3 divide. In *Jameel v Wall Street Journal* [2003] EWCA Civ 1694; [2004] E.M.L.R. 6, the point was approached from two different directions.

First, at [10] Simon Brown L.J. advised judges to bear in mind the observations of Lord Nicholls on the inherent imprecision of language in *Bonnick v Morris* [2002] UKPC 31; [2003] 1 A.C. 300 [20]:

"Language is inherently imprecise. Words and phrases and sentences take their colour from their context. The context often permits a range of meanings, varying from the obvious to the implausible. Different readers may well form different views on the meaning to be given to the language under consideration."

Secondly, he emphasised the high threshold of exclusion which must be satisfied:

" . . . every time a meaning is shut out (including any holding that the words complained of either are, or are not, capable of bearing a defamatory meaning) it must be remembered that the judge is taking it upon himself to rule in effect that any jury would be perverse to take a different view on the question. It is a high threshold of exclusion. Ever since Fox's Act 1792 the meaning of words in civil as well as criminal libel proceedings has been constitutionally a matter for the jury. The judge's function is no more and no less than to pre-empt perversity. That being clearly the position with regard to whether or not words are capable of being understood as defamatory or, as the case may be, non-defamatory, I see no basis on which it could sensibly be otherwise with regard to differing levels of defamatory meaning" [14].

It is at the sometimes unclear dividing line between level 2 and level 3 meanings that the Court of Appeal has particularly discouraged exclusionary rulings: in *Jameel v Wall Street Journal* (above), Simon Brown L.J. referred at [19] to the scope for the border between the two levels to become blurred, and in *Jameel v Times Newspapers Ltd* [2004] EWCA Civ 983; [2004] E.M.L.R. 31 [18], Sedley L.J. observed, in differing from Gray J. (who had ruled out a level 2 meaning), that the distinction between level 2 and level 3 meanings is a fine one. (By contrast, Gray J. set out the "real distinguishing features" of the two levels of meaning in *Jameel v Times Newspapers Ltd* [2003] EWHC 2609, QBD in terms which were cited without disapproval by Simon Brown L.J. in *Jameel v Wall Street Journal* (above) at [20], and by Sedley L.J. in *Jameel v Times Newspapers Ltd* [2004] EWCA Civ 983; [2004] E.M.L.R. 31, on appeal from Gray J.'s ruling, at [19] and [23].)

Moreover, judges should be wary of ruling out a meaning unless there is sound reason to do so (e.g. where the scope of a defence of justification depends on it, and it is desirable to control the evidence which may properly be adduced at trial: see *Jameel v Wall Street Journal* (above) at [16]). A recent example of a case where an exclusionary ruling was necessary is provided by *Armstrong v Times Newspapers Ltd* [2004] EWHC 2928, QBD (that part of Eady J.'s ruling was not challenged when the case went to the Court of Appeal ([2005] EWCA Civ 1007)).

It is important to note the particular role that the repetition rule may play in ruling out a pleaded meaning even when the meaning may not be perverse. The repetition rule is a rule of law designed to prevent a jury from deciding that a particular class of publication, conveying rumour, hearsay or repetition of an allegation, is true or alternatively carries some lesser meaning than the original allegation would bear (see *Stern v Piper* [1997] Q.B. 123, 135–136 and para.11.4 of the Main Work). If a defendant endorses or repeats a defamatory allegation made by a third party, he cannot be heard to say that his words bear some lesser meaning than that borne by the words which he is repeating. The repetition rule thus:

" . . . necessarily circumscribes the considerable latitude a jury otherwise has in relation to ascribing a meaning or meanings to defamatory words. Where it so operates, it might be more accurate to describe the role of the judge in delimiting the possible meanings as not so much 'pre-empting perversity' as precluding an otherwise possible meaning through the implementation of a rule of public policy. It may not be 'perverse' to ascribe to a particular article the meaning 'A said that B murdered C'. It is nonetheless not permitted to plead it as a *Lucas-Box* meaning for the reason that a defendant is required, if choosing to justify, to plead and prove that 'B murdered C' " (*Hamilton v Clifford* [2004 EWHC 1542, QBD, *per* Eady J. at [33]).

Add to note 9: See *Jameel v Wall Street Journal* [2003] EWCA Civ 1694; [2004] E.M.L.R. 6 at [6], [9]–[16]; *Oliver v Chief Constable of Northumbria* [2003] EWHC 2417, QBD; [2004] E.M.L.R. 32 at [17]; *Armstrong v Times Newspapers Ltd* [2004] EWHC 2928, QBD at [14]–[16].

Add to note 10: For the approach to be adopted to determination of meaning by a judge sitting alone without a jury, see *Miller v Associated Newspapers* [2005] EWHC 557, QBD at [24] *et seq.*

Add to note 13: In *Lennon v Scottish Daily Record* [2004] EWHC 359 (QB); [2004] E.M.L.R. 18, Tugendhat J. suggested that the ordinary reader should now be credited with having achieved a level of education not accessible to earlier generations, and should therefore be taken as being more discriminating and better able to understand what he or she reads. The judge founded that proposition, which may not command universal acceptance, on an observation of Eady J. in *Lukowiak v Unidad Editorial S.A.* [2001] E.M.L.R. 46, to the effect that ordinary citizens are now perceived by the courts to have stronger stomachs and more discriminating judgment than was traditionally recognised. However, Eady J.'s observation was made in the context of discussion of the defence of *Reynolds* qualified privilege and the social changes which have given rise to a right in the general public to be kept informed by the media about matters of public interest.

Add to note 14: See *Jameel v Times Newspapers Ltd* [2004] EWCA Civ 983; [2004] E.M.L.R. 31 at [12].

Add to note 16: See *Lennon v Scottish Daily Record* [2004] EWHC 359, QBD; [2004] E.M.L.R. 18, and note 13 above.

Add to note 19: See *Jameel v Times Newspapers Ltd* [2004] EWCA Civ 983; [2004] E.M.L.R. 31, where at [16] Sedley L.J. referred to the "unaddressed tension" between the principle that the range of possible meanings is to be derived from the article as a whole, read through the eyes of a reasonable reader, and the principle that if the article contains a defamatory statement (the bane), that will define its meaning unless it is very plainly negatived (the antidote) in the same article, and speculated that the tension may require resolution in a proper case (that is to say, one where the two principles yield different answers).

Jurisdiction. *Add to note 23*: Such applications are now commonplace, and **30.6** are often coupled with applications for summary judgment under CPR Pt 24 or to strike out under CPR, r.3.4(2) (see, e.g. *Armstrong v Times Newspapers Ltd* [2004] EWHC 2928, QBD and *Hewitt v Grunwald* [2004] EWHC 2959, QBD).

Add to note 24: In *Jameel v Wall Street Journal* [2003] EWCA Civ 1694; [2004] E.M.L.R. 6, both parties invited the judge to rule on the meaning pleaded by the claimant.

30.7   **Appeals.** The Court of Appeal continues to be willing to look again at exclusionary rulings by first instance judges, especially on the blurred frontier between level 2 and level 3 meanings (as to which, see para.30.5 of this Supplement) (see *Jameel v Wall Street Journal Europe* [2003] EWCA Civ 1694; [2004] E.M.L.R. 6 and *Jameel v Times Newspapers Ltd* [2004] EWCA Civ 983; [2004] E.M.L.R. 31).

Add to note 26: See *Jameel v Wall Street Journal Europe* [2003] EWCA Civ 1694; [2004] E.M.L.R. 6; *Jameel v Times Newspapers Ltd* [2004] EWCA Civ 983; [2004] E.M.L.R. 31.

SECTION 3. SUMMARY DISPOSAL AND SUMMARY JUDGMENT

(a) *Summary disposal under the Defamation Act 1996*

30.12   **Judgment for claimant.** *Add to note 43*: Claimants' applications have been rarer still since 2003. An example of a successful application is *Downtex v Flatley* [2003] EWCA Civ 1282, where the claimant persuaded the Court of Appeal to hold that a defence of qualified privilege was bound to fail. The court accepted that the summary procedure should not involve the conduct of a mini-trial where the defence is fact-sensitive and there is reason to think that further facts may emerge or require investigation at trial before a fair or final conclusion can be reached, but held that it would be wrong to shy away from a determination where there is sufficient material before the court (on the pleadings or in evidence) to allow the court to form a confident view on the prospects of success, and where there is no reason to suppose that the defendant will be able to advance his case significantly at trial (*per* Potter L.J. at [31]).

30.13   **Defendants' applications.** The summary disposal process seems to have fallen out of fashion with defendants, for whom the current practice is to apply for summary judgment under CPR Pt 24 (and, if appropriate, for a determination of meaning under CPR 53 PD para.4.1) and/or to strike out under CPR Pt 3.4(2). For the likely reasons for this, see para.30.24 of the main work.

30.14   **Realistic prospect of success.** *Add to note 51*: The decision of the Court of Appeal in *Cream Holdings v Banerjee* was overturned by the House of Lords ([2005] 1 A.C. 253), with the result that the effect of s.12(3) of the Human Rights Act 1998 is to prevent the court from making an interim restraint order unless satisfied that the applicant's prospects of success at trial are sufficiently favour-able to justify such an order being made in all the circumstances of the case.

Add to note 52: See *Downtex v Flatley* [2003] EWCA Civ 1282 at [30].

Add to note 54: The words of Lord Woolf M.R. were cited with approval by Lord Hope in *Three Rivers D.C. v Bank of England (No.3)* [2003] 2 A.C. 1 at 260, [94]–[95]. His Lordship said this:

> "For the reasons which I have just given, I think that the question is whether the claim has no real prospect of succeeding at trial and that it has to be answered having regard to the overriding objective of dealing with the case justly. But the point which is of crucial importance lies in the answer to the further question that then needs to be asked, which is—what is to be the scope of that inquiry? The method by which issues of fact are tried in our courts is well settled. After the normal processes of discovery and interrogatories have been completed, the parties are allowed to lead their evidence so that the trial judge can determine where the truth lies in the light of that evidence. To that rule there are some well-recognised exceptions. For example, it may be clear as a matter of law at the outset that even if a party were to succeed in proving all the facts that he offers to prove he will not be entitled to the remedy that he seeks. In that event a trial of the facts would be a waste of time and money, and it is proper that the action should be taken out of court as soon as possible. In other cases it may be possible to say with confidence before trial that the factual basis for the claim is fanciful because it is entirely without substance. It may be clear beyond question that the statement of facts is contradicted by all the documents or other material on which it is based. The simpler the case the easier it is likely to be to take that view and resort to what is properly called summary judgment. But more complex cases are unlikely to be capable of being resolved in that way without conducting a mini-trial on the documents without discovery and without oral evidence. As Lord Woolf said in *Swain v Hillman*, at p. 95, that is not the object of the rule. It is designed to deal with cases that are not fit for trial at all."

Reasons why the claim should be tried. *Add to note 57*: See *Downtex v*   **30.15**
Flatley [2003] EWCA Civ 1282 and notes 43 and 54 above.

    Time for application. *Add to note 63*: See *Downtex v Flatley* [2003] EWCA   **30.16**
Civ 1282 at [31].

    Practice and procedure. It appears that CPR, r.53.2(3)(a) may not prevent the   **30.21**
making of an application under s.8 of the Defamation Act 1996/Pt 53, combined with an alternative application under Pt 24, as long as the s.8 application is disposed of before the Pt 24 application is heard (*Downtex v Flatley* [2003] EWCA Civ 1282 at [3]). However, the point was not argued.

Add to note 81: See now *Downtex v Flatley* [2003] EWCA Civ 1282 at [3], where the practice of combining a s.8 application with one under Pt 24 was noted by the Court of Appeal without disapproval. However, the s.8 application must be heard and disposed of before that under Pt 24 can be heard.

Add to note 82: See note 81 above. *Downtex v Flatley* (above) appears to suggest that Gray J.'s doubts about the propriety of successive applications under s.8/Pt 53 and Pt 24 may have been ill-founded, although the point was not argued. (*Cf. Hassan v Holburn* [2004] EWCA Civ 789, where Sedley L.J. referred to the defendants as having been obliged at first instance (before Mitting J.) to elect between seeking summary disposal under s.8 and summary judgment under Pt 24. However, it is unclear whether the point was argued before the judge.)

(b) *Summary judgment under CPR Part 24*

30.23   **The Part 24 rubric.** *Add to note 86*: See note 54 above and *Three Rivers D.C. v Bank of England (No.3)* [2003] 2 A.C. 1 at [94]–[95].

Add to note 89: See *Downtex v Flatley* [2003] EWCA Civ 1282 at [31] (a summary disposal case, followed in the summary judgment context by Tugendhat J. in *Wood v Chief Constable of West Midlands* [2003] EWHC 2971, QBD; [2004] E.M.L.R. 17, upheld [2004] EWCA Civ 1638; [2005] E.M.L.R. 20); *Three Rivers D.C. v Bank of England (No.3)* [2003] 2 A.C. 1 at [94]–[95]; *Armstrong v Times Newspapers Ltd* [2005] EWCA Civ 1007.

Add to note 90: The power to make a conditional order for security for costs under r.24.6 was considered by the Court of Appeal in *Musa King v Telegraph Group Ltd* [2004] EWCA Civ 613; [2005] 1 W.L.R. 2282 (reported as *King v Telegraph Group Ltd (Practice Note)*), but the appeal against Eady J.'s refusal to make an order was not pursued. Nonetheless, Brooke L.J. stated at [91] that he had no doubt that Eady J. had been right to refuse to make an order. See also para.31.48 of the Supplement.

30.26   **Burden on applicant for summary judgment.** *Add to note 96*: Following May L.J.'s reference in *Alexander v Arts Council of Wales* to the *Galbraith* test in criminal proceedings, Tugendhat J. has expressed the test in these terms:

> "Because this is a libel action, where the claimant has a right to trial by jury, the test I must apply on these applications is closely analogous to the test used in criminal trials in the light of *R v Galbraith* [1981] 1 W.L.R. 1039. This is re-emphasised by May L.J. in *Alexander v Arts Council of Wales* [2001] 1 W.L.R. 1840, 1852. It is: Could a jury properly directed, and seeking dutifully to comply with the relevant directions, conscientiously reach a conclusion that the applicants were actuated by malice or not? If so, I should leave it to the jury, or at least to a later stage, to determine. But if I am able to conclude that a properly directed and conscientious jury could only decide the issue in favour of the appellant, then it will be my duty to close off that issue so as to save time and money in accordance with the objectives of the Civil Procedure Rules. If that is established, then there is no issue for a jury to decide" (*Meade v Pugh & Hamilton* [2004] EWHC 408, QBD at [18]).

Add to note 98: In *Miller v Associated Newspapers Ltd* [2003] EWHC 2799, QBD; [2004] E.M.L.R. 33 at [13], Eady J. directed himself in these terms:

> "Specifically in the context of the right to jury trial, judgment should not be given at any stage which has the effect of depriving the parties of a jury decision in any case where the defence may depend at least in part on a finding of fact which would be properly open to that tribunal: see, *e.g. Wallis v Valentine* [2003] E.M.L.R. 8 at [13] and *Branson v Bower* [2002] 2 Q.B. 737 at 744. Thus, even if a judge thinks that a particular factual conclusion for which one side contends is somewhat far-fetched, it is the jury's credulity rather than the judge's that must be kept in mind. The parties should therefore be given the benefit of the doubt: see, *e.g. Spencer v Sillitoe* [2003] E.M.L.R. 10 at [31]

and *Bataille v Newland* [2002] E.W.H.C. 1692 (Q.B.) at pp.6–7." (So also in *McKeith v News Group Newspapers Ltd* [2005] EWHC 1162, QBD; [2005] E.M.L.R. 32 at [50].)

Subject matter of applications under Pt 24. There have been a number of   **30.27**
claimants' applications for summary judgment, including several in cases where qualified privilege has been pleaded. Applications succeeded in *Miller v Associated Newspapers Ltd* [2003] EWHC 2799, QBD; [2005] E.M.L.R. 32; [2004] E.M.L.R. 33, in *McKeith v News Group Newspapers Ltd* [2005] EWHC 1162, QBD, both cases of *Reynolds* privilege, and in the non-*Reynolds* case of *Wood v Chief Constable of West Midlands* [2003] EWHC 2971, QBD; [2004] E.M.L.R. 17 (upheld on appeal: [2004] EWCA Civ 1638, [2005] E.M.L.R. 20). The claimant's application for summary judgment in a *Reynolds* privilege case failed before the Court of Appeal in *Armstrong v Times Newspapers Ltd* [2005] EWCA Civ 1007 (having succeeded at first instance). Other claimants' applications include *Hamilton v Clifford* [2004] EWHC 1542, QBD (succeeded in application for summary judgment on justification and fair comment, but failed on qualified privilege), *Hewitt v Grunwald* [2004] EWHC 2959, QBD (failed in application for judgment on qualified privilege and justification), and *Jameel v Times Newspapers Ltd* [2005] EWHC 1219, QBD (succeeded in application for judgment on justification).

It is noteworthy that in *Miller v Associated Newspapers Ltd* (above), Eady J. criticised the tendency to plead *Reynolds* privilege in vague terms and then to try to avoid Pt 24 sanctions by resorting to the dicta of Bingham M.R. in *E v Dorset County Council* [1995] 2 A.C. 233, to the effect that in an area of developing jurisprudence an order striking out should not have been made: "That is an important principle, but it is not to be regarded as a mantra which will guarantee a way around the disciplines of pleading" [7]. He would have been surprised "if their Lordships believed, after the exposition of the law and practical guidance offered in *Reynolds* itself and shortly afterwards in *Turkington*, that the law itself was still in a state of development" [33].

Add to note 1: Defendants' applications succeeded in *Meade v Pugh & Hamilton* [2004] EWHC 408, QBD; *Crossland v Wilkinson Hardware Stores Ltd* [2005] EWHC 481, QBD (in which the defendant also succeeded on the issue of consent), but failed in *Creative Resins International Ltd v Glasslam Europe Ltd* [2005] EWHC 777, QBD.

Add to note 2: A defendant's application succeeded in *Crossland v Wilkinson Hardware Stores Ltd* [2005] EWHC 481, QBD, but failed in *Creative Resins International Ltd v Glasslam Europe Ltd* [2005] EWHC 777, QBD.

Add to note 5: A defendant's application failed in *Jameel v Times Newspapers Ltd* [2003] EWHC 2609, QBD. (This part of Gray J.'s judgment was not taken to the Court of Appeal: [2004] EWCA Civ 983.) However, a later application by the claimant succeeded ([2005] EWHC 1219, QBD). (It is not clear in this case, as in a number of others, whether the application was simply to strike out, or—as is now usual—whether it was also for summary judgment.)

30.28   **The approach which the court will take.** The Court of Appeal had an opportunity to consider the proper approach to follow on summary judgment applications in *Armstrong v Times Newspapers Ltd* [2005] EWCA Civ 1007, a case in which the claimant had obtained summary judgment from the judge in respect of the defence of *Reynolds* privilege. The claimant's notice of application gave only the most general grounds for the application, namely that the defendants had no real prospect of successfully establishing a *Reynolds* defence, and the defendants decided that there was no need to put in evidence. Shortly before the hearing, the claimant served a substantial skeleton argument which raised issues as to the truth of a number of matters asserted in the defence. Had the claimant set out the grounds of the application for summary judgment in the notice, the defendants would have been able to decide what evidence to adduce, in order to show the judge that there were evidential issues fit for trial, but as it was, the claimant's approach was "entirely unsuitable", for the reasons given by Lord Hope in *Three Rivers DC v Bank of England (No.3)* [2003] 2 A.C. 1 at [95] (set out at note 54, para.30.14 above), and the defendants faced a mini-trial for which they were inevitably unprepared. The Court of Appeal allowed their appeal and restored the defence of qualified privilege.

30.30   **Practice and procedure.** In the light of the decision in *Armstrong v Times Newspapers Ltd* [2005] EWCA Civ 1007, the application notice should set out the grounds for the application in clear terms: generalities risk taking the respondent by surprise.

Add to note 11: In *Downtex v Flatley* [2003] EWCA Civ 1282 at [3], the practice of combining a s.8 application with one under Pt 24 was noted by the Court of Appeal without disapproval. However, the s.8 application must be heard and disposed of before that under Pt 24 can be heard. The case appears to suggest that Gray J.'s doubts about the propriety of successive applications under s.8 and Pt 24 may have been ill-founded, although the point was not argued. (See note 82, para.30.21 above.)

Section 4: Striking Out Pleadings

30.31   **Striking out pleadings: CPR, r.3.4(2).** It has now become the general practice for applications for Pt 24 summary judgment to be coupled with applications to strike out under r.3.4(2). At the same time, there appears to have been a decline in applications for summary disposal under s.8 of the Defamation Act 1996. The emergence of a standard practice may be the explanation for the fact that the judges have not always found it necessary of late to spell out in their judgments the formal basis of the application. Even the basis on which judgment is given sometimes borders on the ambiguous (see, e.g. the language used in *Wood v Chief Constable of West Midlands Police* [2003] EWHC 2971, QBD; [2004] E.M.L.R. 17 [59]: "No useful purpose would be achieved by not giving summary judgment that the plea of qualified privilege be struck out", and by the Court of Appeal in the same case ([2004] EWCA Civ 1638; [2005] E.M.L.R. 20 at [17])). The position remains, nonetheless, that evidence is admissible on the application for summary judgment, but generally not (at least where the attack is made under r.3.4(2)(a)) on the application to strike out, although the distinction is not often referred to in judgments. A reminder of that rule is to found in *Hewitt v Grunwald* [2004] EWHC 2959, QBD, where it was agreed that the strike-out application under r.3.4(2), on which evidence was not admissible, would be dealt with first, while the Pt 24 application would be adjourned to give the defendants an opportunity, if they wished, to put in evidence.

Add to note 15: For a more recent example of this principle, see *Collins Stewart v Financial Times Ltd* [2004] EWHC 2337; [2005] E.M.L.R. 5 at [24].

Add to note 18: See, for example, Eady J.'s determination in *Armstrong v Times Newspapers Ltd* [2004] EWHC 2928, QBD to isolate the "real issues" in the action and to excise superfluous material, and *McKeith v News Group Newspapers Ltd* [2005] EWHC 1162, QBD; [2005] E.M.L.R. 32 at [17]. (The judge's decision in *Armstrong* was later reversed ([2005] EWCA Civ 1007), but in this respect his approach was commended by the Court of Appeal at [53].)

Applications by claimant. As stated above, the current practice for combining applications to strike out with applications for summary judgment, and the difficulty in some cases of determining precisely on which basis an order has been made or refused, make it hard to point confidently to recent applications decided in accordance with r.3.4(2). However, claimants' applications which appear to have been decided under that rule include *Hamilton v Clifford* [2004] EWHC 1542, QBD (justification and fair comment), *Hewitt v Grunwald* [2004] EWHC 2959, QBD (qualified privilege and justification: application failed), *McKeith v News Group Newspapers Ltd* [2005] EWHC 1162, QBD; [2005] E.M.L.R. 32 (*Lucas-Box* meanings). **30.33**

Add to note 21: See *Hamilton v Clifford* [2004] EWHC 1542, QBD, where a *Lucas-Box* meaning was struck out because it offended against the repetition rule, and where the particulars of justification were struck out because they did not support the pleaded level 2 *Lucas-Box* meaning of reasonable grounds to suspect, and *Jameel v Times Newspapers* [2005] EWHC 1219, QBD, where a plea of justification based on a level 3 *Lucas-Box* meaning was struck out because it was inadequately supported by the pleaded particulars.

Add to note 22: *Musa King v Telegraph Group Ltd* was later considered by the Court of Appeal, which reinstated two paragraphs of the particulars of justification, subject to amendment of the *Lucas-Box* meanings: [2004] EWCA Civ 613; [2004] E.M.L.R. 23. On meanings at level 2 (reasonable grounds to suspect) and level 3 (grounds to investigate), see para.30.5 above and in particular *Jameel v Wall Street Journal* [2003] EWCA Civ 1694; [2004] E.M.L.R. 6 and *Jameel v Times Newspapers Ltd* [2004] EWCA Civ 983; [2004] E.M.L.R 31.

Add to note 27: See *Miller v Associated Newspapers* [2003] EWHC 2799; [2004] E.M.L.R. 33; *Wood v Chief Constable of West Midlands Police* [2003] EWHC 2971; [2004] E.M.L.R. 17, affirmed [2004] EWCA Civ 1638; [2005] E.M.L.R. 20, *McKeith v News Group Newspapers Ltd* [2005] EWHC 1162, QBD; [2005] E.M.L.R. 32 (all three of which may have been decided on a summary judgment basis); *Armstrong v Times Newspapers Ltd* (decision to rule out qualified privilege overturned by Court of Appeal ([2005] EWCA Civ 1007)).

Add to note 30: See *Hamilton v Clifford* [2004] EWHC 1542, QBD.

Add to note 31: Or the court may allow the application to strike out, while still permitting the pleader to reformulate his pleading (see, e.g. *Howe v Burden* [2004] EWHC 196, QBD).

30.34   **Applications by defendant.** The general *caveat* stated at para.30.33 above about the difficulty in pointing confidently to recent applications decided in accordance with r.3.4(2), as opposed to Pt 24, applies equally here. However, most of the cases cited at notes 1, 2 and 5 under para.30.27 above included an application under r.3.4(2).

    Note *Collins Stewart v Financial Times Ltd* [2004] EWHC 2337; [2005] E.M.L.R. 5 at [24], a successful defendant's application to strike out part of an enormous special damage plea based on the loss of value in shares of one claimant (the parent company of the other claimant), on the basis that it represented a measure of damage which was unsound in law, and that the claim was untriable and a waste of the resources of the court.

30.37   **Claimants' applications for abuse of process.** In *Jameel v Wall Street Journal Europe* [2003] EWCA Civ 1694; [2004] E.M.L.R. 6, the defendant appeared to be contending that an unappealed decision by Eady J. in *Al Rajhi v Wall Street Journal* [2003] EWHC 1776, QBD was wrong, thus prompting a vigorous intervention by counsel for Mr Al Rajhi, whereupon the defendant hastened to explain that it did not intend to secure a decision of the Court of Appeal that the unappealed decision in *Al Rajhi* was wrong. Counsel for the claimant argued that it would be an abuse of process for the defendant to argue the appeal before the court on any basis other than that Eady J. had been right to rule as he did in *Al Rajhi*; but Simon Brown L.J. disagreed [26]. He had no doubt that it would be an abuse of process for the defendant to succeed in the present appeal and then apply out of time for permission to appeal the *Al Rajhi* decision, but that was not the defendant's intention: it sought only to argue the appeal on its merits without being handicapped by what may or may not have been a correct decision in *Al Rajhi*, and there was no objection to that.

30.38   **Defendants' applications for abuse of process.** The doctrine of abuse of process was extended by the Court of Appeal in *Jameel (Yousef) v Dow Jones* [2005] EWCA Civ 75; [2005] 2 W.L.R. 1614, to the case of a libel published minimally in England and Wales by a foreign publisher, where no substantial tort had been committed within the jurisdiction. There had been two developments which made the court more receptive to a submission that pursuit of a libel action might be an abuse of process: one was the introduction of the Civil Procedure Rules, which required a more flexible and pro-active approach of the court, and the other was the coming into force of the Human Rights Act 1998, which (by s.6) required the court to administer the law in a manner compatible with Convention rights. "Keeping a proper balance between the Article 10 right to freedom of expression and the protection of individual reputation must . . . require the court to bring to a stop as an abuse of process defamation proceedings that are not serving the legitimate purpose of protecting the claimant's reputation" [55]. Even if the claimant succeeded at trial, there would be a gross disproportion between the minimal vindication achieved and the huge cost which would have been entailed. Referring to Eady J.'s well-known metaphor in *Schellenberg v BBC* [2000] E.M.L.R. 296, the court found that "The game would not merely not have been worth the candle, it will not have been worth the wick" [69]. (It is curious that the Court of Appeal should have given Eady J.'s phrase such a ringing endorsement less than a year after he disavowed it as an "off the cuff remark in an *ex tempore* judgment . . . specifically with reference to the very unusual facts of that case", and as one which it would "not be right to elevate . . . into a general principle of some kind to be applied in other libel actions" (*Howe v Burden* [2004] EWHC 196, QBD).)

Add to note 61: See *Vassiliev v Amazon Inc.* [2003] EWHC 2302 (Comm). *Pedder v News Group Newspapers Ltd* is now reported at [2004] E.M.L.R 19.

Add to note 62: See *Powell v Boladz* [2003] EWHC 2160, QBD, where the defendant applied unsuccessfully to strike out a claim on the grounds, *inter alia*, that the claimant sought not to vindicate his reputation but to achieve a collateral purpose. (See also note 64 below.)

Add to note 63: Where a claimant genuinely seeks vindication, but that vindication will be minimal in view of the tiny publication of the libel in this jurisdiction, and achieved at a cost out of all proportion to the result, the claim may be dismissed as an abuse (*Jameel (Yousef) v Dow Jones* [2005] EWCA Civ 75; [2005] 2 W.L.R. 1614).

Add to note 64: *Pedder v News Group Newspapers Ltd* is now reported at [2004] E.M.L.R. 19.

Add to note 66: Such an application failed in *Powell v Boladz* [2003] EWHC 2160, QBD, where Tugendhat J. considered in detail the law so far as concerns the proper purpose of proceedings in defamation, delay in prosecution of an action, and the requirements of Art.6 of the ECHR for the requirement of a fair trial within a reasonable time.

Schellenberg's case. Eady J.'s approach in *Schellenberg* was followed with   **30.40** approval by the Court of Appeal in *Jameel (Yousef) v Dow Jones* [2005] EWCA Civ 75; [2005] 2 W.L.R. 1614 at [57], [69], where the Court of Appeal developed the judge's well known reference to the game not being worth the candle, asserting that in *Jameel's* case "The game will not merely have been worth the candle, it will not have been worth the wick". (By contrast, note Eady J.'s own earlier attempt to downplay the phrase as one which should not be elevated into a general principle to be applied in other libel actions (*Howe v Burden* [2004] EWHC 196, QBD at [5]).)

30.41   *Wallis case. Add to note 85*: In *Jameel (Yousef) v Dow Jones* [2005] EWCA Civ 75; [2005] 2 W.L.R. 1614 at [58] the Court of Appeal regarded *Wallis* as an "extreme" case.

30.42   **Developing jurisprudence.** The law of *Reynolds* qualified privilege may no longer be regarded as an area of developing jurisprudence: in *Miller v Associated Newspapers Ltd* [2003] EWHC 2799; [2004] E.M.L.R. 33, Eady J. referred to the dicta of Bingham M.R. in *E v Dorset County Council* [1995] 2 A.C. 233, to the effect that in an area of developing jurisprudence an order striking out should not be made, and to attempts to use that principle as a device to avoid summary judgment on a weak *Reynolds* plea, and stated that he would be surprised "if their Lordships believed, after the exposition of the law and practical guidance offered in *Reynolds* itself and shortly afterwards in *Turkington*, that the law itself was still in a state of development" [33].

CHAPTER 31

INTERLOCUTORY MATTERS

SECTION 1. DISCLOSURE

Norwich Pharmacal case. As to an order against a mere witness, see *Mitsui*   **31.5**
v Nexen Petroleum [2005] EWHC 625 (Ch) at [24], where Lightman J (*obiter*)
said this:

"... it is clear that the exercise of the jurisdiction of the court under *Norwich
Pharmacal* against third parties who are mere witnesses innocent of any participation
in the wrongdoing being investigated is a remedy of last resort ... The jurisdiction is
only to be exercised if the innocent third parties are the only practicable source of
information".

However, he also repeated the general rule that the respondent to the application
must be mixed up so as to have facilitated the wrongdoing, and must be able or
likely to be able to provide the information necessary to enable the ultimate
wrongdoer to be sued, and (had it been necessary) he would have dismissed the
application on the ground that this hurdle had not been surmounted. So also in
Carlton Film Distributors v VCI [2003] EWHC 616 (Ch); [2003] F.S.R. 47 at
[11], Jacob J. observed (following *P v T* [1997] 1 W.L.R. 1309) that *Norwich
Pharmacal* "extends to cases where there is a good indication of wrongdoing, but
not every piece of what the claimant needs to plead a case is fully in position".

Add to note 8: In *Carlton Film Distributors v VCI* [2003] EWHC 616 (Ch);
[2003] F.S.R. 47, relief was available in a contractual dispute.

P v T Ltd See now *Mitsui v Nexen Petroleum* [2005] EWHC 625 (Ch) and   **31.6**
Carlton Film Distributors v VCI [2003] EWHC 616 (Ch); [2003] F.S.R. 47. It
should be noted that *P v T Ltd* was cited with approval in *Ashworth Hospital
Authority v MGN Ltd* [2002] UKHL 29; [2002] 1 W.L.R. 2033 at [57], where

Lord Woolf C.J. referred to it as a case where relief was granted because it was necessary in the interests of justice albeit that the claimant was not able to identify without discovery what would be the appropriate cause of action.

31.10   **Offer of amends.** *Add to note 21*: *Abu v MGN Ltd* is now reported at [2003] 1 W.L.R. 2201.

Add to note 22: *Rigg v Associated Newspapers Ltd* is now reported at [2004] E.M.L.R. 4.

Add to note 25: Eady J.'s decision was upheld by the Court of Appeal: *Milne v Express Newspapers Ltd* [2004] EWCA (Civ) 664; [2005] 1 W.L.R. 772.

31.11   **Use of disclosed documents.** *Add to note 28*: On a related but different point, the court may also refuse disclosure to third parties of pleadings and witness statements: see *Chan U Seek v Alvis Vehicles* [2004] EWHC 3092 (Ch); [2005] E.M.L.R. 19. The *Guardian* newspaper wanted to obtain the documents with a view to running a story about the case. It sought an order after the end of the trial, which ruled out an application under CPR, r.32.13(1) (witness statements open to inspection during the course of the trial unless the court otherwise directs). The order was made under CPR, r.5.4(5)(b), which allows third parties, with the court's permission, to obtain copies of documents on the court file. Given the importance of the open justice principle, Park J. required (but was not given) specific reasons why the respondent would be damaged by publication of a document on the court file.

SECTION 2. FURTHER INFORMATION AND INTERROGATORIES

(a) *General*

31.17   **Necessity.** The need to avoid extravagant use of requests for further information was considered by the Court of Appeal in *Musa King v Telegraph Group Ltd* [2004] EWCA Civ 613; [2005] 1 W.L.R. 2282 (reported as *King v Telegraph Group Ltd (Practice Note)*) at [63], where Brooke L.J. observed that the emphasis in the Practice Direction to Pt 18 was "on confining this part of any litigation (in which costs tended to get out of control in the pre-CPR regime) strictly to what is necessary and proportionate and to the avoidance of disproportionate expense", and recalled Lord Woolf M.R.'s remarks in *McPhilemy v Times Newspapers Ltd* [1999] 3 All E.R. 775, 792–794.

SECTION 3. SECURITY FOR COSTS AND MAINTENANCE

31.46   **The greater scope of security under the CPR.** Tugendhat J. refused to make an order under CPR, r.3.1(3) or (5) for a defendant to bring money into court because of alleged failures to comply with rules of court: following *Olatawura v Abiloye* [2001] EWCA Civ 998; [2003] 1 W.L.R. 275, he held that there was no want of good faith on the defendant's part and that the failures alleged, even if made good, did not amount to the repeated breaches required before the court will exercise this jurisdiction (*Sarayiah v Suren* [2004] EWHC 1981, QBD at [112–115].

Modern principles for the exercise of the wider jurisdiction to order **31.47**
security. The principles which now govern orders for security are well illustrated by the judgment of Eady J. in the libel case of *Al-Koronky v Time Life Entertainment Group Ltd* [2005] EWHC 1688, QBD, a case in which the claimants resided out of the jurisdiction in Sudan, which is not a contracting state (i.e. a party to the Brussels or Lugano Conventions or a Regulation state).

As Eady J. pointed out at [26], modern authority shows a shift of emphasis from the former practice in a number of respects. In particular, no assumption must be made that an order for security will follow from proof of residence in a non-contracting state (*Nasser v United Bank of Kuwait* [2001] 1 W.L.R. 1868, CA): instead, it must be established that any costs order made in favour of the defendant would not be enforceable, or would be substantially more difficult and therefore more expensive to enforce, in that jurisdiction. Furthermore, if the court finds that it may be effectively impossible to enforce an order for costs, that would provide an objective justification for the court to make an order for payment of the full amount of the costs likely to ordered against a claimant if unsuccessful (*Texuna International Ltd v Cairns Energy plc* [2004] EWHC 1102 (Com), Gross J.). That puts an end to the old rule of thumb practice of ordering a specific proportion (often two-thirds) of the costs likely to be incurred up to the relevant stage of the litigation.

The fact that the claimant is impecunious is not a ground for awarding security, but it is a factor which must be relevant to the likely difficulty of enforcement. On the other hand, the court must be alert to prevent the power to order security from being used as an instrument of oppression by stifling a genuine claim. Those conflicting considerations must of course be balanced in the light of the parties' Art.6 rights, having regard to necessity and proportionality. However, it cannot be assumed in the claimant's favour that an order for security will have a stifling effect: that must turn on the evidence, which the court may expect to include evidence that there do not exist third parties who can reasonably be expected to put up security for the defendant's costs (*Brimko Holdings Ltd v Eastman Kodak Co.* [2004] EWHC 1343 (Ch)).

In the *Al-Koronky* case, there was uncontradicted evidence that enforcement in Sudan would fail, and in the exercise of his discretion (taking account, in particular, of the failure of the claimant to state clearly that the claim would be stifled if security was ordered) the judge ordered security for costs in the sum of £375,000 down to the conclusion of disclosure. That amounted to 87 per cent of the sum sought.

The libel context. *Musa King v Telegraph Group Ltd* [2004] EWCA Civ 613; **31.48** [2005] 1 W.L.R. 2282 (reported as *King v Telegraph Group Ltd (Practice Note)*) reached the Court of Appeal in May 2004 ([2004] EWCA (Civ) 613; [2005] 1 W.L.R. 2282). Although the appeal had been brought in part on the footing that Eady J. had been wrong not to make a conditional order for security under CPR, r.24.6, at the hearing of the appeal the defendant did not press that argument, and the court held that it had no doubt that Eady J. had been right, for the reasons that he gave:

"While experience has shown that courts can readily detect on paper those cases which have no real prospect of success—and also those where it is possible that a claim may succeed but improbable that it will do so—to go any further than this in the pre-trial assessment of the merits of an action, at whatever early stage of the proceedings the application is made, would be to lure the court into dangerous territory and to open the way to very undesirable satellite litigation" (*per* Brooke L.J., [91]).

Instead, the court suggested that the solution to cases where a claimant is funding litigation by conditional fee agreement without after the event insurance is to make a prospective costs capping order under CPR, r.3.2(m).

"In my judgment the only way to square the circle is to say that when making any costs capping order the court should prescribe a total amount of recoverable costs which will be inclusive, so far as a CFA-funded party is concerned, of any additional liability. It cannot be just to submit defendants in these cases, where their right to freedom of expression is at stake, to a costs regime where the costs they will have to pay if they lose are neither reasonable nor proportionate and they have no reasonable prospect of recovering their reasonable and proportionate costs if they win" (*per* Brooke L.J., [101]).

SECTION 4. CONSOLIDATION, JOINDER AND SEVERANCE

31.61 **Addition and substitution of parties.** There is power under CPR, r.19.2(3) to set aside a wrongful joinder: see *Sarayiah v Suren* [2004] EWHC 1981, QBD, a slander action in which three defendants had been joined ex parte notwithstanding that they had good limitation defences and notwithstanding that joinder was (as Tugendhat J. found) unnecessary.

SECTION 5. MODE OF TRIAL

31.63 **Prolonged examination of documents.** *Add to note 8*: So in *Collins Stewart v Financial Times Ltd* [2004] EWHC 2337, QBD, [2005] E.M.L.R. 5, a case with complex general and special damage claims, where it was common ground that a judge alone should try the special damage claim, Tugendhat J. held that the necessary directions of law to the jury on general damages would be difficult to understand and would require prolonged consideration. Moreover, since juries do not give reasons, it would impossible for the judge trying the special damage claim to know what view the jury had taken on issues of fact in assessing general damages, and there would be a risk of double or under compensation and of inconsistent verdicts. The judge therefore ordered a split trial, with liability to be tried by judge and jury and damages (general and special) by judge alone.

Add to note 9: See *Maccaba v Liechtenstein* [2004] EWHC 1580, QBD, where although the documents included Hebrew phrases and required some expert evidence on Jewish law, it was not apparent that the jury would have to examine a large number of the documents, and any problems of comprehension were surmountable. This was a classic case for trial by jury, since the main issue at trial would be which account of events was true. By contrast, in *W v Westminster City Council* [2004] EWHC 2866, QBD, the substantial volume of documents in the trial bundle was likely to require careful study, and trial by judge alone was ordered.

Residual discretion. If the discretion stage is reached, the overriding objective   **31.65** under the CPR is relevant to the exercise of the residual discretion under s.69(3) of the Supreme Court Act 1981 (*W v Westminster City Council* [2004] EWHC 2866, QBD). It may be thought unlikely that the overriding objective (which is concerned *inter alia* with saving expense, dealing with the case in ways proportionate to such factors as the amount of money involved, ensuring it is dealt with expeditiously, and allotting to it an appropriate share of the court's resources) will often lead the judge to exercise his discretion in favour of trial by jury.

Add to note 18: see also *Jameel (Mohammed) v Wall Street Journal* [2005] EWCA Civ 74; [2005] 2 W.L.R. 1577 at [70], where the Court of Appeal observed that the division between the role of the judge and that of the jury where *Reynolds* privilege is in issue is not an easy one, and questioned whether jury trial was desirable at all in such cases.

Separate trail of liability and quantum. *Add to note 20*: See also *Collins*   **31.66** *Stewart v Financial Times Ltd* [2004] EWHC 2337, QBD; [2005] E.M.L.R. 5, where liability was ordered to be tried by judge and jury and damages (both general and special) by judge alone.

CHAPTER 32

THE TRIAL: THE CLAIMANT'S CASE

SECTION 1. COMMENCEMENT OF TRIAL

32.2   **Opening statement.** In the Australian case of *John Fairfax Publications Pty v Rivkin* [2003] HCA 50; 201 A.L.R 77 McHugh J. (at [74]) made some perceptive observations about the advantages offered to plaintiff's counsel when opening the case:

> "Skilled counsel, appearing for plaintiffs in defamation trials exploit this [tendency for people selectively to perceive when interpreting data what they expect and hope to see] and other biases by delaying bringing the contents of the publication to the jury's attention until they have injected the plaintiff's preconceptions and assumptions into the collective mind of the jury. They begin by discussing the publication in general terms without going to the details. They plant in the collective mind of the jury an expectation that what they will read will be the imputations for which the plaintiff contends. Jurors then tend to see in the publication what they expect to see."

SECTION 2. EVIDENCE FOR THE CLAIMANT: INTRODUCTION

32.3   **General.** The power of the court under CPR, r.32.3 to allow a witness to give evidence through a video link should be noted. When the use of video conferencing (VCF) in civil proceedings is being considered a judgment must be made not only as to whether it will achieve an overall cost saving but as to whether its use will be likely to be beneficial to the efficient, fair and economic disposal of the litigation (PD 32, para.33). In *Polanski v Conde Naste Publications Ltd* [2005] UKHL 10; [2005] 1 W.L.R. 637 the claimant, who had brought proceedings for libel against the publishers of an American magazine, applied to be permitted to give his evidence at trial by VCF, as he was at risk if he came to London for the trial of being arrested and extradited to the USA, from which he had fled before sentencing after pleading guilty to having unlawful sexual intercourse with a

13-year-old girl. The judge made the order sought, but it was rescinded by the Court of Appeal. The House of Lords (by a majority of three to two) allowed an appeal and restored the judge's order holding that the administration of justice was not brought into disrepute by the permitting of a fugitive to have recourse to one of the court's current procedures which would enable him in a particular case to pursue his proceedings while remaining a fugitive, and that the general rule was that in respect of proceedings properly brought in England a party's unwillingness to come into this country because of his fugitive status was a valid reason, and could be a sufficient reason for making a VCF order. The majority were also of the view that the court was not bound to make an order excluding a witness's statement as evidence if he did not attend for cross-examination. Such an order should be made only if, exceptionally, justice so required. The principle underlying the Civil Evidence Act 1995 was that in general the preferable course was to admit hearsay evidence, and let the court attach to the evidence whatever weight may be appropriate. This applied to jury trials as well as trials by judge alone.

SECTION 3. PROOF OF PUBLICATION

Internet publication. In *Barrick Gold Corporation v Lopehandia*, Ont. CA, **32.7** 71 O.R. (3d) 416; (2004) Ont. Rep. Lexis 142, Blair J.A. described internet communications as follows:

"Communication via internet is instantaneous, seamless, interactive, blunt, borderless and far-reaching. It is also impersonal, and the anonymous nature of such communications may itself create a greater risk that the defamatory remarks are believed. The internet has greater potential to damage the reputation of individuals and corporations as a result of these features than does its less pervasive cousins."

Add to note 24:

(i) the proposition that a text on the internet is published at the place where it is downloaded was accepted without argument in *King v Lewis* [2004] EWCA Civ 1329; [2005] E.M.L.R. 45. See also *Carter v B.C. Federation of Foster Parents Association* [2005] BCCA 398 referred to in para.6.5 of this Supplement.

(ii) Although it may be a matter of inference that the posted material will have been downloaded and read by persons within the jurisdiction, especially if a substantial number of "hits" can be proved, it is a rebuttable inference.

In *Jameel (Yousef) v Dow Jones & Co. Inc.* [2005] EWCA Civ 75; [2005] 2 W.L.R. 1614 the words complained of were posted on a subscription website. The particulars of claim alleged that there were between 5,000 and 6,000 subscribers within the jurisdiction. The defendant was able to show that the offending material had only been accessed by five subscribers within the jurisdiction, two of whom did not know of the claimant and had no recollection of reading his name, and the other three were connected with the claimant. The Court of Appeal struck out the claim as an abuse of the process:

"If the claimant succeeds in this action and is awarded a small amount of damages, it can perhaps be said that he will have achieved vindication for the damage done to his reputation, but both the damage and the vindication will be minimal. The cost of the exercise will have been out of all proportion to what has been achieved. The game will not merely not have been worth the candle, it will not have been worth the wick" (at [69]).

32.12 **Foreign language.** *Add to note 44*: this was held not to be essential in *Sing v Jinggut* (2003) 6 M.L.J. 433 where the court refused to strike out particulars of claim in which only the translation of the words complained of had been included and not the words in the language in which they had been published (mandarin).

32.14 **Variance between words alleged and words proved.** *Add to note 50*: *Buchanan v Jennings* [2004] UKPC 36; [2005] 1 A.C. 115:

"[w]here an oral statement is complained of, it is rarely possible (in the absence of a recording, a transcript or a very careful note) for a plaintiff to establish the precise words used by the defendant. But the law does not demand a level of precision which is unattainable in practice. The plaintiff must plead the words complained of, but it is enough if the tribunal of fact is satisfied that those words accurately express the substance of what was said" [5].

SECTION 4. IDENTIFICATION OF CLAIMANT

32.17 **Claimant not expressly named.** "Where the claimant is named in the libel no difficulty can arise." This perhaps should no longer be expressed in such absolute terms following the dicta in *Jameel (Yousef) v Dow Jones* [2005] EWCA Civ 75; [2005] 2 W.L.R. 1614 that, "[w]here a common name is included in an article, the name itself will not suffice to identify any individual who bears that name." (at [45]).

32.22 **Evidence of reputation.** *Add to note 77:* See also *Jameel (Yousef) v Dow Jones* [2005] EWCA Civ 75; [2005] 2 W.L.R. 1614 which followed *Shevill v Press Alliance* [1996] A.C. 959 and also approved Eady J.'s view expressed in *Multigroup Bulgaria Holding v Oxford Analytica* [2001] E.M.L.R. 737 that an article defaming an identifiable individual would give rise to a cause of action even when no one reading the article had prior knowledge of the victim. (See further, para.32.45 of this Supplement.)

SECTION 5. DEFAMATORY MEANINGS

32.24 **Context.** *Add to note 85*: In *Galloway v Telegraph Group* [2004] EWHC 2786, QBD; [2005] E.M.L.R. 7 the claimant was complaining of parts of newspaper articles spread over two days. The judge indicated how meaning should be approached:

" . . . when judging the meaning of the April 23 articles, it is necessary to bear in mind that many readers will have had a general impression of their reading from the day before. It is legitimate to take that into account when assessing the meaning of the second day's coverage. The reverse is not the case, since it is not permitted when attributing a meaning or meanings to a published article to refer to subsequent material" (at [50]).

SECTION 6. EVIDENCE OF MALICE

Definition. *Add to note 11*: In *Miller v Associated Newspapers Ltd* [2004] **32.31** EWHC 2799, QBD; [2004] E.M.L.R. 33 at [10] Eady J. stated, "If a particular publication passes the [*Reynolds*] privilege test, it is very difficult to envisage circumstances where there would be room for it to be overridden by malice".

No honest belief. *Add to note 18*: In *Rackham v Sandy* [2005] EWHC 482, **32.32** QBD Gray J. allied himself with the analysis of Gleeson L.J. in *Roberts v Bass* that the essence of malice was improper motive, rather than absence of honest belief, but acknowledged that the point was of limited practical significance since knowledge of falsity will almost always establish the existence of an improper motive. (See para.16.4 of this Supplement).

Add after reference to note 22: Tugendhat J. in *Crossland v Wilkinson Hardware Stores* [2005] EWHC 481 pointed out that meaning and malice were often linked as it was common for a claimant to pitch the meaning high and then say that the defendant could not have believed that meaning. In such cases it was important that the words were given their ordinary meaning.

Extrinsic evidence. *Add to note 33*: In *Meade v Pugh & Hamilton* [2004] **32.35** EWHC 408, QBD Tugendhat J. emphasised that spite or desire to injure must be the dominant motive (at [27]).

Irrelevant material. *Note 52.* In para.14.61 of this Supplement are references **32.38** to recent cases in which the effect of irrelevant statements in the context of privilege and malice has been considered.

Evidence to defeat offer to make amends defence. *Add to note 83*: The **32.44** decision has been upheld by the Court of Appeal ([2004] EWCA Civ 664; [2005] 1 W.L.R. 772). The words "had reason to believe that the statement complained of . . . was . . . false" were to be construed as importing the concept of recklessness from *Horrocks v Lowe*, namely indifference to the truth or falsity of the words complained of.

SECTION 7. EVIDENCE TO SUPPORT CLAIM FOR DAMAGES

Damage presumed. In *Jameel (Yousef) v Dow Jones* [2005] EWCA Civ 75; **32.45** [2005] 2 W.L.R. 1614 the Court of Appeal rejected a submission that the presumption of damage was incompatible with Art.10 of ECHR (freedom of expression), and confirmed that it remained part of English law. However, it also concluded that if a claimant brought an action in circumstances where his reputation had suffered no, or minimal, actual damage, it might constitute an interference with freedom of expression that was not necessary for the protection of the claimant's reputation, which might render the action susceptible to being struck out as an abuse of the process (which is what in fact the Court did). It might therefore be advisable, and perhaps necessary, for a claimant, where there has been very limited publication, to lead evidence of damage to reputation or evidence from which such damage can be inferred.

See also *Jameel (Mohammed) v The Wall Street Journal* [2003] EWCA Civ 74; [2005] 2 W.L.R. 1577 in which an appeal against Eady J.'s decision ([2003] EWHC 2945, QBD), that the principle of presumption of damage applied to a foreign corporation not trading within the jurisdiction and corporations generally, and had not been swept away as a result of the Human Rights Act 1998 and Art.10 of ECHR, was dismissed.

32.47   **Injury to reputation.** Where the claimant was a company which had been restructured and renamed since publication of the libel, the court in assessing damages could disregard the element of vindication for the future, that is the ability of the company in future by reference to the award to demonstrate that there was no substance in the libel (*Downtex plc v Flatley* [2004] EWHC 333, QBD).

32.48   **Injury to feelings.** *Add to note 2*: See also Eady J. in *Nail v News Group Newspapers* [2004] EWHC 647, QBD; [2004] E.M.L.R. 20 at [27].

32.49   **Actual damages.** A (plc) company cannot claim special damages on the basis of the difference between its actual market capitalisation following publication of the alleged libel and its potential market capitalisation without the alleged libel, as there may have been many factors influencing fluctuations in the market capitalisation, and the suggested measure of damages was too uncertain to be acceptable as a legal basis for assessing damages. Further the investigation required to assess the loss in market value attributable to the alleged libel would render the case untriable. These were part of the rulings of Tugendhat J. in *Collins Stewart v Financial Times Ltd* [2004] EWHC 2337; [2005] E.M.L.R. 5 who struck out a claim for £230,626,320 damages based on the fall in the market value of the shares of the second claimant, Collins Stewart plc. The Judge also held that the proposition that the losses suffered by the first claimant, Collins Stewart Ltd, a wholly owned subsidiary of plc, and the subject of the defamatory article, would be reflected in the losses suffered by the shareholders of the second claimant, was not sustainable. (See further the discussion in para.8.16 of this Supplement.)

32.51   Aggravated damages.

"[T]he defining characteristic of an award of aggravated damages is that its function is to provide a claimant with compensation for injury to his or her feelings caused by some conduct on the part of the defendant or for which the defendant is responsible . . . It seems to me to follow that aggravated damages are in principle not available to a corporate claimant ... The reason is that ... a company has no feelings to injure and cannot suffer distress" (Gray J. at [30], [31] in *Collins Stewart v Financial Times Ltd* [2005] EWHC 262, QBD).

Add to note 16: In *Collins Stewart v Financial Times Ltd* [2005] EWHC 262, QBD, Gray J. expressed a different view, that there are sound reasons both of principle and of practice why a claimant, whether an individual or a corporation, should not be permitted to seek to recover increased damages in respect of the publication of subsequent articles which are not themselves the subject of complaint (at [27]). The judge did not seek to distinguish between injury to feelings caused by the subsequent articles, for which on old authority damages are recoverable, and injury to reputation, for which, it is generally accepted, no additional award should be made.

SECTION 10. EVIDENCE DIRECTED AT DEFENDANT'S CASE OF QUALIFIED
PRIVILEGE

Evidence that is admissible on qualified privilege. The ruling in *GKR* **32.57**
Karate Ltd v Yorkshire Post (No.1) [2000] E.M.L.R. 396 was that it was not relevant to [*Reynolds*] qualified privilege whether the publication was true or not, or to speculate what further information the publisher might have discovered if he had made more extensive enquiries. Thus evidence directed to these matters would be inadmissible. However, in *Jameel v Wall Street Journal* [2003] EWCA Civ 1694; [2004] E.M.L.R. 6 the Court of Appeal upheld Eady J.'s decision in a case where there was a *Reynolds* privilege defence that evidence was admissible for the purpose of demonstrating that the defendant's sources were in fact unlikely to have told the defendant what it alleged it was told, or at least unlikely to have conveyed the information as clearly as the defendant alleged:

"The [claimant's] evidence in the present case is that Mr Dorsey, the main author of the article, received his information from five different confidential sources all of which he believed to be credible, and that a further confidential check was made in Washington by Mr Glenn Simpson, a staff writer who contributed to the article. Is the evidence here designed to demonstrate that those sources were not as reliable as objectively it might have appeared to the [claimant] at the time, or is it designed rather to show that the sources are in fact unlikely to have told the [claimant] what it says it was told (or at least unlikely to have conveyed the information as clearly as the [claimant] claim it was conveyed)? The former purpose would, as *GKR Karate* makes plain, be impermissible; the latter, however, seems to me entirely unjustifiable" (Simon Brown L.J. at [31]).

The source of the information is one of the ten circumstances in Lord Nicholls' non-exhaustive list (see *Reynolds v Times Newspapers* [2001] 2 A.C. 127 at [205]). The claimant, it is submitted, must be able to lead evidence on other matters in the list, if they are in dispute, such as whether comment was sought from him, and whether the article contained the gist of his side of the story. But the area of admissible evidence from the claimant must surely extend wider than this in the face of the Court of Appeal's observations in the *Jameel* appeal from the judgment at the trial [2005] EWCA Civ 74; [2005] 2 W.L.R. 1577, that the presumption of falsity should not be applied when considering issues of fact that were relevant to *Reynolds* privilege. (See further, discussion of the Court of Appeal decision in para.14.88 of this Supplement.) The expectations apparent in the judgment of May L.J. in *GKR Karate* that the *Reynolds* privilege defence combined with the court's powers of case management under the CPR would enable many defamation actions to be disposed of without having "to trudge expensively through" a mire of evidence, as can happen in justification cases, are unlikely to be realised.

CHAPTER 33

THE TRIAL: THE DEFENDANT'S CASE

SECTION 3. EVIDENCE FOR THE DEFENDANT: GENERAL

Context of alleged libel or slander. *Add to note 23*: In *Galloway v Telegraph* **33.4**
Group [2004] EWHC 2786, QBD; [2005] E.M.L.R. 7 Eady J. accepted as part of
the context two documents found in the Foreign Ministry in Bagdad reproduced
in full in the defendant's newspaper on the same day as one of the articles
complained of, but not the subject of complaint. The defendant was said to attach
great weight to the documents and the judge agreed that it was necessary to take
them into account when considering meaning.

SECTION 4. PROOF OF JUSTIFICATION

Evidence of justification in mitigation if defence not pleaded. *Add to note* **33.12**
49: See also *Galloway v Telegraph Group* [2004] EWHC 2786, QBD; [2004]
E.M.L.R. 7, Eady J. at [203].

Note 50: *Burstein* is further discussed in paras 33.42 and 33.43 of the Main
Work.

Evidence admissible on other issues. It should be noted that it is impermis- **33.14**
sible to seek to prove the truth of the defamatory words as part of the plea of
qualified privilege. In *Armstrong v Times Newspapers Ltd* [2004] EWHC 2928,
QBD, Eady J. struck out part of the particulars in support of a *Reynolds* privilege
defence which sought to incorporate by reference all paragraphs of the particulars

of justification. This ruling was not challenged on appeal ([2005] EWCA Civ 1007) which was successful in respect of other orders of the single judge.

33.18   **Reasonable grounds to suspect.** The principles where a defendant is justifying a meaning that there were reasonable grounds to suspect the claimant to have committed some discreditable act—now commonly labelled a "level 2 meaning"—were first set out by Eady J. in *Musa King v Telegraph Group* [2003] EWHC 1312, QBD (see [32]), repeated by him three days later in *Al Rahji Banking & Investment Corporation v Wall Street Banking Corporation* [2003] EWHC 1358 at [27], referred to with implicit approval by the Court of Appeal in *Musa King* on appeal ([2004] EWCA Civ 613; [2004] E.M.L.R. 23 at [22]), and reiterated once more by Eady J. in *Miller v Associated Newspapers* [2005] EWHC 5457, QBD at [33]. These principles (set out in full in para.11.6 of this Supplement) can be regarded as governing the pleading and proof of a level 2 meaning. See further discussion in the additions to the note 60 of para.27.10 in this Supplement.

Add to note 68: By contrast, in *Miller v Associated Newspapers* [2005] EWHC 21, QBD the defendant was allowed to plead in support of justification of a "level (1) meaning" (actual guilt) representations made by the claimant some time after the publication of the alleged libel on the basis that they were lies and should be treated as tantamount to admissions.

SECTION 5. PROOF OF FAIR COMMENT

33.19   **Fact or comment.** An analysis of how this issue should be determined was undertaken by Gray J. in *Oliver v Chief Constable of Northumbria* [2003] EWHC 2417, QBD; [2004] E.M.L.R. 32 at [22–33]; and see para.12.12 of this Supplement. See also *Haines v Television New Zealand* [2004] NZAR 513: " . . . a statement of fact without reference to any other facts on which it was based could not be opinion or comment".

SECTION 6. PROOF OF PRIVILEGE

33.25   **"Reynolds" type privilege.** The evidential burden has been given emphasis by the statement of the Court of Appeal in *Jameel (Mohammed) v Wall Street Journal Europe Sprl (No.3)* [2005] EWCA Civ 74; [2005] 2 W.L.R. 1577 at [59] that it was not appropriate for the jury to apply the presumption of falsity when considering issues of fact that were relevant to *Reynolds* privilege. Some of the implications of this were considered in *Jameel* at [60–61]. It was pointed out that where an issue is raised as to whether those responsible for the publication of an article have accurately described the information supplied to them by their sources, the question of whether the information allegedly supplied was true or false would have obvious relevance.

Of equal significance are the court's observations (in *Jameel* at [27]) on the importance of evidence of the publisher about his subjective belief:

"[it] seems to us that, in seeking to demonstrate that a publication accords with the requirements of responsible journalism, a publisher will almost certainly wish to adduce evidence of subjective belief of those responsible for the publication. To demonstrate that it was reasonable to believe that a defamatory article was true, the writer is likely to be called to give evidence of why he thought it was true. To demonstrate that it was reasonable to believe that a third party was conducting an investigation, or inquiry, or monitoring, the writer is likely to be called to explain why he believed this to be the case. To demonstrate that it was reasonable not to appreciate that an article bore a defamatory meaning [see *Bonnick v Morris* [2002] UKPC 31; [2003] 1 A.C. 300] the writer is likely to be called to say that he did not appreciate this."

The conclusion was, at [29] " . . . it may be necessary or at least admissible for a defendant to allege and prove subjective belief in order to establish a defence of *Reynolds* privilege". (See also discussions in paras 14.88 and 32.57 of this Supplement.)

SECTION 8. EVIDENCE IN MITIGATION OF DAMAGES

Categories of evidence. In addition to those listed in the Main Work the **33.28** European Court of Human Rights would seem to have added an additional category, namely the means of the defendant. For in its decision in *Steel & Morris v United Kingdom (2005)*, Application No.64816/01; [2005] E.M.L.R. 15 the Court held that the award of damages (a total of £76,000) was disproportionate and amounted to a breach of Art.10 because, although relatively moderate by contemporary standards in defamation cases in England and Wales, they were very substantial when compared to the modest incomes and resources of the two defendants. If this is now to be regarded as the correct approach in English law it would be appropriate and advisable in many cases for a defendant to lead evidence as to his means. However, it has been an axiomatic principle of the common law that in assessing damages for the commission of a tort, no regard is given to the means of the defendant, which is generally an irrelevance: "It is also well-settled that financial compensation (unlike any penalty) is to be awarded without regard to the parties' means", Eady J., *Cleese v Clark* [2003] EWHC 137, QBD; [2004] E.M.L.R. 3 at [38]. (The exception, referred to by Eady J., is punitive or exemplary damages, where the objective is to punish the defendant, and the punishment must be related to his resources.) If this fundamental rule is to be disturbed, the consequences will be radical and far-reaching. It is suggested that practitioners should await an authoritative ruling from an English court on the effect of *Steel & Morris*—which may be explained as applying only to exemplary damages—before preparing cases for trial on the basis that evidence of the defendant's means will be admissible as relevant to damages. (See further discussion at para.9.2 of this Supplement.)

(a) *Claimant's bad reputation*

Reputation in relevant sector. *Add to note 11*: By contrast, in *Shave v West* **33.32** *Australian Newspapers* [2003] WASC 83 where the plaintiff was a government minister and the defamatory allegation that he had given misleading evidence at an official inquiry, the court refused to strike out a plea that the plaintiff had a reputation as a Minister who had inadequately and incompetently discharged his duties. It was stated that the scope of the relevant sector of a plaintiff's reputation was not limited by the scope of the imputations pleaded, and that the various facets of a politician's life were constantly under scrutiny.

33.33   **Evidence of subsequent bad character.** *Add to note 13*: In Australia at least there is some doubt as to whether this is a rule strictly applicable in all circumstances—see review of case law and discussion in *Anderson v Ah Kit* [2004] WASC 194.

(b) *Facts relevant to the contextual background in which the defamatory publication was made*

33.42   **The *Burstein* case.** *"Spiedel v Plato Films"*: the correct spelling of the plaintiff is *"Speidel"*.

33.43   **Aftermath of *Burstein* decision.** There have been few cases where judges have had to consider what is encompassed in the term "directly relevant contextual background" and how it should be applied to particular circumstances. But in *Turner v News Group Newspapers Ltd* [2005] EWHC 892, QBD; [2005] E.M.L.R. 25 the judge (Eady J.) was required to assess compensation under the offer to make amends procedure (ss.2–4 of the Defamation Act 1996). Compensation under that procedure is to be determined "on the same principles as damages in defamation cases" (s.3(5)). Accordingly, the judge ruled that directly relevant background context was as pertinent to the assessment of compensation under the offer to make amends procedure as to the assessment of damages in a normal action. The article complained of was about couples who indulged in "swinging", defined as "hooked on sex with strangers" and featured the claimant and one of his former wives (second defendant) whom it was alleged was pressurised by the claimant to have sex with strangers at a Coventry club. The first defendant acknowledged that this was untrue but sought to rely on three categories of material in mitigation of damages under the *Burstein* rule: the involvement of the claimant and his former wife in fetish functions at a Coventry club; the claimant's encouragement of his former wife in her career as a model to pose for explicit photos; and the fact that the claimant had "slagged off" his former wife in a newspaper feature. The judge accepted that what was admissible under *Burstein* must be narrower than what would have been allowed under the draft cl.13 of the Defamation Bill (1996), rejected by the legislature, which was in these terms: "all facts affecting or liable to affect [the claimant's] reputation . . . in relation to the sector of his life to which the defamatory statement relates". Notwithstanding, he ruled that the first two categories were admissible under *Burstein* since the allegations complained of concerned the circumstances in which the claimant and his wife attended the Coventry Club and the supposed pressure on her to indulge in sexual activities with other people. As the former wife's career as a model was not a matter mentioned or alluded to in the words complained of, it has to be said that the line between facts liable to affect reputation in the sector of the claimant's reputation to which the defamatory statement relates and facts part of the "directly relevant background context" would appear to be a thin one, and it may be difficult in any particular case to determine on which side of the line the discreditable facts fall.

As to the third category—the "slagging off" of his former wife in a newspaper feature—Eady J. made no decision as to whether the *Burstein* rule applied but admitted the disputed material as bearing on the issue of the extent of the claimant's hurt feelings: "his self-invited exposure in the tabloid newspapers is relevant to the extent with which he values his privacy and would, or would not, suffer hurt feelings by tabloid exposure on the subject of his marital relations" (at [25]).

It should be noted that in *Turner* the judge reiterated his statement in *Abu v MGN* [2002] EWHC 2345; [2003] 1 W.L.R. that neither party should be able to take the other party by surprise by introducing new material (relevant to compensation) after an offer of amends has been accepted, and also ruled that seeking to rely upon discreditable actions of the claimant under the *Burstein* rule, provided the defendant was acting reasonably, was not to be regarded as aggravating conduct which would increase the amount of compensation (at [55]).

(f) *Apology or other amends*

Effect of apology. The quality and effect of an apology has come under close   **33.52** scrutiny in assessments of compensation under the *offer to make amends* procedure. In *Cleese v Clark* [2003] EWHC 137, QBD; [2004] E.M.L.R. 3 the judge described the apology as published without "great enthusiasm or generosity of spirit" and therefore it had done little to mitigate the hurt to the claimant's feelings. In *Nail v Newsgroup Newspapers* [2004] EWHC 647, QBD; [2004] E.M.L.R. Eady J. stated:

> " . . . there is no point in endlessly haggling or niggling about the size or location of an apology. The important thing is to achieve vindication as quickly and effectively as possible . . . I believe that the important elements of the apology are that it was published relatively quickly after the proceedings were issued, at the top of the page, and that it was relatively eye-catching" [69].

In *Campbell-Jones v Guardian Media Group* [2005] EWHC 893, QBD; [2005] E.M.L.R. 24 the judge remarked that it was a case for a speedy, unequivocal and prominent apology, but what the claimant obtained was an apology published three months after the offending article which the claimant might justifiably have considered "off-hand" in its terms. In *Turner v News Group Newspapers* (see para.33.43 of this Supplement) the claimant's criticism of the apology, that it did not include words to the effect that the first defendant had agreed to pay damages, was rejected on the grounds that it would not have improved the claimant's position.

Chapter 34

THE TRIAL: FUNCTIONS OF JUDGE AND JURY

34.4   **Two or more meanings reasonably possible.** *Add to note 24*: See also on this point observations of Sedley L.J. in *Jameel v Times Newspapers* [2004] EWCA Civ 983; [2004] E.M.L.R. 31 at [16]:

> "There seems to me to be an unaddressed tension between the principle that the feasible range of meanings is to be derived from the article as a whole, read through the eyes of a sensible person, and the principle that if the article contains a defamatory statement or imputation, that will define its meaning unless it is very plainly negatived in the same article."

See further, para.3.29 of this Supplement.

34.14   **Fair comment.** *Add to note 60*: In *Anderton v Ah Kit* [2004] WASC 194 there was a ruling that the welfare of animals kept privately and not open for public inspection was not a matter of public interest for the purposes of fair comment. See also para.12.28 of this Supplement.

34.15   **Privilege.** *Add to note 73*: This passage was cited by Gillard A.J.A. in *Herald & Weekly Times v Popovic* (2003) VSCA 161 in which he concluded that where the defence is qualified privilege in accordance with the ruling in *Lange v Australian Broadcasting Corp.* (1997) 189 C.L.R. 520, the question whether the defence has been established is one for the judge, but any disputed primary facts relevant to the issue are for decision by the jury. The "primary facts" were defined as "the actual happening of a particular event, what was said or done, but not the inferences or conclusions to be drawn from those primary facts" [111]. Thus whether the conduct of the publisher in publishing the matter was reasonable—an ingredient of the statutory defence of qualified privilege under the law of the State of Victoria—was for the judge to decide as it was not a primary fact.

The difficulties to which the task of distinguishing between the roles of judge and jury in *Reynolds* privilege cases may give rise led Lord Phillips M.R. in *Jameel (Mohammed) v Wall Street Journal Sprl* [2005] EWCA Civ 74; [2005] 2 W.L.R. 1577 to remark, at [70], "the division between the role of judge and that of the jury when *Reynolds* privilege is in issue is not an easy one; indeed it is open to question whether jury trial is desirable at all in such a case". (See further extensive discussion in para.14.88 of this Supplement.)

34.18   **Malice.** *Add to note 89*: See also Tugendhat J.'s paraphrasing of May L.J.'s test in *Meade v Pugh & Hamilton* [2004] EWHC 408, QBD at [18] quoted in full in para.30.26 of this Supplement.

CHAPTER 35

THE TRIAL: THE FINAL STAGES

SECTION 1. SPEECHES

Generally. *Add to note 2*: In *John Fairfax Publications Pty Ltd v Rivkin* [2003] **35.1**
HCA 50; 201 A.L.R. a complaint that the trial had been unfair as the judge had
not allowed plaintiff's counsel to reply to the defendant's final speech, where the
defendant had called no evidence, was rejected. McHugh stated, "[i]t is a
fundamental rule of the common law jury trial of a civil cause that, if counsel for
the defendant does not call evidence, he or she has the last address" (at [71]), but
here this must be subject to the court's overriding discretion.

SECTION 2. SUMMING-UP

Deficiencies in summing-up. *Note 19*: The reference in the final sentence **35.4**
should read "para.36.4. n.40, below". The "substantial body of authority"
included in this note was described in *Jameel (Mohammed) v Wall Street Journal*
[2005] EWCA Civ 74; [2005] 2 W.L.R. 1577 as giving strong support "to the
proposition that this court will not entertain a complaint of misdirection in a
defamation action if counsel has failed to avail himself of the chance of raising
the matter at the trial" (at [64]), a proposition which the Court of Appeal applied
to a particular ground of appeal. (See further discussion at para.36.4 of this
Supplement.)

SECTION 5. COSTS

Introduction. *Note 48*: In any defamation action, in which the claimant has **35.11**
brought the action under a conditional fee agreement (CFA) without taking out
an after-the-event (ATE) insurance policy, attention must be given to the judgment of Brooke L.J. in *Musa King v Telegraph Group Ltd* [2004] EWCA Civ
613; [2005] 1 W.L.R. 2282 (reported as *King v Telegraph Group Ltd (Practice
Note)*). It had been originally contended by the defendant in this case that if a
claimant embarked on a libel action on a CFA without ATE cover the court
should treat this conduct as an abuse of the process if the prospects of success,

viewed objectively, were less than evens. Such conduct was likely to have a chilling effect on journalism because the media would feel constrained to "buy out" such claims at an early stage rather than face the prospect of paying heavy legal costs, win or lose. It was suggested that the court should give summary judgment to the defendant or make some form of conditional order. Eady J. declined to do so, and on appeal the defendant abandoned this approach and invited the court to effect "dynamic case management" by capping the costs at this stage. The court decided that it had no power to make quite a different type of order from the type the judge had been asked to make. However, the court accepted that the case had exposed a situation which was a cause of concern namely that in defamation actions CFAs could result, particularly where the litigation was extravagantly conducted, in obvious unfairness to defendants which was bound to have a chilling effect on a newspaper exercising its Art.10 rights to freedom of expression. It therefore indicated how the court's powers might be exercised to deal with the problem. In summary, where defamation proceedings are initiated without ATE cover, the defendant could apply at the allocation stage for a "costs capping order" which would be a direction that the recoverable costs would be limited to a specified amount. A costs judge would determine the sum which was reasonable and proportionate to fix as the recoverable costs of the action. The power of the court to make such orders was derived from s.51 of the Supreme Court Act 1981 and CPR, r.3.2(m).

In *Matadeen v Associated Newspapers Ltd*, unreported, March 17, 2005, Master Eyre acceded to the defendant's application for a costs capping order in a libel claim by a claimant litigating under a CFA in respect of an article in the *Evening Standard*.

See also *Turcu v News Group Newspapers* [2005] EWHC 799, QBD; [2005] All E.R. (D) 34 in which Eady J. described the defendant's position when faced with a claimant with the benefit of a CFA as "wholly unenviable" (at [6]), and remarked, " . . . there must be a significant temptation for media defendants to pay up something, to be rid of litigation for purely commercial reasons, without regard to the true merits of any pleaded defence" [7].

35.17 **Amount of costs.** *Add to note 76*: In *Gazley v Wade & News Group Newsapers* [2004] EWHC 2675, QBD it was held that the costs judge was not in error in ruling that it was not reasonable for the claimant to instruct London libel specialists as his solicitors rather than a local firm in Norwich in respect of his defamation claim against a national newspaper.

Add to note 78: In *Miller v Associated Newspapers Ltd* [2005] EWHC 773, QBD indemnity costs were ordered against the unsuccessful claimant after a Pt 36 payment was not accepted on the grounds that the claimant had been unreasonable in not accepting the payment. But in *Rackham v Sandy* [2005] EWHC 1354, QBD an order for costs on an indemnity basis against a defendant who had rejected the claimant's Pt 36 offer and against whom a finding of malice had been made was refused because of the financial consequences on the defendant, which made it unjust to make such an order.

35.19 **Costs against co-defendants.** In *Rackham v Sandy* [2005] EWHC 1354, QBD, the claimant was ordered to pay the two successful defendants' costs as it had been the claimant's choice to join them as defendants.

CHAPTER 36

APPEAL

Section 1. General Principles

Application for permission to appeal. *Add at end of note 3*: See also *Pell v Express Newspapers* [2004] EWCA Civ 46 and *Jameel (Mohammed) v Wall Street Journal Europe Sprl* [2005] EWCA Civ 74; [2005] 2 W.L.R. 1577 at [54]–[68]. **36.1**

Where permission to appeal is granted. *Add at end of note 22*: Note that in *Lloyd Jones v T Mobile (UK) Ltd* [2003] EWCA Civ 1162; (2003) 49 E.G. 130 at [26], the Court of Appeal granted permission to appeal on condition that the appellant should not be entitled to the costs of the appeal, even if it succeeded. The appellant was a large corporation which had incurred substantial costs in relation to the appeal because the matter was important to its business. The respondents, by contrast, were individual objectors to the installation of a telephone mast. The ostensible rationale of this decision was to prevent the respondents being caused financial oppression by the appeal and thereby to ensure that the parties were on an even footing. **36.2**

Add at end of paragraph: The Court of Appeal has no power to make a quite different type of order from the order the judge was asked to make if it is satisfied that the judge's approach cannot be faulted, unless the parties agree to such a procedure being adopted (new note 34A).

New note 34A: CPR, r.52.11(3); *Musa King v Telegraph Group Ltd (Practice Note)* [2004] EWCA Civ 613; [2005] 1 W.L.R. 2282 (reported as *King v Telegraph Group Ltd (Practice Note)*) at [54].

Security for costs. *Add to note 35*: The Court of Appeal has power under CPR, r.52.10 to make an order for security in respect of the costs of the proceedings below: *Dar International FEF Co. v Aon Ltd* [2003] EWCA Civ 1833; [2004] 1 W.L.R. 1395. **36.3**

36.4   **Raising a point not taken below.** *Add to note 38*: See also *Jameel (Mohammed) v Wall Street Journal Europe Sprl* [2005] EWCA Civ 74; [2005] 2 W.L.R. 1577 at [54]–[57].

Add to note 40: See also *Jameel (Mohammed) v Wall Street Journal Europe Sprl* [2005] EWCA Civ 74; [2005] 2 W.L.R. 1577 at [64]:

> "[Counsel for the claimants] referred us to a substantial body of authority in footnote 40 to paragraph 36.4 of the 10th Edition of *Gatley on Libel and Slander*. This gives strong support to the proposition that this court will not entertain a complaint of misdirection in a defamation action if counsel has failed to avail himself of the chance of raising the matter at trial. We consider that this principle is particularly significant in the present case. The only remedy for a misdirection is a re-trial . . . We would be very reluctant to permit a point to be raised on appeal which could and should have been taken below in circumstances such as this. Were it plain that the misdirection had resulted in a miscarriage of justice we might have been persuaded to grant permission to appeal none the less. But that is far from the case . . . ".

36.5   **Retrial.** *Add to note 46*: In this context, see also CPR, r.52.10(3): "In an appeal from a claim tried with a jury the Court of Appeal may, instead of ordering a new trial—(a) make an order for damages; or (b) vary an award of damages made by the jury". The position in relation to the Court of Appeal's power to order a retrial where the lower court comprised a judge and jury is correctly stated in para.36.5 of the Main Work, subject to the following proviso: that where the Court of Appeal can remedy the flaw in the result of the trial proceedings by exercising one of its powers under CPR, r.52.10(3), then, consistently with the overriding objective, it is likely to do so. With regard to the Court of Appeal's powers under CPR, r.52.10(3), see also para.36.30 of the Main Work.

SECTION 3. WRONG CONCLUSION OF LAW

36.10   **Wrongly withdrawing a question from the jury.** *Add to note 63*: Conversely, in *Downtex v Flatley* [2003] EWCA Civ 1282, the Court of Appeal decided that the judge had wrongly *failed* to rule out a defence of qualified privilege. At [38], Potter L.J. expressed concern that:

> "it would be an inappropriate exercise in this court to reverse the considered view of a first instance judge in a specialist jurisdiction in that there were insufficient facts before him . . . to justify the giving of summary judgment . . . In such cases, the approach of this court is usually, and rightly, to refuse to become engaged in the detail of a matter in which (as in the case of the exercise of a judicial discretion), the outcome largely depends on a process of evaluation in relation to which opinions may vary from judge to judge."

Nonetheless, in the *Downtex* case itself the Court of Appeal did not let this concern stand in its way, decided that the judge *had* had sufficient facts before him to rule summarily on the viability of the defence of qualified privilege, and so determined it in favour of the first claimant. For an account of why *Downtex* is a problematic case, see para.14.1 of this Supplement.

Section 5. Unreasonable Verdict

Where the verdict would be set aside. *Add to note 23*: For the current **36.20** position in New South Wales, see *John Fairfax Publications Pty Ltd v Rivkin* [2003] HCA 50; (2003) 201 A.L.R. 77.

Section 6. Excessive or Inadequate Damages

Province of the jury. *Add to note 37*: For the position in Ontario, see *Barrick* **36.25** *Gold Corp. v Lopehandia* (2004) 71 O.R. (3d), Ont. CA.

Section 9. Discovery of Fresh Evidence

Criteria for allowing new trial on basis of discovery of fresh evidence. *Add* **36.38** *to note 92*: Another procedural appeal point in relation to which the court, post-CPR, has followed the old RSC practice is the question of when the court will permit fresh evidence to be admitted concerning matters *that have occurred* since the date of the trial or hearing under appeal. CPR, r.52.11(2), unlike its predecessor in the RSC, RSC Ord.59, r.10(2), contains no express qualification permitting the admission of such evidence only in the most exceptional of circumstances, having regard to the need for finality in litigation. See *Hughes v Singh, The Times*, April 21, 1989, for the position under the RSC. In *Bentley and Skinner (Bond Street Jewellers) Ltd v Searchmap Ltd* [2003] EWHC 1621 (Ch) at [20], Lightman J. treated the principles stated in *Hughes v Singh* as continuing in effect post-CPR.

APPENDIX 1

FORMS AND PRECEDENTS

C SETTLEMENT OF ACTION

A. Steps up to and Including Issue of Proceedings **A1.1**

Note 1: Substitute "Civil Procedure Vol.1 (2005)" for "Civil Procedure, Vol.1(2003)".

Offer to Make Amends: Qualified Offer to Make Amends Pursuant to Defamation **A1.4**
Act 1996, s.2

Note 2: *Cleese v Clark* is now reported at [2004] E.M.L.R. 37. *Milne v Express Newspapers* has now been appealed to the Court of Appeal ([2004] EWCA Civ 664; [2005] 1 W.L.R. 772).

Particulars of Claim **A1.16**

Replace para.2 of the Particulars of Claim with the following:

"2. The Defendant is a self-employed journalist specialising in postwar European history and the author and/or editor of a website set up or caused to be set up by him in or about [*date*] on the World Wide Web system of the Internet. The said website is entitled "Modern History Bulletin Board" and its address is http://www.[*website address*].co.uk. At all material times the said website has been open to general access by any user of the World Wide Web. In the circumstances, it is to be inferred from the open access of the site and the wide interest in modern history amongst sections of the population including history pupils, students and lecturers that the words complained of in paragraph 3 were published to a substantial but unquantifiable number of readers [new note 26A]."

Add new note 26A: In cases where the publication complained of is alleged to have been published via the internet, a claimant may wish to identify in the particulars of claim individuals whom he claims downloaded and read it. Otherwise, except in cases where it is plain and obvious that publication has taken place, the claimant should plead an inferential case of publication, setting out the facts and matters relied on in support of that case. See *Loutchansky v Times Newspapers Ltd (No.2)* [2001] EWCA Civ 1805; [2002] Q.B. 783; *Jameel (Yousef) v Dow Jones & Co. Inc.* [2005] EWCA Civ 75; [2005] 2 W.L.R. 1614; *Pritchard Englefield (a firm) v Steinberg* [2005] EWCA Civ 288 and *Hewitt v Grunwald* [2004] EWHC 2959, QBD at [72]–[74].

A1.17   Particulars of Claim

Add at the end of note 27 See also *Jennings v Buchanan* [2004] UKPC 36; [2005] 1 A.C. 115 at [5].

A1.27   Defence

Add to paragraph 4 of the Defence in cases where the defendant's subjective belief is relevant:

"(8A) The [journalist] believed in the truth of the matters published and/or their implications, namely that the Claimant [*fill in the belief held*]. This belief was reasonable based upon the matters [the journalist] found out prior to publication and was told by his sources. The basis upon which that belief is held is set out below [*set out particulars*]"

Add to paragraph 4 of the Defence in cases where the defendant's subjective belief is not relevant:

"(8A) The [journalist]'s belief as to the truth or otherwise of the publication complained of is irrelevant to the claim for privilege. The Defendant was under a duty to pass on the matters published whether or not he believed them to be true [*set out particulars*]."

Note 50: Substitute "Civil Procedure Vol.1 (2005)" for "Civil Procedure, Vol.1(2003)".

Add at end of note 50: The Court of Appeal in *Jameel (Mohammed) v Wall Street Journal Europe Sprl (CA, No.2)* [2005] EWCA Civ 74; [2005] 2 W.L.R. 1577 at [18] directly addressed the question: "What must a defendant plead and prove to establish *Reynolds* privilege?" In answer to this question, see the detailed discussion in this Supplement at para.27.19A.

A1.30   Reply

Replace note 54 with: See *Milne v Express Newspapers* [2004] EWCA Civ 664; [2005] 1 W.L.R. 772.

Libel

Add to paragraph 2 of the Reply: "2.4A In respect of paragraph 4 above, it is denied that the Defendant held that belief pleaded. Alternatively, it is denied that the belief held was a reasonable one for the following reasons: [*set out the reasons why.*]"

Add to note 55: *Bonnick v Morris* is reported at [2003] 1 A.C. 300.

LIBEL AWARDS

Add A3.8A

Wood v Chief Constable of West Midlands Police [2004] EWCA Civ 1638; [2005] E.M.L.R. 20
The claimant and H, trading as VSG, were in motor salvage for the insurance industry. H was arrested and charged with handling stolen motor vehicles, unconnected with VSG. Prior to H's trial, a senior police officer wrote letters to members of the insurance world, including to a client of VSG, advising of H's arrest and of his attempt "to disguise his criminal activities with a veil of legitimacy", thereby referring to VSG. The letters did not name W, but he sued in libel complaining that the letters implicated him, as H's partner in VSG and its public face, in the alleged criminal activity of H. The police unsuccessfully raised qualified privilege. At the trial, the client of VSG to whom a letter was sent gave unexpected evidence that the letter was never received and an amendment to plead slander was sought and allowed. The Court of Appeal dismissed the appeal and upheld the jury award of £45,000.

Add A3.8B (NB: not jury award under appeal but compensation following offer of amends)

Nail v News Group Newspapers Ltd [2004] EWCA Civ 1708; [2005] 1 All E.R. 1040
In 1998 HarperCollins published a biography of the claimant entitled "Nailed". He decided not to sue at that time, on legal advice. In 2002 extracts from "Nailed" were

published in the *News of the World* and the book attracted new consumer interest, selling about 100 copies. The claimant sued the *News of the World* over the offending article and, separately, HarperCollins in respect of the editions of the book sold in 2002. An offer to make amends having been accepted by the claimant, Eady J. awarded the claimant £7,500 in compensation for the book and £22,500 for the article. The claimant appealed. The appeal was dismissed. Section 3(5) of the 1996 Act requires the judge to determine compensation on the usual principles applied in defamation cases. He is not required to speculate what a putative jury might award. If an early unqualified offer to make amends is made and accepted and an agreed apology published, this is bound to be substantial mitigation. The judge's use of the word "rewarded" was superficially open to mis-interpretation but there was no distinction between the inevitable mitigation of using the procedure and a "reward" for using it, provided that the mitigating factors were not brought into play twice. The judge had not applied a double discount. He had based his assessments on conventional principles and in amounts that were not so low to justify interference by the Court of Appeal.

Add A3.12

The Gleaner Company Ltd v Abrahams [2003] UKPC 55; [2004] 1 A.C. 628
The plaintiff, a former Jamaican Minister of Tourism, had been accused of taking bribes. A plea of justification had stood on the record for some seven years before it was struck out in the absence of pleaded facts to support it. An apology was then published, but the plaintiff produced strong evidence of a ruined career, public humiliation and prolonged stress. The Privy Council declined to interfere with an award of £533,000 general damages made by the Jamaican Court of Appeal in substitution of a jury award of £1.2m. The Jamaican Court of Appeal declined to follow the English practice derived from *John v MGN Ltd* [1997] Q.B. 586 of using personal injuries damages as a reference point in the quantification of libel damages, and the Privy Council held that they had not erred in this respect. It was a question of policy "open to legitimate differences of opinion" and did not, in Lord Hoffmann's view, involve any question of legal princi-ple.

Add A3.13

Galloway v Telegraph Group Ltd [2004] EWHC 2786, QBD; [2005] E.M.L.R. 7
The defendant published articles on April 22 and 23, 2003 said to have been based on documents found in badly damaged government buildings in Baghdad, accusing the claimant, a former Labour Member of Parliament and prominent anti-war campaigner, of having received money from Saddam Hussein's regime and having been granted special deals in the United Nations oil for food programme. The articles published on April 23 also reported that the documents indicated that the claimant had demanded more money from Saddam Hussein's regime but had been rebuffed and also raised questions about his ownership of various properties including a villa in the Algarve. The defendant disputed the meaning attributed to the articles by the claimant and pleaded *Reynolds* qualified privilege. Eady J., sitting without a jury, held that the articles were not protected by qualified privilege. Since there was no plea of justification it was not part of the court's function to rule directly upon the truth or otherwise of the underlying allegations and had to presume the words were false. The allegations were serious; there had been no apology; and some of the conduct at trial had been aggravating. The claimant was awarded £150,000. The defendant has been given permission to appeal to the Court of Appeal.

Add A3.14

Walsh v Carpenter, unreported, April 25, 2005
The claimant sued for libel over an allegation made in an email published to one person to the effect that he had been dismissed from his employment for "financial irregu-larities". Eady J., sitting without a jury, awarded damages of £18,000. The allegation

was serious; the defendant had been motivated by malice and had refused to retract the allegation; he had repeated the allegation in his evidence, even though he had made no attempt to justify it.

Add A3.15

Rackham v Sandy [2005] EWHC 482, QBD

The claimant sued over a letter written by three defendants in their capacities as the CEO, finance director and legal director of a company and sent to four members of the board of the company, making allegations of poor corporate governance by the claimant. The defendants had first raised their concerns with the chairman of the company, but he had not dealt with them. The defendants obtained and followed legal advice from solicitors on the letter prior to it being sent. The second defendant was not involved in the writing of the letter. He approved it after it was read over the telephone to him while he was on holiday. The defendants relied on the defence of qualified privilege. The claimant admitted that the publication was made on an occasion of qualified privilege. Gray J., sitting without a jury, held that this was a case where there was an established relationship between the publishers and the publishees and the court should be slower to find malice in such cases. The judge found that the second and third defendants had not been actuated by any improper motive in sending the letter. The first defendant was found to have written the letter in order to procure the removal of the claimant from the board and to save his own position. The claimant was awarded judgment against the first defendant and £2,000 damages. Gray J. considered that the allegations in the letter complained of were of some gravity but the circulation of the letter had been very limited. The judge also considered that the action was brought because no acceptable apology was offered to him rather than because his feelings had been hurt by the libel and that, in the circumstances, the reasoned judgment in his favour would provide vindication.

Add A3.16 (N.B. compensation following an offer of amends)

Turner v News Group Newspapers Ltd [2005] EWHC 892, QBD; [2005] E.M.L.R. 25

A former wife of the claimant was featured in an article in the *News of the World* concerning "swinging" and sex parties. It was said that she had been introduced to the swinging scene by her husband (who was not named but identifiable to some readers) and that their marriage broke up after he pressured her to have sex with other men. An offer to make amends was made by the defendant, coupled with a lengthy "*Burstein*" mitigation plea. An apology was published but compensation not agreed. At the compensation hearing, the defendant relied on an amended "*Burstein*" plea in mitigation while the claimant relied on both forms of the "*Burstein*" plea as matters aggravating the injury, disentitling the defendant from any, let alone a "healthy" discount, for making an offer of amends. Eady J. awarded the claimant £9,000 in compensation after applying a discount of 40 per cent having regard to the offer of amends. Reliance in preparation for a s.3(5) hearing on material which may increase the claimant's hurt will not automatically be held against a defendant. At least some of the material relied on by the defendant at the hearing was admissible under the "*Burstein*" principle. It was not always necessary to establish a direct causal link between such material and the publication complained of. The claimant has been given permission to appeal to the Court of Appeal.

Add A3.17 (N.B. compensation following an offer of amends)

Campbell-James v Guardian Media Group plc [2005] EWHC 893, QBD; [2005] E.M.L.R. 24

The claimant complained about an article published in the *Guardian* in September 2004 headed "UK officers linked to torture jail" which falsely linked him with the notorious abuses at Abu Ghraib prison in Iraq in 2003. Colonel Campbell-James accepted an offer to make amends made by the defendant under s.3 of the Defamation Act 1996. Eady J. considered the allegation to be very serious: "anyone who truly bore a degree of responsibility for such atrocious abuse of power, even indirectly, would rightly be reviled and made the subject of criminal charges or, at least, military discipline". The judge also noted Col. Campbell-James's distress at being accused of something which he found "personally abhorrent". There was solid evidence before the court of a serious security risk to Col. Campbell-James and his family following the article. The *Guardian* was criticised for waiting three months before publishing an apology and correction, when there should have been "an immediate and generous acknowledgment of error". Its attitude was described as "remarkably casual". Eady J. considered £90,000 to be the correct notional starting point for damages which would have been awarded at trial and 35 per cent to be the appropriate percentage reduction taking into account the offer of amends and apology. The claimant was accordingly awarded £58,500 in compensation.